DAVID COLEMAN ....al psychologist, broadcaster and author. A graduate of University College Dublin, David has been a practising clinical psychologist, working with children, teenagers and their families, for over twelve years. David has become well known in Ireland as the presenter of the hit RTÉ television series *Families in Trouble*, and more recently *Teens in the Wild*, both of which were enjoyed by huge audiences nationwide. David also presents *21st Century Child*, a landmark venture for RTÉ that follows twelve Irish families for six years from the birth of their babies. A natural communicator, David's style is universally acclaimed as accessible and approachable. David has successfully transferred his skills to radio, where he is the dependable weekly contributor to *The Moncrieff Show's* parenting slot every Wednesday on Newstalk 106–108fm. David is also the bestselling author of *Parenting is Child's Play*, a guide to raising young children. A firm and continuing favourite with Irish parents, the book was published by Penguin Ireland in May 2007. He is also a weekly expert contributor to the Parenting Section of *Health Plus*, the *Irish Times'* supplement every Tuesday. This is his second book.

for
Michèle, Conall, Megan and Éanna

DAVID COLEMAN

PARENTING IS CHILD'S PLAY
the teenage years

PENGUIN
IRELAND

PENGUIN IRELAND

Published by the Penguin Group

Penguin Ireland, 25 St Stephen's Green, Dublin 2, Ireland (a division of Penguin Books Ltd)

Penguin Books Ltd, 80 Strand, London WC2R 0RL, England

Penguin Group (USA) Inc., 375 Hudson Street, New York, New York 10014, USA

Penguin Group (Australia), 250 Camberwell Road, Camberwell, Victoria 3124, Australia
(a division of Pearson Australia Group Pty Ltd)

Penguin Group (Canada), 90 Eglinton Avenue East, Suite 700, Toronto, Ontario, Canada M4P 2Y3
(a division of Pearson Penguin Canada Inc.)

Penguin Books India Pvt Ltd, 11 Community Centre, Panchsheel Park, New Delhi – 110 017, India

Penguin Group (NZ), 67 Apollo Drive, Rosedale, North Shore 0632, New Zealand
(a division of Pearson New Zealand Ltd)

Penguin Books (South Africa) (Pty) Ltd, 24 Sturdee Avenue, Rosebank, Johannesburg 2196, South Africa

Penguin Books Ltd, Registered Offices: 80 Strand, London WC2R 0RL, England

www.penguin.com

First published 2010

1

Copyright © David Coleman, 2010

Illustrations copyright © Anna Hymas, 2010

The moral right of the author and of the illustrator has been asserted

Set in Din, Fh_Nicole, Thug and Trade Gothic

Printed and bound in Italy by Printer Trento, srl.

A CIP catalogue record for this book is available from the British Library

ISBN 978–1–844–88215–1

CONTENTS

INTRODUCTION

I have worked with and counselled hundreds of teenagers and their families over the last twelve years. In so many ways this has put me in a lucky and privileged position. I get to be the person who can try to understand things from that teenager's point of view. I can help them to negotiate relationships with their parents and their peers. I can support and guide them through the maze of conflicting messages from family, friends, teachers and the global media. I have been lucky enough to be allowed to share in the complexities of their lives. Teenagers will sometimes talk to me when they remain closed to everyone else around them. This happens because my job is to create a space and a forum for them to express and deal with the troubles that have the potential to trip them up in their daily lives.

I am sometimes tempted to assume that all teenagers are rebelling and recalcitrant. Thankfully, I know the reality is different.

But, although I know teenagers and their issues, I still feel a small amount of anxiety at the thought of writing a book about parenting them. I half expect any teenager who picks up this book from their parents' bookshelf to snigger and dismiss most of what I am saying. This, in fact, is a ridiculous anxiety. It is based not on the reality of most teenagers, but instead on my insecurity at being challenged for taking a position of authority on the subject of their lives. I'm guessing, however, that my anxiety probably mirrors the anxiety of many parents as they move into this phase with their children. We really do fear having our authority challenged.

Adolescence is often hyped as a time of plummeting parental control and increasing parent–child conflict. It is portrayed as a time when respect is replaced by rejection and communication is replaced by cynicism. In the face of such negative anticipation it is unsurprising that many of us dread the shift into adolescence. My working life with teenagers, by the nature of the distress already ingrained in the families, has been continually focused on problems, difficulties and discord. I am sometimes tempted to assume that all teenagers are rebelling and recalcitrant. Thankfully, I know the reality is different. The majority of teenagers move through the transition from childhood to adulthood with enough struggles to make the process real, but not enough struggles to alienate them from their parents.

From my experience with teenagers and families, one of the key determining factors in a successful transition through adolescence centres on the quality of the relationships that parents have formed with their teenagers when they were children. Interacting with your child and showing yourself to be loving, caring, reliable, respectful, authoritative and fair will pay dividends during the teenage years. A solid and secure relationship base provides the ideal launching platform for adolescence and increases dramatically the likelihood of a safe landing into adulthood.

Another key factor is your recognition that your parenting styles have to develop and progress during their adolescence. The styles and strategies that may have proved very successful during the toddler years and even the primary school years will not necessarily be successful during the teenage years. Parents need to accord their teenagers greater responsibility, expect greater levels of trust to be reciprocated and negotiate the consequences for the mistakes that will inevitably be made. Throughout all of that, parents need to foster mutual respect and growing independence – a hard task!

I sometimes picture the parenting journey as a parent and child walking to a chosen destination along the road. This journey has several stages.

A solid and secure relationship base provides the ideal launching platform for adolescence and increases dramatically the likelihood of a safe landing into adulthood.

During infancy and babyhood the parent is entirely responsible for choosing both the destination and the route to be followed. During this phase they carry their baby along the road.

In toddlerhood their child insists on walking alone and often decides to go backwards along the route already travelled, especially if another baby is added to the family. The parent must now continue to choose both route and destination and invariably must hold the hand of their child, leading them clearly in the desired direction to keep everyone moving forward.

Middle childhood, as it is called, or the primary school years provide parents with the opportunity to let go of their children's hands for short periods. Before they let go they continue to keep an eye on the destination and will often let their child choose from the safety of two routes that they have already explored and are happy with. For the child the sense of exploration can be exciting, but at times the parent builds walls on both sides of the path to help their child avoid distraction and to keep the boundaries of the journey clear. They will also explain in great detail the journey to be taken and will keep showing a map of the route to the child, so they know where they are expected to go. If needed, parents will take their children by the hand again to lead them.

Once those children move into adolescence, however, it becomes harder and harder for parents to dictate either the road that must be followed or the destination that must be reached. The guiding walls along the road that they had constructed are either jumped over by their teenager, or jumped upon to see what other kinds of roads and destinations are out there. Teenagers will scoff and scorn at any hand that is offered by their parents to guide them.

Once teenagers start to choose their own route, parents can easily feel frustrated and let down that the route they had chosen for their child is being ignored. They can be scared about the dangers of the road their son or daughter chooses to walk along. Parents now feel like they are hurrying along behind their child, trying to remind them of where to go and how to get there. It can often feel as if there is not enough space on the road for them and their teenager because all of the teenager's friends are bustling along too (probably whispering in the ear of the teenager to ignore the parents' directions and follow theirs).

So adolescence could become a time when parents give up because they no longer feel heard, responded to or respected. The temptation to holler after your child's departing back, 'Don't come back to me if you find you are getting lost!' might be strong. But giving up is not an option favoured by parents. We are a hardy bunch and we know in our hearts that we will keep trying. So at times we do follow, while at other times we get back to a position of leading and directing, despite our child's rejection or dismissal of that guidance. At times we try to erect, or to re-erect, the boundaries to keep our teenagers safer. At times we acknowledge that we have done all we can to describe the road ahead, including the pitfalls, and we recognize that we have done all we can do to show them how to reach what we have always believed is a good destination. At that point we wait, we trust and we go to help when we are called.

In my own imaginings of the outcome of this journey for parents, children, teenagers and the adults they eventually become, I am always struck by the anecdotal evidence that at some stage most parents are rewarded by the experience of their son or daughter reaching a destination that is equivalent to the one that the parent planned at the start. Of course, the route they took and the hurts and excitement along the way may have been radically different from what the parents expected, but then, that is what teenager-hood is all about: finding your own way to who you will become in the world. Our job as parents is to support that journey of discovery as best we can.

This book is intended as a support to you while you offer that support to your teenager. Ultimately, we are all just doing the best we can for our children. As long as our parenting is aimed at being 'good enough', then it will be good enough for our children to get them from childhood to adulthood, safely.

So the aim of the book is to give you all of the background information you require to understand your teenagers better, to communicate with them more effectively and to know more about their developmental tasks during adolescence. In case you run into difficulty with specific problem areas, I have also provided information and advice to help you respond to the main teenage issues of alcohol, drugs, self-harm and so on.

Parenting is not an easy occupation. Indeed, it can be so hard at times that it overwhelms us and the issues and stresses insinuate themselves into every aspect of our being. I have long been of the opinion that in order to mind our children and our teenagers, we have to be able to mind ourselves. That means that we have to manage our stress by having a proper diet, regular exercise, knowing how to relax and so on. Importantly, we also need support. We need to know that other people are having the same stresses and struggles with their teenagers. We need to know that we are not alone and that there are things we can do. This book is about giving you support. It is about reassuring you that you are not going mad and that yes, this is the life of the parent of a teenager and here are some things you can do to make a difference. So if the going is getting tough, have a nice cup of tea . . . ring your best friend to cry down the phone . . . read some relevant chapters . . . and then get back on in there!

So if the going is getting tough, have a nice cup of tea . . . ring your best friend to cry down the phone . . . read some relevant chapters . . . and then get back on in there!

I. SEARCHING FOR IDENTITY

the who, why and what of becoming an adult

It often comes as a complete shock to parents that their children are suddenly teenagers. Of course, the transition to teenager is never really a sudden event, but nonetheless it's hard to get your head around the fact that your child is now acting, and possibly thinking, very differently. Just as you got the hang of being the parent of a child, suddenly you have to change and adapt what you know to become the parent of a teenager.

Obviously we've all lived through our own teenage years, but it can be very hard to remember our own behaviour and thoughts at that time when faced with a surly teen who's sure we are the least cool parent on the planet. So, the focus of this chapter is to give an overview of what adolescence is all about and what the job of being a teenager is. One of the central themes of adolescence is the search for identity; in psychological terms, this is often referred to as identity formation. During this time in their life, your child is working hard on trying to identify who they are, what they believe in and where they might be going in life. This means that they are building up their own expectations and their own goals, which often seem to be in total contrast to, and in conflict with, the ideals, expectations and goals you might have for them.

Like every developmental phase, identity formation is a process and not an event. In other words, your child's identity will change and solidify over time rather than suddenly appearing, newly minted, one morning. Parts of our identities are formed genetically at conception, parts are developed through childhood and adolescence is simply the next stage of that development.

What marks adolescence out in terms of identity formation is how much that search for identity seems to occur in opposition to the values, beliefs and identities of the child's family. This can often feel hurtful and dismissive for you, the parents, who find it hard to accept that your son or daughter is now rejecting so much of what you may have stood for. My intention is to give you a helpful insight into what your teenager is trying to do during this potentially turbulent time of adolescent development.

THIS CHAPTER LOOKS AT . . .

The five major changes that occur in the teenage years
- *Physical growth and puberty*
- *Cognitive development*
- *Becoming independent*
- *Sexuality*
- *Moral and ethical development*

THE FIVE MAJOR CHANGES

In my experience, there are five key areas of development for teenagers who are forming their identities:

1. their physical growth
2. their cognitive development
3. becoming independent
4. the development of their sexuality
5. their moral and ethical development

It is through these key developments that teenagers grow, mature and find out who they are.

The parents' job is to provide opportunities for individuation – which is the process of becoming separate from us and less dependent on us – and opportunities for connectedness – which is the process of maintaining a secure base of support and caring. In this way, we let our children go out into the world to explore it, but safe in the knowledge that we are still here to help them recover from the knocks and bumps they will experience physically, emotionally and psychologically.

There is no way to discuss these topics of personal development without delving into the theories underlying them, so I'll come clean and warn you now that the next few sections are full of psychology! What I have tried to do is to include some real-life stories of teenagers that I know or have known (and their relationships with friends and families) in order to illustrate what these developmental shifts might look like in the real world. The case studies are all of youngsters I have worked with, and to protect their anonymity I have changed their names and also changed elements of their stories to make them unrecognizable. While you don't know who these youngsters are, you may well know teenagers just like them and, with a bit of luck, you will be able to recognize your own son or daughter and their progress, too.

PHYSICAL GROWTH AND PUBERTY

In the early years of adolescence, i.e. from about the ages of ten to fourteen years, your teenager starts the process of physically growing and taking on their adult body. Certainly we have seen that girls, as a general rule, will start puberty earlier than boys. Many girls have begun the physical changes of puberty at ten years of age, while boys don't start until about thirteen.

The kinds of changes to expect in early puberty are growth in height and weight. Both boys and girls will grow pubic and underarm hair. Boys will additionally start to grow hair on their faces, and their leg

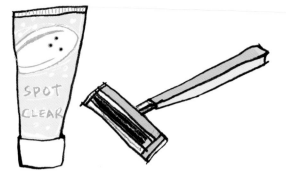

and arm hair will thicken and darken. Along with more hair comes more oil, as the hair follicles will be producing more sebum. The oil glands of the skin become larger as well as producing more oil. It is the sex hormones that are responsible for telling the skin to produce more oil. As the larger oil glands get blocked, we see spots, pimples and acne. So these are, in fact, a sign of the sexual maturity that is also occurring (not that many teenagers will see spots in a positive light). If your son or daughter is badly affected by acne, consult your GP to get advice or a referral to a dermatologist.

Your teenager will also be perspiring more and as the perspiration dries, it could lead to a strong odour. Your teenager may need to be reminded of their personal hygiene. I remember a friend of mine, with a fourteen-year-old son, complaining for about a year at his refusal to shower regularly and the subsequent smell the family had to suffer. She then described how he discovered girls and suddenly was regularly draining the hot-water tank in his eagerness to be clean and fresh!

Boys will also have physical growth of their penis and testicles. This often coincides with an unconscious and uncontrollable erection-practising system. It is as if their body is just making sure that everything is in good working order, and so they get frequent erections. Erotic distraction is not needed at this age to get an erection, so there are times when we need to be discreet and understanding if they don't jump up from the sofa as soon as we ask them to do something. The other things most boys experience at some stage are 'wet dreams', which is when semen is ejaculated, unconsciously, during the night. This too has the potential to be embarrassing for boys and so forewarned (telling them this might happen, along with giving them advice about dealing with the dirty laundry) is forearmed from everyone's perspective and normalizes this experience.

Another significant step for boys is the deepening (or breaking) of their voice. This is rarely a single moment; usually there is a period of time where their voice oscillates between higher and lower octaves. This often brings much frustration and embarrassment as the occasional squeaks seem designed to diminish their impending manhood.

Most youngsters will be aware of these physical changes and will be expecting them. In fact, their non-arrival may be a greater source of anxiety than their arrival. I am a big fan of making sure that teenagers know what to expect.

Girls will experience breast growth and the arrival of menstruation. Typically, mums step in to describe what menstruation will involve, both physically and emotionally, and to describe the options and practicalities for hygiene and self-care. Some mothers advise their daughters to record the dates on which their periods arrive so they can chart their cycle into the future. Similarly, parents need to take an interest in and at least discuss the growth of their daughter's breasts, if only to ensure they periodically get fitted for the right kind of bra. Depending on your own experience, you may choose to mark this moment as a very significant transition from one aspect of childhood to adulthood.

Most youngsters will be aware of these physical changes and will be expecting them. In fact, their non-arrival may be a greater source of anxiety than their arrival. I am a big fan of making sure that teenagers know what to expect. Later in the book I deal with relationships and sexuality in much greater detail (see Chapter 7), including the information to be described in the 'facts of life' conversations you will have. Knowing this practical stuff about physical growth and development can really help to reduce anxiety for both sons and daughters. So, even though you may believe that they are aware of what changes are to come, and even though you might want to avoid having 'the talk', it is still really important to ensure that they have the information by checking it out with them. The younger they are when you describe the changes to come, the less embarrassing it might feel for them and for you.

As teenagers move through middle adolescence (fifteen to sixteen years) and then into late adolescence (seventeen to twenty-one), the rate of growth and physical change slows significantly. Girls, for example, will probably only grow about two inches taller from the time of their first menstrual period, and by about seventeen or eighteen years most girls are fully developed. Boys, on the other hand, continue to have height and weight gain, as they put on muscle mass and broaden out right up into their early twenties.

➔ Cillian: Size does matter

I knew a lad whom I will call Cillian. Cillian was brought to see me when he was fifteen years old, because his lone parent, his mum, was struggling to cope with his anger and aggression, especially towards her. I had received a letter from their family GP describing the situation at home, including information that his mum had a significant problem with bipolar disorder. Bipolar disorder is when a person alternates between the symptoms of depression and the symptoms of mania. In the manic period, thinking is often speeded up and the person can become quite paranoid; it might also appear as an extreme giddiness or elation. The important bit of this for Cillian was that his mum had been hospitalized on a few occasions because of her mental health and he had to be minded by relatives.

When I met him, I was surprised. I had created an image in my head of a tall and formidable young man who was full of physical aggression and bluster, which he used to mask his stress and distress of living with his mum's mental health problems.

The boy I met was small, slim and very immature-looking physically. Indeed, if his mum had told me that Cillian was eleven or twelve, I would have believed her. In our first session he was belligerent towards me and the fact that I couldn't possibly know what his life was like and so couldn't help him. Near the end of the session he accused me of staring at him and demanded to know did I think there was 'something f**king wrong' with the way he looked. I didn't get into it then and there because the time was so limited.

As the sessions continued, Cillian's manner with me softened and eventually, after about four sessions, we finally got to talk about how he felt about the fact that he looked (and therefore was misperceived as) immature and that he tried to compensate for that by being a 'real man'. We had further conversations about 'real men' and what they looked, sounded and acted like. We talked about how he didn't have a 'real man' to father him and how he actually had to take on a fatherly role in minding his mother when she became unwell, including ringing the psychiatric team who arranged for her to be forcibly removed to hospital on one occasion of mania when she was in real danger of harming herself.

Sure, Cillian had issues with his mum and her mental health. He felt overly responsible for her and unconsciously that angered him greatly. But he also had a huge feeling of inadequacy that was directly linked to his small stature and his physical immaturity. He couldn't wait to grow up.

COGNITIVE DEVELOPMENT

Cognitive development refers to the development of the ability to think and reason. Children (six to twelve years old) develop the ability to think in concrete ways (concrete operations), such as how to combine (addition), how to separate (subtract or divide), how to order (alphabetize and sort) and how to transform objects and actions (change things, such as five 20c pieces =€1). They are called 'concrete' because they are performed in the presence of the objects and events being thought about.

Adolescence marks the beginning of the development of more complex thinking processes (also called formal logical operations), including abstract thinking (thinking about possibilities), the ability to reason from known principles (i.e. to form their own, new ideas from something that is known), the ability to consider many points of view according to varying criteria (i.e. to compare or debate ideas or opinions), and the ability to think about the process of thinking. These are huge steps.

As an example, I can remember asking two sisters, one aged seven and one aged thirteen, who they were most like in their family. The seven-year-old described how she was most like her brother because she had the same hair colour as him and they both had freckles on their faces. The thirteen-year-old described how she was most like her mum, whom she felt thought similarly and believed in the same things as she did. The comparison, for me, was striking: the concrete and practical similarities between the younger sister and her brother, and the similarities of concept and thought between the older sister and her mother.

In practice you will see the effect of the ability to think abstractly in things like your teenager being able to plan effectively into the future. In fact, even their interest in a future develops during adolescence. In their early adolescence their focus remains on the here and now or, at best, the near future. As they move into later adolescence, however, their future career becomes more tangible and they begin to think about their future role in life.

Their ability to reason and the ability to think about and argue from various points of view may or may not be very evident in your teenager. You may have noticed that the rows you have with them take on a more debate-like feel. They are still likely to let their emotions overwhelm them at times (don't we all!), but nonetheless their ability to draw on principles like fairness and equality seems more practised and more understood at a theoretical level, rather than just a gut feeling of things being unfair. Because of their new-found logicality and rationality of thinking, they will pick holes in your reasoning if you are not careful. So your daughter may point out the hypocrisy of your appeals to not drink alcohol by alluding to your own drinking habits or the age at which you stopped haranguing her older sister about her drinking habits.

→ Gemma: The ability to be insightful

Gemma was a sixteen-year-old girl who played violin to a very high standard. She had clear intentions of becoming a concert musician and already played with a youth orchestra. She also self-harmed by cutting herself on her forearms with a razor blade. This was why I was asked to see her.

When we met, I was struck by how pretty she was and, from the description given by her mother, how very talented she was too. On the face of it she had a lot going for her and so I was genuinely interested to know why she self-harmed. However, when I asked her, she said that she didn't know why, she just did it. We spent the rest of the session exploring the frequency with which she cut herself, her thinking before, during and after the cutting, her mood before, during and after the cutting and the other things going on in her life. Gemma had almost no insight into her thoughts or feelings in relation to the cutting. She tried really hard in the session, but just could not seem to grasp her motives for harming herself.

She was well able to describe her life, however. It turned out that her life was very stressful because her parents had very high expectations of her musically and academically. They pushed her hard to study and to practise. She spent many hours each day pursuing her future career and ensuring that she had a fall-back educational platform. The more she talked about it, the more intense, focused and driven she appeared. I also noticed that she physically tensed up in the chair while she was talking about this stuff. It was almost as if she was holding on to her future so tightly, she couldn't let go.

As we finished I asked her how she relaxed when her music and study were complete each day. She looked at me blankly and said, 'I don't know.' The manner in which she said it was very reminiscent of how she had responded to my questions about self-harming. I devised my own theory about why she might cut herself and stored it away as a possible insight to share with her at some point in the future.

The following week she came in to me and sat down opposite me. 'Remember last week when you asked me why I cut myself and I said, "I don't know?"', she asked. I replied that I did indeed remember. 'I was thinking about it during the week. I think I cut myself to relax. It is like a release. When I cut all the tension goes away. My life is very tense you know. It was only when you asked me how I relax that it all started to make sense. I was going home and I started to make all these links in my head between the amount of pressure I feel and my need to cut myself. There is a very strong correlation you know between my stress and my self-harming. The more I am worked up, the more blood I let run free.'

I was amazed by her new-found insight and impressed by her thinking and how she had interconnected many things from her life. Her theory exactly matched the one I had formulated at the end of the last session. It was in stark contrast to her 'I dunno' comments of the first session. Our work became focused on teaching her alternative and healthy relaxation techniques and looking at how her thinking can easily slip into 'all-or-nothing' patterns, where she sets high standards in line with those set by her parents and then feels unable to accept any deviation from that. The key for Gemma was her ability to think about and correlate several disparate concepts and make the leap in understanding from how she had an emotional need for release to how she played that out physically.

BECOMING INDEPENDENT

It is the movement towards independence that most typifies the struggle of adolescence. It is the process by which teenagers' identities emerge and are shaped by both the outside influences of their family and their friends and also by the internal influences of their own personality and way of thinking. In the early stages of adolescence we begin to see that teenagers have a greater ability to express themselves verbally, but are still more likely to express their feelings by action rather than by words. That's why we see them sulking, having tantrums, fighting with the family, slamming doors and stomping off.

> In the early stages of adolescence we begin to see that teenagers have a greater ability to express themselves verbally, but are still more likely to express their feelings by action rather than by words.

It is also in these early stages that close friendships gain more importance, which is matched by a greater distance from their parents. In a way, young teenagers are beginning to realize that their parents aren't perfect. Now, the reality is that we have always known we're not perfect, but when your children are small, they do assume that you are perfect and that you know everything. I call this position of all-knowing and all-power 'omnipotence'. At times, your omnipotence may have been challenged by the knowledge of their teacher. You probably remember that time when it was first stated to you by your child that their teacher is right and suddenly you are wrong and know nothing. This is a process that re-emerges strongly in adolescence. But in adolescence, it's almost as if your teenager becomes confident in their own knowledge and doesn't even need to present you with an alternative source of authority, such as the teacher, to tell you that you are wrong.

This is a complicated time for your teenager because although they have an innate drive to pull away from you, they also miss their contact with you. Psychologically, they experience the loss of their relationship with you. While they remain your son or your daughter, they are moving to a time where they are no longer your child.

As teenagers move onward to the middle and later years of adolescence, their opinion of their parents can be further lowered and they may withdraw from us even further. They are quite likely to complain that we are interfering with their independence and not giving them the space and the freedom they require. This is a complicated time for your teenager because although they have an innate drive to pull away from you, they also miss their contact with you. Psychologically, they experience the loss of their relationship with you. While they remain your son or your daughter, they are moving to a time where they are no longer your child. They feel sad about this, even though they may not be able to put words to where this sadness comes from.

This may be just one factor in the moodiness that is so typical of teenagers' movement towards independence. Particularly in the early and middle years of adolescence, youngsters have a lot of self-doubt that coincides with a huge amount of self-involvement. They spend a lot of their time, figuratively, navel-gazing. For example, they may have unrealistically high expectations of themselves and yet worry about failure; they may be extremely concerned with their appearance and their own body, but also feel great dissatisfaction and dismay with how they are developing physically; they may desperately want to be part of a particular peer group and yet be anxious about exclusion and rejection. As I've mentioned above, they may cruelly reject you and yet feel really sad about the loss of their relationship with you. This is the time, therefore, when they may choose to focus more on their inner experiences, and in middle adolescence they might choose to record these complicated feelings and thoughts in a diary.

Part of the searching that goes on, at this stage, is for other people to love in addition to their parents. At various stages throughout this book I will be talking about the idea of having a mentor for your child, somebody who is outside your immediate family circle to whom they can look up and who they will continue to respect and admire, even if their admiration for you is waning. Role models become very important for young teenagers. This is another reason why the global media is so important. Music and television provide huge numbers of role models of varying quality for teenagers to aspire to. Even the title of one of the shows, *Pop Idol*, reflects the underlying intention to produce a winner at the end of the show who will be idolized. I think that the variety and dubious morals of some of these celebrity role models can cause a big problem for parents. The alternative values, beliefs and behaviours that are espoused and lived out by some celebrities give very conflicting messages that can be very influential for your teenager and serve only to weaken further your own influence.

So in addition to these potentially far-removed role models, you might also want to encourage your teenager to look closer to home to some mentors or role models that you can believe in, too.

This is also the beginning of a stronger peer-group influence on how they look, what they wear, where they go and what they do. Indeed, in the later stages of adolescence their peer group is likely to have solidified and they will identify strongly with being part of that group. And they will be beginning to form relationships with boyfriends and girlfriends, trying out this notion of loving other people. I have two chapters later in the book, one looking at peer friendships (see page 126) and one looking at sexual relationships (see page 148), that delve into these topics in greater depth.

Although your teenager is moving towards maturity and, consequently, moving towards independence, they are obviously not there yet. As a result, when they are under pressure and are stressed, you may find that they return to very childish behaviour. That might be the re-emergence of their tantrums or things like fear of the dark, anxieties about social situations or just wanting to curl up on the sofa, suck their thumb and watch a movie.

In fact, it is only when they reach late adolescence, from about seventeen years of age onwards, that they seem firmer and clearer about their identity. This is also the time when they should be able to think through their ideas and to express those ideas in words. Hopefully you will see that they can make independent decisions, including being able to compromise when needed. With luck they will be more self-reliant and clearer about their goals for the future.

→ Michael: A challenging journey to healthy independence

I first met Michael when he was thirteen. His parents came to me in a very distressed state because Michael had played truant from school and had been caught drinking alcohol in a local park with three older boys. They described Michael as always being a bit of a handful, even when small, but nothing this bad had ever happened until he started secondary school. His mum, in particular, felt that she had no influence on him and that all of their interactions involved screaming fights, followed by Michael storming off and doing his own thing anyway. Michael's dad felt that there still were times when he could connect with Michael, but also admitted that the level of conflict between Michael and his mother was so great that he felt caught in the middle. He described that inevitably he would side with his wife at the expense of his own relationship with Michael because he felt he had to, to avoid even bigger rows with her. The more his parents talked, the more discord became apparent in their own relationship. By the end of the session the only two positive things they could say about Michael were that he was a great hurler and loved horse-riding, and show-jumping in particular.

I didn't realize at the time that both parents were playing down their own conflict – in fact, they were already in the process of legally separating. Within a couple of weeks of starting to work with the family, Michael's dad withdrew from the process and, I found out later, moved to the UK.

Needless to say, Michael felt incredibly disillusioned and let down when his father left. Michael himself was very open with me and talked freely about how much he hated school, how pointless he felt it was and how much easier it was to drift into the company of the older lads, who seemed to really respect him because he mitched school regularly and refused to bow down to authority. He felt his mum was really out of touch and he partly blamed her for his dad leaving.

It turned out that my relationship with Michael and his mum continued on and off over a number of years. The centre of the difficulty was Michael's relationship with his mum and his absent dad. Michael felt that his mum was a total embarrassment to him. For example, he hated the fact that she would drive around at night until she found him to bring him home. He was completely dismissive of her and would regularly slander her, call her names and try to put her down. His mum, despairingly, told me that this was the manner in which her ex-husband had also spoken to her.

His mum felt that Michael was deliberately provocative, nasty and thoughtless. She hated the manner in which he would blatantly defy her and openly challenge her to discipline him for his defiance. She explained that she had resorted, on occasion, not just to screaming at him but also to striking out at him. But there was one time when he was fifteen that he pushed her in retaliation, and she realized only then that he had the potential to harm her if she persisted in hitting him. There were many times over the years of my contact when I was fearful that their relationship was about to break down entirely, to the point that Michael would have to come into the care of the HSE. However, Michael and his mum always seemed to manage to pull things back from the brink and find some way of moving forward.

During the time I knew him, Michael's success on the hurling field grew. Every year, in fact, he made the trials for the county underage team. When he was fifteen, he got his first chance to play at county level. He also spent two evenings a week working for nothing at the local stables and had a great relationship with the owner, who was a hard but fair taskmaster and was infectious in his love of all things horse-related. If anything, these two interests were the most stabilizing influences in Michael's life. His success in, and his commitment to, these two activities was in stark contrast to the constant trouble in school, his delinquent drinking and his conflict with his mum.

I was never really sure quite what help I was to Michael and his mum. Many of our sessions were taken up with the litany of problems that Michael was causing and the poor quality of the relationship between his mum and him. Perhaps, in fact, I was just an observer to his prolonged and extreme movements towards independence. Michael was a boy who experienced a very significant loss of the relationship with his dad, and I think he acted this out by fighting with his mum and the school authorities. I know I invested many hours in trying to advise and guide him, giving him strategies for understanding and dealing with his anger and trying to influence him to choose better options, such as his hurling or horse-riding over his 'drop-out' down time with some very dubious 'mates'. I always wanted things to come good for him because he was such a genuine youngster and seemed almost classically 'misguided'.

He certainly rejected his mum in favour of his peer group and I think his decision to hang out with the undesirables of the town was partly a punishment for her. Luckily for Michael, he had more than one peer group with which to align himself. He had his 'drop-out' friends and he had some 'regular' friends from hurling and horse-riding. Mind you, some of his 'regular' friends were being advised by their parents to steer clear of him because of his potential to be a bad influence. Ultimately, in fact, Michael himself dropped his delinquent friends when they began to move from drinking into regular drug-taking. The final shift came when one of his closest friends started to deal drugs. This was the point at which Michael decided he actually had a future that he didn't want to throw away. He refocused his energies, and that was the year he successfully made it on to the county hurling team and began to believe in himself again.

When I finished meeting with Michael and his mum he was aged sixteen. He had left school with a very poor Junior Certificate, but with the intention of sitting his Leaving Certificate. He had researched, on his own initiative, two local colleges that ran Leaving Certificate programmes and had applied to both. The owner of the local stables where Michael worked was employing him full-time over the summer and would regularly ring Michael's mum to tell her how committed and industrious he was in the stables. Michael and his mum still had rows, but, crucially, his mum believed in Michael and saw that he had a future that he was focusing on. Despite the stresses in their own relationship, she was a great practical support, driving him to training and shows around the country.

I think that because she managed to hang in there with him through those dark years of disaffection with school and authority, she gave him that base that allowed him to return to a place of relative safety. They were worrying and turbulent years and I am glad that they eventually settled for him and his mother. I often wonder will I see Michael playing at senior inter-county level or will he come to notice on the show-jumping circuit. I hope he achieves both.

God knows it can be hard enough just to talk to your teenager, so talking to them about their sexuality may be a step too far.

SEXUALITY

God knows it can be hard enough just to talk to your teenager, so talking to them about their sexuality may be a step too far. In fact, if the truth be told, most of us don't even like to acknowledge the sexual development of our children. We would love to think that they maintained their naivety and their innocence for as long as it is possible. We look at some of the clothes and the mannerisms of pre-teen television stars and rue the early sexualization of children. Unfortunately for us, no matter the age at which it starts, we can't stop the juggernaut of their sexual development and the consequent development of their sexuality. Our children will become fully sexual beings and that happens during adolescence.

Of course, teenagers will come to sexual maturity at different stages. As I mentioned earlier, in terms of their physical development, girls tend to mature sexually at a younger age than boys. With so much change going on and with such differences between friends in terms of how their bodies are growing, or not, most boys and girls will keep a low profile in terms of sexual development. Therefore, in those early teenage years, both boys and girls are likely to be shy about the changes to their bodies. They will look for more privacy and will probably be more modest in how they present themselves. Early sexual development can be a real challenge. Girls who mature and develop breasts, for example, at a younger age tend to draw unwanted attention when they don't feel quite ready to cope with being sexual. Having said that, some youngsters love the thrill of a new body shape and want to show it off, particularly in front of the opposite sex.

Most young teenagers worry about whether they are normal, both in terms of their physical development and their sexual feelings. This anxiety intensifies in middle adolescence, although it might be more clearly expressed as a concern about their sexual attractiveness. Both girls and boys are likely to be experimenting with their own bodies, by masturbating. They will also probably be having more frequent short-term relationships with boyfriends and girlfriends, again more in the manner of practice and trial and error.

The main conflict for boys and girls is often felt in trying to make sense of their sexual orientation. Because both wider society and teenagers' peers are still predominantly negatively disposed to homosexuality, it is probably harder for any young person who wonders if they're gay. They probably feel a lot of internal conflict between the reality of their sexual feelings and their desire to fit in with what they too might perceive as 'normal' heterosexual orientation. By the age of fifteen or sixteen most boys and girls will usually be clear about their sexual orientation, even if they don't get to express it through sexual relationships with others.

Helping teenagers to make sense of their developing sexual identity is a real struggle for parents. There is certainly a sense of taboo about the issue that can be a real block for both parents and their teenagers. In the chapter where I discuss relationships and sex (Chapter 7), I have included my thoughts about how you can make this process easier. The strongest piece of advice I would give is to begin talking, not just about physical and sexual changes to their bodies and the facts of life but also about relationships, from an early age. Try to tie sexuality into relationships. By being clear about your understanding of sex and relationships and about your values and your beliefs, you will give your teenager a yardstick against which to compare and measure their own experiences.

We parents can often be quite dismissive of the real feelings of love and passion that teenagers feel. Some of our dismissal comes from our own knowledge of just how intense teenage relationships can be and yet how divorced from the reality of a truly sustainable relationship they are. It's tempting to remind our sons and daughters that they actually haven't got a clue about what real relationships involve. There is a huge amount of physicality involved in teenage relationships and this creates quite a magical bubble, which it is very tempting for us to burst.

However, your teenager will move to a stage where they are more concerned with serious relationships and where they have greater capacity for tender and sensual love. If we are too dismissive too often, we may deny teenagers the reality of their experience.

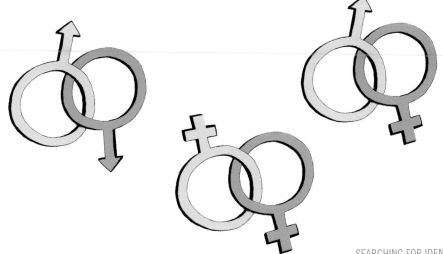

→ Sinéad: Communicating fully about sexuality

As you can imagine, not many teenagers come to me to talk about sex. In fact, despite sex and sexuality being such an integral part of our humanity, it is often a very peripheral part of the therapeutic work that I do. However, there was one girl who was referred to me specifically because sexual behaviour was a big worry for her mum. While I would hope that this girl's experience will not be representative of most teenagers, it does show just how difficult it can be for teenagers to make sense of complex sexual feelings.

I was introduced to Sinéad when she was thirteen years old. Her mum brought her to me because her behaviour seemed totally out of control. Sinéad regularly stayed out all night, hiding from her mother, and refused to abide by any house rules. Of greatest concern to her mum, however, was that Sinéad had a fifteen-year-old boyfriend with whom she claimed she was having a full sexual relationship. Her mum fully believed Sinéad, but did not know who this fifteen-year-old was. During the initial meeting her mum also described that when Sinéad was seven she had been touched, on a few different occasions, on her vaginal area by a neighbouring ten-year-old boy. At that time Sinéad had explained that she was only playing a game. Her mum was terribly upset and gave out severely to Sinéad for letting this boy play such a game with her. She told Sinéad how 'dirty' the game was and that boys are bad and bold and that Sinéad was bold, too, for letting him touch her in that way.

According to her mum, Sinéad was really upset and then sulky for days afterwards, but then settled. In fact, for a few years nothing untoward or noteworthy happened for Sinéad or her mum. Things were good. However, when Sinéad was eleven she began her periods and quickly developed breasts and a very 'shapely' figure, according to her mum. Indeed, when I first met Sinéad she could easily have been mistaken for a fifteen- or sixteen-year-old. The thing that really struck her mum was that almost as soon as puberty kicked in, Sinéad's behaviour began to deteriorate. She became sullen and oppositional and began to disrespect the house rules.

When I first met her, Sinéad projected every inch of that sullen and distrustful teenager that her mum described. It took two sessions for her veneer to soften and for her to show me the world as she saw it. While a lot of our early sessions were focused on her rows with her mum, there wasn't a great deal of connection between Sinéad and me. It was only when I commented about the notable 'telling off' that her mum described when Sinéad was seven that she really looked at me. Then her eyes filled with tears and she looked away again.

Gently we returned to that incident and the incident of touching that had preceded her falling out with her mum. Sinéad was able to describe, in time, how she had blocked that experience from her memory and that it had stayed blocked there until the day her mum spoke to her about her period, when it came. She remembered her mum talking about 'down there', which was the same expression she had used when giving out to Sinéad about being touched. Sinéad recalled feeling a huge amount of shame and then fierce anger towards her mother, all in a short space of time.

By Sinéad's reasoning, the severity of her mum's reaction when she was seven meant that her body must be bad and that she too was bad because she attracted this ten-year-old boy to do 'bold' things with her. This one experience had created a deep well of hurt and shame. Her developing sexuality and the trigger of her mum's reference to 'down there' seemed to have led that well to flood, and it had been flooding actively since she was eleven. It was as if her body and sexual self were again potentially betraying her through their development. As a direct response, she shifted to promiscuity as her means of blocking down and numbing those feelings of shame and hurt. She blamed her mum, too, and so part of her dynamic was to punish her by having numerous sexual relationships with boys.

Sinéad refused to come back and see me after this session. I guess that she felt over-exposed and vulnerable, having talked so openly at age thirteen about her sexuality and sexual feelings. In deference to her vulnerability I spoke with her mum and shared my insights into the possible explanation for her promiscuity and her angry, acting-out behaviour. Her mum was shocked that the incident aged seven had the potential to be so meaningful still. She also felt very guilty about her reaction then, wryly commenting on the fact that if she had known what was to come in terms of Sinéad's sexual behaviour, she would never have over-reacted as she did.

She rang me several months later to say that she and Sinéad had had a very tearful conversation about that incident a few weeks after our last session. She had apologized to Sinéad for her reaction back then and had explained that she was just so fiercely protective of Sinéad, that she didn't want anyone to ever hurt her sexually. Sinéad, apparently, told her that she was deeply ashamed but also terribly hurt by her reaction. Crucially, her mum then responded by saying that none of what had happened was Sinéad's fault. This conversation was a turning point. According to her mum, Sinéad had subsequently settled in school, was coming home at night and had dumped her boyfriend. I don't know how things continued from there.

MORAL AND ETHICAL DEVELOPMENT

I am sure that, at times, it seems like your teenager has no morals or ethics at all. We can easily wonder whether they know the difference between right and wrong. Children of all ages will test limits, but teenagers will also question the rules in a more meaningful way. Of course, even this ability to question the rules reflects a greater cognitive ability and also underlines the fact that they realize that there are rules for the common good that allow societies and groups to function. One of the jobs of teenagers is to try out different roles and to experiment with different ways of being. That means that they may try things that they know go against those rules. This includes things like drinking alcohol, taking drugs, shoplifting or other forms of stealing, lying and so on.

In their early teenage years most youngsters are not guided by their conscience because this is still developing. Rather, they are guided by rewards and consequences for different actions. It is only as they reach fifteen or sixteen and beyond that we might see more consistent evidence of their conscience at work. Around this time they may also develop ideals that they may cling to fiercely and that they might be keen to argue about.

By the time we have reached adulthood, we have usually come to the decision that we are happy to follow social rules and cultural traditions. We will have reached this conclusion either through blind acceptance or because we have searched elsewhere and decided that these are as good as any others as a means to live our life. In the past, I do think that there was a strong element of blind acceptance, particularly in terms of religious values and morals, which many people went on to struggle with at different stages of their adult lives. In theory, these are the very issues that teenagers should be trying to make sense of and decide upon themselves. So by the time our teenagers are reaching their late adolescence, they should be more accepting of the social institutions and cultural traditions within which they live. Ideally, therefore, with their fully developed conscience, they will also self-regulate their behaviour and be mindful of their personal dignity.

The more choice that there is between value systems, belief systems and expectations of personal and group behaviour, the harder it is for teenagers to decide which values and morals they will hold as their own. Some never decide.

But since we don't live in an ideal world, there will be some teenagers who will grow up into adults who continuously challenge the status quo (maybe not a bad thing) or who refuse to accept the social rules and regulations and don't internalize the values that underpin those rules. As with several other areas of development, the conflicting messages that come through the global media make this a more confusing issue for teenagers. The more choice that there is between value systems, belief systems and expectations of personal and group behaviour, the harder it is for teenagers to decide which values and morals they will hold as their own. Some never decide.

We consistently find that most youngsters who may actively challenge and dismiss their parents' point of view and the values that their parents try to live by will actually come to hold very similar value systems in their own adulthood. I think this happens because one of the strongest influences for teenagers is what they see happening around them and how the people close to them act and behave. So if we role-model values like honesty, mutual respect, trust and fairness, then our influence will come to bear on our teenagers. We need to have an element of faith that our voices and our actions will be noticeable and influential in the midst of all the competing voices for the moral and ethical development of our teenagers.

Patricia: The anxiety of a conscience

Patricia was referred to me with exam-related anxiety. She was seventeen years old and at the start of her Leaving Certificate year. According to the letter from her GP, she had had a panic attack about an end-of-week test and had been unable to go into school. The GP also informed me that she had diabetes and that her mother had a progressive neurological disease. On the face of the referral information, my initial thoughts were that she would probably need some anxiety-management techniques and perhaps some help with planning her study in advance of the Leaving Certificate.

What transpired, however, was that Patricia not only was experiencing exam-related anxiety but was also feeling very anxious in social situations. For example, she spoke to me in the quietest, almost whispering voice. She never made eye contact in the first two sessions and for the duration of every session sat with her hands clasped in her lap and her back and shoulders stooped. I commented, early in her first session, that she seemed anxious or at the very least uncomfortable even being in the room. She denied this and, in fairness to her, she answered everything that I asked her, even though she volunteered nothing spontaneously.

What I discovered through my questioning was that Patricia was an extremely conscientious and diligent student. She had huge worries about her mother's health and how the neurological disease might continue to progress. She was exacting in the application of her own insulin schedule for her diabetes and had never, to the best of her knowledge, caused either her mother or her father any concern or distress due to misbehaviour. In fact, she later admitted that she was anxious during her first session, but that she felt she must respond to the questions simply because it would be impolite not to. Here was a girl who was afraid to do anything wrong.

On the face of it, she was every parent's dream teenager: never a day's bother, diligent, respectful and caring. Patricia had obviously internalized some very high expectations of herself and also what was expected of her by other people. She was crippled by these expectations, however. Her fear that she might fail in any undertaking, including friendships, meant that she avoided any situation that might involve risk. Her exam anxieties were about failure, too. In the end, my work with Patricia, contrary to almost every other teenage client that I have ever worked with, focused on getting her to deliberately make mistakes and to experiment. I was hoping that she would come to realize that the world did not end because she was human and consequently imperfect.

Perhaps it was because the intervention was so bizarre that it actually worked. Patricia and I had a good laugh at the outcome of some of her 'experiments'. It was almost as if those around Patricia did not know how to react when she did things 'wrong'. Teachers, for example, did nothing when she told them she hadn't done her homework. (I actually don't think they realized what they were hearing because she'd been so consistent over the previous five years.)

Not having to live by every rule, not having to attain impossibly high standards was very freeing for Patricia. She learned to relax with imperfection. Just like every other teenager, she needed to make some mistakes to realize what she truly valued.

IN CASE OF EMERGENCY . . . KEY POINTS TO REMEMBER

→ Your child's identity will change and solidify over time rather than suddenly appearing, newly minted, one morning.

→ Your job is to provide opportunities for individuation – which is the process of becoming separate from us and less dependent on us – and opportunities for connectedness – which is the process of maintaining a secure base of support and caring.

→ Girls, as a general rule, will start puberty earlier than boys. Many girls have begun the physical changes of puberty at ten years of age, while boys don't start until about thirteen.

→ Even though you may believe that they are aware of what changes are to come, and even though you might want to avoid having 'the talk', it is still really important to ensure that they have the information by checking it out with them.

→ Adolescence marks the beginning of the development of more complex thinking processes.

→ In their early adolescence their focus remains on the here and now or, at best, the near future. As they move into later adolescence, however, their future career becomes more tangible and they begin to think about their future role in life.

→ In adolescence, it's almost as if your teenager becomes confident in their own knowledge and will feel more confident to tell you that you are wrong.

→ Although they have an innate drive to pull away from you and to challenge you, they also miss their contact with you and psychologically, they experience the loss of their relationship with you.

→ Role models become very important for young teenagers.

→ No matter the age at which it starts, we can't stop the juggernaut of their sexual development and the consequent development of their sexuality.

→ The main conflict for boys and girls is often felt in trying to make sense of their sexual orientation.

→ Begin talking, not just about physical and sexual changes to their bodies and the facts of life but also about relationships, from an early age.

→ In their early teenage years most youngsters are not yet guided by their conscience because this is still developing. Rather, they are guided by rewards and consequences for different actions.

→ Most youngsters who may actively challenge and dismiss their parents' point of view and the values that their parents try to live by will actually come to hold very similar value systems in their own adulthood.

2. EFFECTIVE COMMUNICATION

the search for a meaningful 'chat'

Feeling rejected, perhaps ostracized, by your teenager opens up a whole new area of hurt for parents. Can you recall a time of asking your teenager, pleading with them, perhaps, in respect of some behaviour or other: 'Why are you doing this to me?' Perhaps it was their refusal to attend a family gathering, perhaps it was their decision to drop out of school or to remain friends with a child you didn't like. Their response may have been to grunt, turn away or simply ignore you.

The reason that they didn't or, more likely, couldn't answer the question is because they probably didn't actually know what the answer was. They may have had a sense that their behaviour was hurtful for you, but that wasn't a good enough reason to change what they saw as central to who they were at that moment. Perhaps they were defining themselves in their relationships with peers or with school and that seemed more important than the hurt experienced by you.

Yet how can they voice the confusion they may have felt between what they believe to be right and true for them and your desires? How can they deal with the feelings of their parents when they may not even be fully aware of their own feelings? These things are not easy for teenagers. This chapter will show you how, as the parent, you can facilitate your child to talk about and to express some of what is inside. The next chapter will deal specifically with connecting to their emotions.

The miscommunication happens on both sides and it matters least who is at fault for not communicating effectively.

In this chapter on communication I have also focused on skills you can use to improve your ability to listen. I believe that at the heart of a lot of conflict between teenagers and their parents is miscommunication. The miscommunication happens on both sides and it matters least who is at fault for not communicating effectively. What does matter is the potentially devastating outcome of increasing hostility and an inability to resolve problems by talking it out.

We might like to believe that teenagers just stop talking during adolescence, but this isn't true. They do talk, and they talk at great length sometimes, but more often just not to us. Sometimes this is because they feel they may not get a fair hearing. Sometimes this is because they are afraid of how we might respond. Sometimes this is because they know what they are talking about is so outrageous that their shame or guilt prevents them. So, we need to find ways to allow them to say this to us, as well as to others.

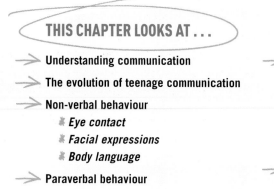

THIS CHAPTER LOOKS AT . . .

→ Understanding communication

→ The evolution of teenage communication

→ Non-verbal behaviour
  * *Eye contact*
  * *Facial expressions*
  * *Body language*

→ Paraverbal behaviour

→ Active listening
  * *Focused attention*
  * *Encouraging*
  * *Reflecting/echoing*
  * *Summarizing/clarifying*
  * *Open questions*

→ A typical teenage scenario

UNDERSTANDING COMMUNICATION

When I think of communication, I think of many more things than simply talking. We have developed many other skills to help us to get our message across. Typically, we use things like non-verbal behaviour and paraverbal behaviour to add extra meaning to what we are saying. Non-verbal behaviour refers to all the things that we do while we're talking, which might include things like eye contact, making gestures, facial expressions and so on. Paraverbal behaviour refers to all the aspects of speech apart from the words that we're using, which includes things like the tone of our voice, the loudness of our voice and the rate or rhythm with which we speak.

Researchers at Cornell University, in America, did some very interesting work that showed that when we are communicating under pressure, we pay less attention to what the person is saying and much more attention to how they are saying it and what they are doing when they are saying it. In fact, 93 per cent of the meaning that we take from the communication comes from the non-verbal and paraverbal behaviour of the person who is speaking. That means that only 7 per cent of the meaning we take from that communication comes from the words we use. In other words, in a typically pressured family communication, such as a row or an argument, what you are saying to your son or daughter doesn't really matter because they are hardly attending to it. You may be trying to tell them some important things about their safety, but they are not attending to the words, instead they are focused on how you look and how you sound while you are saying the words. So while you're giving out to them, they are looking at you and simply thinking, 'Oh, she's angry now!'

Once we realize what's happening, it's easy to see that it's a good idea for us either to take the stress out of the communication so that more attention can get paid to the words that we are using or, alternatively, to be fully in charge of our non-verbal behaviour and the tone of our voice to ensure that we are understood correctly. We rely on non-verbal behaviour and paraverbal behaviour to give us important additional information to help us put the words into context. So, for example, if I were to say to you, 'You are such a devil,' with a big smile on my face and giving you a wink, you would understand that I am joking and that I quite like your 'devilish' ways. If, on the other hand, I were to say to you, 'You are such a devil,' with a frown on my face and a tone of desperation and annoyance in my voice, you would understand that I really do believe you are a devil and that I have had enough of your devilish behaviour.

The non-verbal and paraverbal aspects of communication are so interwoven with speaking that we become very used to having that additional information when we are trying to interpret what is being said to us. Without it, it can be very easy to misunderstand what we are being told.

THE EVOLUTION OF TEENAGE COMMUNICATION

One of the most striking things about teenage communication is that the advent of mobile phones and instant messaging over the internet places far greater emphasis on the words alone. There is no opportunity to read someone's facial expression or hear the tone of their voice in a text message or in a comment on their Bebo page.

There has been a real and very significant shift in communication patterns for teenagers. This much greater emphasis on written communication means teenagers have had to create acronyms in order to add some additional contextual information to what they are texting or instant messaging to each other. So you will see acronyms like 'LOL' (laughing out loud), 'ROFL' (rolling on the floor laughing), 'PML' (pissing myself laughing) and many more. You will also see 'emoticons', which are little faces with emotional expressions like happy, sad, angry, surprised and so on, which can be placed at the end of a sentence or after a particular word. Again, their function is to give you a sense of the tone and the context in which you are to interpret what has been written.

Even with these clues, however, I think it's easy to misinterpret and misunderstand what is meant by texts we receive or by comments that get left on social networking sites. Perhaps this is why teenagers complain about cyber-bullying. It may be that the bare words on a screen get misinterpreted because their context is not clear. Mind you, I also think that the relative anonymity and the emotional disconnection of not being present with the person with whom you are communicating also make it easier to be deliberately hurtful online or in a text message.

I know that some commentators and educators are concerned that the heavy use of shorthand in texting and the slang that has been created on social networking sites is changing the way that teenagers use language. There is no doubt that language is used differently, that it is manipulated and shortened, but it is also, perhaps, made more efficient and more effective as a result. The massive technological advances of the last fifteen years have meant that the current crop of teenagers is

The massive technological advances of the last fifteen years have meant that the current crop of teenagers is growing up with a different set of skills when it comes to communication.

growing up with a different set of skills when it comes to communication. This is a challenge for parents. Parents may not feel as proficient or as comfortable with the technology and so can feel excluded from that aspect of their teenager's life. It is perhaps the case that the skills of communicating online are the next evolution in human communication. So there is also a challenge for us parents to allow ourselves to be educated by our teenagers.

Any evolution is a slow process, however, and that means that just as we become more proficient in online communication, we still need to hold onto our current social communication skills. Importantly, our teenagers need those human, face-to-face skills, too. They need to know how to interpret and use non-verbal behaviour and paraverbal behaviour. They need to know how to actively listen and how to engage in a meaningful conversation. So, in a typical 'two-way-street' fashion, we need to be teaching them about talking and listening. Mostly that teaching will be through our role-modelling and our shaping of their responses to us. Occasionally we may have to be more deliberate and direct in explaining to them how to talk to us in a way that makes it easier to listen to them.

NON-VERBAL BEHAVIOUR

I am going to focus on three aspects of non-verbal behaviour: eye-contact, facial expressions and the rest of the body. The most important thing about non-verbal behaviour is to have an awareness that it is occurring. It's very easy to forget, particularly when we're angry, that we are giving all these additional messages (55 per cent of the meaning of what gets communicated during a row comes from non-verbal behaviour). We need to remember to use non-verbal behaviour to our advantage. We need to make sure that it is transmitting the right message that supports what we want to say and that will give our teenagers a sense of inclusion rather than of rejection or heightened conflict.

EYE CONTACT

Eyes are very important in human communication. Looking at a person who is speaking to you is the most powerful way of showing them that you're focusing your attention on them and that you are listening to them. All too often, because we're busy or distracted, we don't take the time to look at our children when they are talking to us. In many ways, looking at the person who is talking to us is one of the most basic social rules in Western European culture. The expectation is that we will look at the person all of the time that they are speaking. Interestingly, they generally won't be looking at us all of the time they are talking to us. What you will notice is that the talker will mostly look elsewhere and only occasionally glance at you. When they do glance, however, they will want you to be looking at them. So speakers won't look at the listener all of the time (in fact, it is a bit freaky if someone does look at you all the time that they are speaking to you). Try this the next time you are conversing and be aware of looking while you listen, but only occasionally glancing while you talk.

Eyes are very important in human communication. Looking at a person who is speaking to you is the most powerful way of showing them that you're focusing your attention on them and that you are listening to them.

Generally, then, it is a good thing to look at your teenager if they are talking to you and to encourage them to look at you when you're talking to them. This simple act will give both of you a greater sense of being attended to and you're more likely to think that what you're saying is being respected and valued. However, there are certain times when it is not helpful to insist on sustained eye contact from your teenager when you are talking to them. Let me explain.

There are two times when a speaker will make sustained eye contact with the listener. The first time is when you're deeply in love with, and very intimate with, the person to whom you are speaking. Typically, you might remember looking at your husband, wife or partner over a candlelit dining table? Hopefully that wasn't too long ago! You probably both felt at ease in sustaining eye contact, whether you were speaking or listening. Indeed, sometimes you probably didn't feel the need to say anything as you gazed lovingly into each other's eyes.

Therefore, there can be times when, if you insist on your teenager looking at you when you tell them something very important, they may feel a forced intimacy and can actually feel more uncomfortable with the communication. If that's the case, they could end up being more distracted by their discomfort and may not be able to pay attention to what you're saying. Later in the book I deal with the 'facts of life' conversation that we should all have with our children. This is a good example of the kind of conversation where insisting on sustained eye contact will definitely lead to discomfort and could actually inhibit your child from listening carefully to what you say. Indeed, just hearing you mention the words 'penis' and 'vagina' will be discomfort enough for them!

The second time that a speaker will make sustained eye contact with the listener is in times of conflict. You are probably familiar with the situations where you have tried to 'stare someone down'. There is an unwritten understanding between you and the person that you are fighting with that whoever looks away first is the loser. I term this experience the 'conflict eye stare'. Getting locked into a stare in this fashion will generally increase the level of conflict between you and the other person. Be wary, therefore, of those times that you find yourself in conflict with your teenager. Forcing them to look at you while you are angry and accusatory may trigger their own anger and heighten the conflict rather than help with the resolution.

FACIAL EXPRESSIONS

It's actually quite hard to know what your face does when you speak. We are usually so focused on what we are trying to say that we leave our facial expressions to the unconscious workings of our brain. What do you think you look like when you're angry? Could you make me your typical angry face if I asked you? I'm guessing that you couldn't. I would also guess that your son or daughter could give me a perfect mimic of what you look like when you're angry. Of course, none of us spends much time looking in the mirror when we're talking, nor do we often get to see ourselves on video. Part of the reason most of us get freaked when we do see ourselves on video is because we really aren't aware of how we portray ourselves while talking.

Because our facial expressions are typically an unconscious behaviour, it takes great awareness and great practice to take back conscious control when we are communicating. The time when having conscious control is most helpful with our teenagers is when we are responding to the things they tell us. Some of the things that they might tell us are shocking, shameful, annoying, disgusting or distressing. You can be sure that your true emotional response to what is being said will register first in your facial expression and only afterwards might you consciously respond in a controlled or deliberate way, perhaps to mask your true feelings. So, if your sixteen-year-old daughter is telling you that she is pregnant, then your shock, and perhaps your shame, will be written all over your face. Your daughter will probably pick up, quite correctly, that you're ashamed and this might colour all of your future conversations about her pregnancy.

Generally, I think it's a good idea to be expressive about our feelings. I think it's good that our children and our teenagers know clearly when we're sad or when we're angry, scared or distressed. Indeed, I usually encourage parents to label their own feelings to teach their children about recognizing feelings. When you describe your feelings, verbally, to your child or teenager they learn the words that are associated with that feeling. This means that they then have the right language that they can use to describe a similar feeling that they might have themselves.

But there are two feelings that I think are really unhelpful for our teenagers to receive as a response from parents. Those feelings are shame and disgust. It adds nothing to their experience to know that we are ashamed or disgusted by them. It can only detract from their self-esteem and will create barriers to supportive communication. You can be pretty sure that if the event they are describing is shameful or disgusting, they are already feeling those feelings and don't need ours to be heaped on top. So, unlike the majority of our feelings, to which we should expose our children, I would encourage you to mask those particular feelings from them. You might need to get a good handle on your facial expressions in order to achieve this. Try speaking to the mirror so you can rehearse!

Our simplest task with our bodily gestures is to use them to encourage our teenagers to talk to us, rather than discourage them from talking to us.

BODY LANGUAGE

Most of us make regular gestures as we speak. Typically, we might shrug our shoulders, wag an index finger, either shake or nod our head, impatiently tap a foot, deliberately turn our back to someone or even walk off and slam the door in our wake. As with all non-verbal behaviour, these bodily gestures are sending information to the person with whom we are communicating. Our simplest task with our bodily gestures is to use them to encourage our teenagers to talk to us, rather than discourage them from talking to us. For example, nodding gives a message of acceptance and/or understanding, whereas shaking your head will give them a clear message that you disagree or are rejecting what they are saying.

Physically turning to face your teenager when they start to talk to you is a powerful and encouraging act. Just like making eye contact, it shows that you're attending to them. Importantly, you can't even make eye contact unless you're facing them. It is interesting, though, that sometimes they will choose occasions to tell us things when they know that we can't attend to them in this physically demonstrative way. Classically, when you are driving the car is a moment that they will often choose to tell you something important. This happens because, while they want you to hear (they have you as a captive audience), they may not want to have to witness your reaction. If they fear scorn, rejection, shame or disgust in response to what they tell you, then it is easier if you are looking out the windscreen and they can turn to look out the passenger window.

When we want to talk to teenagers it's important that we move to where they are. Calling your children is usually a pointless task. Mostly, they have learned that you don't really mean business until you come and get them. What happens for most of us is that the first few times we call our children, they ignore us. Then our frustration builds because we are being ignored and it finally reaches a point at which we stop calling them and we storm into the room where they are, to physically get them. So rather than waste your energy on shouting pointlessly at your teenagers, you may only have to say what you need once if you go to find them first and say it.

You may have heard people talking about the concept of 'personal space'. This refers to the proximity between us and the other person we are talking to. Usually, we need to be physically and emotionally intimate with someone in order to be very close to them when we talk to them. Most of us will have our younger children cuddle up to us while they talk about troubles in their lives. Small children don't really take personal space into consideration and so will regularly get up close, even with strangers on occasions. Teenagers, however, are struggling to come to terms with their changing bodies, with their developing sexuality and with their understanding of relationships. So don't be surprised if your teenager seems to need more personal space than they did when they were smaller. Don't be disheartened if your teenager seeks to be more physically distant from you. It may be that their changing comfort with proximity is indeed a non-verbal message to 'back off', but it might also mean that they are simply trying to work out where they stand (literally and figuratively) with you.

PARAVERBAL BEHAVIOUR

Paraverbal behaviour refers to all of the aspects of speech apart from the words that you use. It incorporates your tone of voice, the rate and rhythm of your speech and the loudness of your speech. Paraverbal behaviour is very difficult to describe in written form. By its nature, it is all to do with sound and how we hear speech. So, I would like you to imagine you are having a conversation with your own teenager. I am going to tell you what to say and I will add in brackets the way in which I want you to say it. If you actually read the conversation out loud, you will find it easier to hear how you change your tone, your inflection and the way in which the words come out. If you feel up to it, I have also given you the manner in which your teenager is probably responding, so you could practise a little play or drama all by yourself.

>**You:** *So how did things go at your friend's house last night? (Genuinely open question, asked in a neutral way)*

>**Teenager:** *Yeah . . . it was cool. (Evasive and somewhat abrupt)*

>**You:** *What DVD did you watch? (Persistent, not willing to be put off or closed out)*

>**Teenager:** *Oh . . . eh . . . eh . . . I'm not sure what it was called. (Caught off-guard, surprised)*

>**You:** *You did watch a DVD. (Said as a statement, inviting them to prove you wrong)*

>**Teenager:** *Yeah, yeah, of course we did . . . sure, what else were we going to do? (Trying to be calm and playing for time)*

>**You:** *I don't know. What else were you going to do? (Provocative and suggesting that you might know that they were up to other things than simply watching a DVD)*

>**Teenager:** *Yes . . . no . . . nothing . . . what's with all the questions anyway? (Flustered and showing a little bit of anger, as if attack might be the best form of defence)*

>**You:** *Oh, no reason particularly . . . I'm just interested to know how you got on last night. (Pretending you have no agenda and feigning a desire to be connected to them)*

>**Teenager:** *Yeah, right. (Completely incredulous and sarcastic)*

>**You:** *Why, is there anything I should be interested in? (Probing)*

>**Teenager:** *Look . . . nothing happened! We just watched a DVD and had a laugh. (Definitive – trying to close off the conversation)*

>**You:** *Okay, you know I just worry about you whenever you go out. (Warm, conciliatory, not really wanting to fight)*

>**Teenager:** *Yeah . . . whatever. (Dismissive) I can look after myself. (Determined and forceful)*

>**You:** *I know you can look after yourself, but I still worry about you because I care about you and because I will always help if you need it. (Genuine warmth and caring)*

>**Teenager:** *Yeah . . . I suppose. Look, I'm not getting mad; I'm just tired because we were up late chatting. (Gentler, more accommodating)*

>**You:** *Yeah, it's always good to have time to talk to friends. But if I'm being truly honest, I worry that you are going to be drinking or smoking dope when you're with your friends. (Harder edge)*

>**Teenager:** *Look, I don't do that stuff. You just have to trust me. (Emphatic)*

>**You:** *Yes I do have to trust you. (Resigned. Wishing that you didn't have to trust, but just know)*

>**Teenager:** *Yeah well . . . all right then . . . I'm going to have a shower to freshen up. (Grateful, thankful that the conversation is coming to an end)*

>**You:** *All right, you know I love you and here I am again, trusting you that you didn't do drugs or anything. But just mind yourself. (Hopeful and suggestive)*

>**Teenager:** *Yeah, I know . . . thanks, I guess. (Genuine)*

I have done something similar in sessions where I get teenagers to take on the role of their parents and vice versa. I get them to play out a scenario like this one, from their real life, but they act as each other. It is often hilarious to hear the mimicry and the subsequent disbelief in either the parent's or the teenager's voice as they think, 'I don't speak like that!' but in reality they do! It is yet another lesson that we really do need to pay attention not just to what we communicate but to how we communicate.

That conversation could have gone any number of ways depending on how the parent chose to respond to the slightly dismissive, angry and defensive tones of the teenager. You may feel that the parent is none the wiser about what happened at the friend's house and you are right. But maybe their goal was never to actually hear about the detail of the night (how realistic is it to expect to hear everything anyway?). But what the parent has achieved by the end is ongoing communication with their son or daughter. The issue of trust and the fact that their relationship does involve mutual trust has also been reconfirmed. These are important and positive outcomes from a conversation, especially as the door to future communication is also wide open.

Hopefully you have had fun acting out the roles above. If you have spoken them out loud, then you will also have a clearer sense of how vital are the paraverbal tone and manner of our speech.

ACTIVE LISTENING

There are several important skills we can use to show our teenagers that we are listening to what they say, which gives them the crucial message that what they say is important, valuable and being attended to. Teenagers regularly complain about not being respected and not being listened to. It is true that sometimes we don't credit their observations, opinions and views about different subjects. But other times, even when we do believe in what they are saying, we find it hard to show them that we are heeding them. Active listening gets around this difficulty. It is also a central skill in negotiating with your teenager, resolving conflicts with them and assisting them to make decisions. Really listening to them is a challenge, too, because when we truly hear what they have to say we might have to respond. This means that we might have to let them influence us rather than us being the people to influence them.

Sometimes we may think that listening is a passive task; after all you are just sitting there while somebody else is doing the work. The reality is that listening is not passive at all. As listeners there are things we can do to encourage the talker to keep talking and to demonstrate that we are hearing them. The particular active listening skills I am going to focus on are: focused attention; encouraging; reflecting/echoing; summarizing/clarifying; and using open questions.

FOCUSED ATTENTION

The first step to showing that you are listening to someone is to focus your attention on them. If you think back to some of the things we talked about in using our non-verbal behaviour, you will recall that the easiest way to give focused attention is to turn to face the person who's talking and look them in the eye. It may mean that you stop whatever other task you were doing. It may mean that you ask other people around to be quiet. It may also mean that you have to be quiet yourself.

> The first step to showing that you are listening to someone is to focus your attention on them.

The experience of being attended to in this way is very powerful for any child or teenager. The reality is that we can't give them our focused attention all of the time, so in the times when we are going to give it to them we may as well be 100 per cent focused. Sometimes, like in the example of driving I referred to above, simply being present and being unable to withdraw or get away from the conversation is enough.

Ensuring focused attention by your teenager to what you are saying is often the antidote to those youngsters who never seem to take 'no' for an answer. If you have been negotiating something with your teenager and you have reached a point at which you have to agree to disagree, you will usually make the final decision. Because they may not like that decision, they are likely to continuously try to re-open the negotiation in the hope of wearing you down and getting you to change your mind. This is a time to sit down with them. Get rid of any other children for a few minutes and ensure that there are no other distractions. Then, looking them in the eye, be clear about your 'no'. Repeat your reasoning for why you are saying 'no' and explain that this is the final discussion of the matter. Because you can be sure they have heard both the decision and the reasons, you are justified in subsequently ignoring all future attempts to talk about the issue further.

ENCOURAGING

When we are listening to someone, we instinctively make encouraging noises and gestures to indicate to the other person that we'd like them to keep talking. Examples of this are nodding your head, smiling, saying 'uh huh' and 'I know'. These may seem like tiny things, but without them the experience of a talker is lessened.

In our society and culture we have become so used to this that sometimes if we don't get this kind of feedback, we think that somebody has stopped listening. The easiest example of this might be when you are on the telephone and suddenly realize that, as you are talking, there is a complete silence on the other end of the line. This is the point at which many of us will stop talking to check if the other person is still there. And in response, the other person quickly goes, 'yeah, yeah I was just listening . . . ' But we don't actually expect listening to be silent.

In some of the workshops that I run for parents and professionals working with children and teenagers, I get them to practise all the skills of communication. One of the exercises involves sitting in pairs, with their backs to each other. One person of each pair is designated as the 'talker' and I ask them to talk about, for example, the last holiday that they were on. The other person is designated as the 'listener' and they are instructed to not make any sound or any movement while the 'talker' is talking (remember they have their back to the 'talker', too). I give all the pairs five minutes to 'chat'.

In the exercise, when the 'listeners' give no encouragement (either verbal or non-verbal), most 'talkers' dry up after about a minute. At the end of the exercise I get the group to discuss the experience. During this discussion, the 'talkers' usually describe how difficult it was to keep talking when they felt the other person wasn't listening. They explain that they didn't feel listened to because they were getting no feedback and, importantly, no encouragement from the listener.

Another great experiment was carried out in an American university. A large class of students were enrolled as active participants. Their lecturers were not informed of the experiment. Before their first lecturer arrived, the students in the lecture theatre were split into two groups; the group on the Right and the group on the Left. The Rights were told to give lots of focused attention and encouragement to the lecturer. They were told to make lots of eye contact, nod in response to the lecturer's comments, be obvious in their note-taking and so on. The Lefts were told to ignore the lecturer, keep their eyes downcast, take no notes and show no sign of interest in what was being said.

Once the lecture was underway, the experimenters observed that very quickly the lecturers reciprocated the ignoring behaviour of the Lefts and focused entirely on the Rights. If they lectured from behind the podium, they were observed to only look up to the right. If they walked while lecturing, they only walked within the confines of the right-hand side of the theatre and, similarly, only looked up to the students on the right. The lecturers were demonstrating, unknowingly, that we invest our communication energy in those that we believe are interested and listening to us.

The message in this for us parents is that if we don't obviously encourage our teenagers to talk to us, they may believe that we are not interested in them. If this is the case, then it can only add to any feelings of alienation from us that might come with individuation. As they drift further away, our communication with them will become more of a struggle.

REFLECTING/ECHOING

When our children and teenagers talk to us, we find ourselves frequently repeating what they are saying. Sometimes it is an exact replication of what they say and other times it is a variation on it. In terms of communication skills, these are known as echoing (repeating exactly) and reflecting (saying back a slight variation of what was said to you). Doing this may seem a pointless task and not much of a way to communicate. In fact, it is a great help to someone talking as it tells them that you have heard them. After all, if you can repeat something, you must have heard it.

With tiny babies we reflect and echo almost constantly. It is part of the turn-taking that we engage in with babies: they 'goo, goo', we 'goo, goo' back at them. Indeed, with small babies we also echo their physical movements.

I rely heavily on echoing and reflecting in my work with teenagers. Most of the teenagers who are brought to see me are reluctant attendees. They usually don't choose to come, but rather have been brought because their parents want them 'fixed'. So when they get to my office, they can often look sullen and are frequently unresponsive or monosyllabic in their responses. The only comforting thing in this is that I am aware of it and am almost expecting it (to the point that a teenager who wants to talk is a very pleasant experience), and so I don't take their lack of engagement personally. But what I do find is that echoing is often the perfect avenue to get a conversation going, even with the most resistant of teenagers. Let me show you how I use it in my work.

We'll use the example of a fifteen-year-old lad called Paul (not his real name) who was brought to me. Usually, after a short meeting with the teenager and his parents together, I invite his parents to leave while I have a chat with the young lad on his own. Paul's parents spent the initial, joint part of the session complaining about Paul's lack of interest in school, his regular truanting, his drinking around the town with other truants and his frequent argumentative and provocative rows with them at home. Paul sat through this with his eyes downcast and his shoulders slumped. He occasionally threw a sharp look at either his mother or father as they described particular examples of his truancy or drinking. He sighed loudly as they described the rows. When I asked him if his parents' description was fair, he managed a 'suppose so' response while looking into his lap.

When his parents left us alone, I asked Paul to tell me about school. There was a long pause while I just waited for his answer. Eventually it came. 'It's all right' was his response. 'It's all right?' I echoed, but note my tone of questioning. 'Yeah, it's all right,' he confirmed. 'So,' I said emphatically, 'school is all right!' Paul looked up at me at this point and I was able to match his gaze with a bit of (I hoped) an encouraging smile. He looked both puzzled and a bit frustrated, but said nothing. 'Is school more all right-good or all right-bad?' I asked. He shrugged his shoulders, 'More bad, I suppose'. Again I echoed, 'So you suppose school is more bad.' Then I added a reflection, 'I'd say there are bad times and that you find it hard to be there sometimes.' In response, Paul seemed a bit cross because he said in an accusatory tone, 'Well, of course! You heard my parents; I'm forever mitching!' I had just stated the obvious, so I could see why he was a bit cross, but I was also pleased because this was the most information he had volunteered spontaneously.

So I went back to echoing, 'Yeah, you're forever mitching.' Then, before he could say anything, I added a little ponder out loud: 'I wonder why that is.' There was a long pause then. I looked at Paul, who seemed to be having a bit of an internal struggle (probably about whether or not to respond). Then he looked back at me. 'I'll tell you why,' he said, 'because school is shit and the teachers are all muppets!' He sat more upright at that point, as if to challenge me to deny his claim. I actually said nothing, just nodded and waited. After a couple of seconds he continued. 'Nobody treats you well there. They treat you like dirt as if you are not as good as them. Just because they're the teachers they think they can say anything to you. I hate when people look down on me like that. I'm just never going to put up with that shit!' and suddenly our session took off . . .

Part of the strength of echoing is the tone of voice you can add to whatever it is that the other person says. You can make your repetition sound understanding or incredulous, warm or critical. Obviously, for it to be encouraging to your teenager, you need to keep your echoes understanding, warm and occasionally questioning, but with a tone that says, 'please-tell-me-more-because-I-am-interested-to-know-this-and-understand-it-better'.

SUMMARIZING/CLARIFYING

This is another skill we commonly use in talking, but of which we're probably not aware. When someone chats away to us, we often will stop them and check bits of the story out. Examples might be, 'Really? He said that?' or 'So first you stood out of your chair and then the teacher gave out to you?' or 'Tell me again the order of events.'

Teenagers rarely tell you about an event as a narrative. In other words, it rarely starts at a beginning, has a definite middle and then comes to an endpoint. What usually happens is that they tell you bits of a story. Depending on the topic, it may only be the bits of the story that you actually ask them about (perhaps they are operating on a strictly 'need to know' basis!). You do have to ask them questions about what you are hearing, either to check the credibility or simply to ensure that you're hearing it right.

If you remember, I spoke about texting and the potential for misinterpreting a text because things like tone of voice or non-verbal behaviours aren't there to provide the context. Even when we are physically present with someone, we can still make errors of interpretation. Summarizing and clarifying allow you to check if your understanding of the story being told to you is correct. The potential for conflict to arise from a misunderstanding or a miscommunication is quite high, so practise checking about the narrative that you heard but also about the meaning of that narrative.

OPEN QUESTIONS

I have a bit of a thing about questions. Even though I have just been advocating asking your teenager questions to clarify what they are telling you, I often feel that questioning them is a bit stressful. There is a social expectation that if you ask someone a question, they must answer it. This puts pressure on the person to whom you pose the question.

When we do ask questions, I believe we should always try to ask open questions. Open questions are questions that have unlimited potential for answering. The opposite of this, a closed question, is a question that requires a simple 'yes/no' answer. It is amazing how often we ask closed questions. For example: 'Did you knock over the milk?' 'Are you Irish?' 'Do you like sugar in your tea?' The same examples rephrased as open questions would be: 'Who knocked over the milk?' 'Where are you from?' 'How do you like your tea?'

A short way to remember the difference is that open questions begin with the five 'w's (and an 'h'): who, what, where, why, when and how. They are important because, as the name suggests, they open up conversations. Closed questions, on the other hand, can close down conversations. When we converse, one of the skills of encouraging someone to talk is to ask questions that seek them to expand on a topic or to clarify a topic. Open questions do this more effectively than closed questions.

When we converse, one of the skills of encouraging someone to talk is to ask questions that seek them to expand on a topic or to clarify a topic. Open questions do this more effectively than closed questions.

A TYPICAL TEENAGE SCENARIO

So, how do you put all of this together in the real world of your communication with your teenager? Talking to teenagers is fraught at times. We feel we get so little spontaneous information from them that we are forever asking them questions, just to feel like we are still involved in their lives. This can leave them feeling harangued and nagged. Not only that, but we frequently ask our teenagers questions that we already know the answer to, and where only one answer is acceptable. This means that our youngsters are in a potentially difficult situation. They know they should answer us, but if the true answer is not what we are expecting, or hoping, to hear, then they may disappoint or anger us. Do they take the risk of being truthful, even though it might get them into even greater trouble? Or do they lie, so that we are not disappointed in them?

We hate the idea of our teenagers lying to us. The reality, though, is that sometimes not knowing the full truth actually protects us. As long as they are safe, we may be better off not knowing how close they came to danger. Also, if we are honest with ourselves, we too tell occasional lies for lots of reasons, like avoiding hurting someone's feelings, or to avoid getting ourselves into trouble, or to protect someone else from getting into trouble, or because we believe that in some way the benefit of lying outweighs the cost of telling the truth. Teenagers make exactly the same judgements in deciding how much of the truth to tell.

So, by way of summarizing what we now know about communication, I have created an example for you. We'll play the example twice, first in an ineffective communication style and then in a more effective communication style.

Imagine the scene – your fourteen-year-old daughter, Yvonne, has just started second year in secondary school. She had a very uneventful first year and you felt she settled in well. Recently, though, she has struck up a close friendship with a girl in her class called Michelle. They have been inseparable since the summer holidays. Then you get a call from Yvonne's year head to say that Yvonne had a huge row with Michelle during Geography class and the teacher thought that Yvonne struck Michelle, who retaliated in kind. The year head had to put the two of them in detention. As far as the school is concerned, the incident is dealt with, but they felt they had to inform you of the incident and the detention.

You are understandably distressed because you have never had a bad report from school. You had been wondering for a while about the influence Michelle has on Yvonne, since Yvonne has been ruder and more provocative in recent weeks. You had a huge row with her at the weekend and you feel she is getting a bit too big for her boots. During the row you told her how you felt about Michelle and you accused Michelle of being a bit underhand and two-faced. Yvonne hasn't really talked to you since.

So, you wait, impatiently, for Yvonne to come home from school. When she comes in, you get straight down to it and I imagine the conversation might go something like this (I have added the unspoken subtext in brackets).

>**You:** *How was school? (I'd like her to tell me in her own words about the fight and the detention)*

>**Yvonne:** *Grand. (She needn't think I've forgotten about the weekend and I have no intention of firing her up again by telling her about the hassle in school today)*

>**You:** *Grand was it? Nothing major to report? (Come on, you know there is stuff to own up to)*

>**Yvonne:** *No. (I'll try gambling that she doesn't know the truth because how could she know anyway?)*

>**You:** *Are you sure? (God, that is such a blatant lie. That makes me so mad but I'll give her one final chance to be truthful, even though she doesn't deserve it)*

>**Yvonne:** *Yeah, I'm sure. (I can't admit to lying now, that'll just make her mad)*

>**You:** *Nothing at all? (I hope she hears the scepticism in my voice!)*

>**Yvonne:** *No. (Uh-oh, there's trouble ahead, she must know something)*

>**You:** *So you didn't have a fight with anyone? (At last we'll get the truth out there)*

>**Yvonne:** *(Just gives a shrug and looks away, knowing that all is lost)*

>**You:** *Look at me while I'm talking to you. I know you were fighting today, and with Michelle, your year head told me. Did you do it? (You know I can't bear be lied to and yet here you are, blatantly lying to my face)*

>**Yvonne:** *Yeah, maybe. (I guess I have no choice but to admit it now, maybe it'll take the sting out of her anger)*

>**You:** *So why are you lying to me, you know I can't bear to be lied to? Lying is the most despicable thing you can do! (I know why you lied; I just want to hear you say it)*

>**Yvonne:** *Dunno (Well if you can't work it out, I'm not telling you)*

>**You:** *And what are you fighting with Michelle for, even though to be honest I don't like her? (I never get anywhere with her lying, I'd better go back to her behaviour in school)*

>**Yvonne:** *Dunno. (Just get the punishment over with, you are obviously not interested in hearing the real story and you probably wouldn't believe me anyway)*

>**You:** *How come you never talk to me any more? You just lie. Well I have had enough of your lies for today. If you can't own up to what goes on, then maybe you should just sit in your room until you feel like telling me the truth for once. Now, go on, get out of my sight.*

>**Yvonne:** *(Screams) You wouldn't listen to me even if I did tell you! (Storms off to her room, slamming doors all the way)*

At this point I guess that Yvonne and you both feel completely wound up. All of your questioning had been designed to catch her in the lie, which you did, but it was to no avail. Your relationship with her is worse than it was. You are no closer to having any insight into her friendship with Michelle or why she is acting so angrily of late. Instead, you and she are further polarized and it will be harder than ever for you to build the bridge back to Yvonne.

We are going to replay the example, but in this second version you are going to try a different tack. Imagine a conversation like this.

>**You:** *I got a call from your year head today. She told me that you had a big fight with Michelle and they put the two of you in detention during the break. What was that all about? (Even though I feel so cross with her these days, I do still see that this is really untypical behaviour)*

>**Yvonne:** *Oh God, I didn't know if you would hear. (I really don't want a replay of the row at the weekend. Why are you getting into this?)*

>**You:** *I'm glad I heard. I was worried about you. (I'm always worried about you, but you think I am just nosy most of the time)*

>**Yvonne:** *Well, there was just stuff going on. (God, please don't make me spell it out – I can't see you liking it)*

>**You:** *There was stuff going on? (I'll let her explain in her own words)*

>**Yvonne:** *Yeah. (Pauses) Michelle was being really bitchy. (Maybe she is really listening this time)*

>**You:** *Michelle was being bitchy and you sound like you got provoked.*

>**Yvonne:** *Well, she was calling me horrible names! (Anybody would have been provoked by her. I hate to admit it, but I think you are right she is two-faced and devious)*

>**You:** *That can't have been nice. Could you not have ignored her? (I thought we had it well drilled in to you to ignore that kind of stuff, responding only ever makes it worse)*

>**Yvonne:** *I did ignore her, but she didn't stop.*

>**You:** *So she was calling you names and even though you didn't retaliate, she didn't stop. I'd say you were getting mad, though.*

>**Yvonne:** *Yeah, she has no right to call me names. (I thought she was a good friend but actually she is just a back-stabber)*

>**You:** *No, she has no right. Even still, it doesn't give you the right to hit her either.*

>**Yvonne:** *Yeah, I guess so. I didn't mean to hit her, but suddenly she started saying nasty things about you and I couldn't let her get away with that!*

>**You:** *Wow, so you were upholding my honour? (I shouldn't be pleased that she hit another girl but it is nice to know that I am still important to her)*

>**Yvonne:** *Yeah, I guess. (I feel a bit embarrassed now – who would have thought that I would put my mum before my friend?)*

>**You:** *You know that I believe hitting other people is wrong, but sometimes we have to make difficult choices. You had to make a choice between being disrespected and trying to make it stop. Not an easy place to find yourself. Was the choice you made the right one?*

>**Yvonne:** *Maybe. It certainly shut Michelle up. But I got a detention and I am on a report card now, so all the teachers will be keeping a closer eye on me.*

>**You:** *I guess you'll just have to make sure to behave well until the report card is over; it is only for a week, isn't it?*

>**Yvonne**: *Yeah, that's all.*

>**You:** *What about you and Michelle?*

>**Yvonne:** *I don't really care about her. If she can be that mean, then maybe we're better off not being friends.*

>**You:** *Maybe indeed. Thanks for standing up for me. I know we fight a bit these days, but I never stop loving you.*

>**Yvonne:** *You're all right. (Let's not get too sentimental here!)*

>**You:** *Right so, I'd better go and get the dinner sorted.*

>**Yvonne:** *Yeah, thanks so.*

>**You:** *Thanks so. (I hope her dad doesn't lose the plot when he comes in)*

In this version, you were explicit about what was alleged to have happened in the class so that both you and Yvonne knew where you were starting from. All the way through you tried to see things from her perspective, or at least to give her a chance to explain things in her own words. By simply repeating and summarizing what Yvonne said, you were able to get a complete picture of what happened, from her viewpoint. Who knows if what you heard from Yvonne was the full truth? What is actually more important is that by not getting into 'truth and lies', you stayed focused on the incident in school and now have a much better understanding of what probably happened. Also, and more importantly, you and Yvonne have reconnected since your fight at the weekend. She is likely to have felt supported and understood by you and therefore is much more likely in the future to come to you with a problem or an issue.

I have used this example to show that you can use lots of different communication skills, from across the range of active listening, to understand and resolve the situation. Both you and your daughter leave the conversation feeling satisfied and listened to and neither of you is frustrated or angry.

IN CASE OF EMERGENCY . . . KEY POINTS TO REMEMBER

→ The calmer you are in talking to your teenager the more likely they are to pay attention to what you are saying.

→ Typically, we use things like non-verbal behaviour and tone of voice to add extra meaning to what we are saying.

→ There is no opportunity to read someone's facial expression or hear the tone of their voice in a text message or in a comment on their Bebo page, so teenagers may be placing far more emphasis on the words alone.

→ Importantly, our teenagers still need those human, face-to-face skills, too. They need to know how to interpret and use non-verbal behaviour and tone of voice.

→ Making eye contact is one of the easiest and most important ways of showing someone that you are listening to them.

→ You can be sure that your true emotional response to what is being said will register first in your facial expression.

→ Our simplest task with our bodily gestures is to use them to encourage our teenagers to talk to us, rather than discourage them from talking to us.

→ We don't actually expect listening to be silent and so it is helpful to make encouraging sounds and gestures like 'uh-huh' or 'I know …' and nodding and smiling.

→ Echoing, simply repeating what has been said to you, is often the perfect avenue to get a conversation going, even with the most resistant of teenagers.

→ The potential for conflict to arise from a misunderstanding or a miscommunication is quite high, so practise checking out what is said by summarizing and clarifying.

→ Avoid trying to trap your teenager in a lie by questioning them about things you already know – be upfront about your knowledge and invite them to explain further what happened from their perspective.

3. UNDERSTANDING FEELINGS

how to make sense of the white-knuckle ride of teenage emotions

Modern society feels like a very changed place, even in comparison to the society that I grew up in. The pressures on young people today, while not necessarily harder, are certainly different. The increased exposure to media like television and the internet has changed the perceptions and expectations of many children and teenagers. The world seems smaller and more accessible, virtually, at least, if not in reality.

Other pressures come to bear on teenagers, pressures associated with their family and pressures from society and their peers. Family separation is a growing problem for many teenagers, and learning to cope with the changed relationships and new family configurations can be a difficult task. Other life changes, like moving house, bereavements and changing school (for example, moving from primary to secondary school), can also be difficult experiences for children and teenagers. Trying to fit in with friends or, worse, being excluded and bullied by peers can also be very hard for teenagers.

The one thing we can be certain of is that your son or daughter will have strong feelings in response to any or all of these experiences. What we can be less certain of is how well they will cope with those feelings. A lot of the examples of things that can happen to teenagers, like those I have given just now, are environmental. That is to say, they are things that happen in the physical and social world of our teens. Internally, your adolescent is also struggling to cope with their own changed body, their emerging sexuality and their changing intellectual and social interests. Again, these personal events and maturing developments will all lead to feelings. If your son or daughter can't make sense of those feelings, then those feelings could get quite stuck. In my experience, youngsters who have intense feelings that are trapped and unprocessed or unresolved tend to blow off the emotional pressure in their behaviour. Consequently, that behaviour is often of the most challenging kind for parents to try to deal with.

What I want to do here is to show you why and how helping your teenager to deal with those feelings can radically reduce their challenging behaviour and allow them to grow and develop into emotionally mature adults who can be more in charge not just of their feelings but of their behaviour, too. Throughout the chapter I will return to this concept of being in charge of, or managing, your feelings. I am not referring in these instances to controlling feelings in a blocking or blunting fashion. Rather, when I talk about this concept of 'being in charge of' feelings, I am referring to being able to understand and regulate those feelings. So rather than raw feelings leading directly to unplanned action, I want your teenager to be able to recognize their feelings and to be attuned to them so that they can respond with feeling as opposed to responding because of feeling.

THIS CHAPTER LOOKS AT . . .

→ **The link between feelings and behaviour**

→ **Emotional congruence**

→ **Regulating emotions**

→ **Emotional intelligence**

→ **The impact of not sorting out feelings**

→ **The impact of stress, pressure and trauma**
    ❋ *Healthy distraction*
    ❋ *Unhealthy distraction*

→ **Emotional support**

THE LINK BETWEEN FEELINGS AND BEHAVIOUR

I think there is a strong inter-relationship between feelings, behaviour, thinking and our physical well-being. In many ways they operate like interconnected cogs in a system, such that when one changes, it has a knock-on effect on the others. Also, they are all affected by the environment around us – experiences we have in the world may affect one or more areas and lead to a shift in thinking, feeling, behaviour or physical health, either separately or all together. When I talk about 'environment' in this context I refer to a range of factors that impact on a person. So it includes things like the physical environment they live in, like the kind of home or school they are part of. It includes the community of friends, family and other people that surround them. It also includes the wider social, political and media influences that may affect someone.

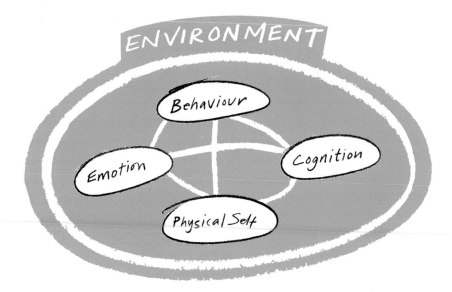

A model for understanding the interconnection between key aspects of our being.

In the diagram above, I have tried to represent this graphically to give you a clearer sense of what I mean. An example may serve the same purpose. Imagine that your fourteen-year-old daughter shoplifted with her friends. This was behaviour that you feel was totally out of character for her. You came to know about it because you got a call from the shop manager to say that their security guard had stopped her outside the shop with €40 worth of make-up that she had not paid for in her bag.

This single incident could trigger a change in mood where your daughter becomes uncommunicative and withdrawn. You know she feels guilty for her actions because she was very upset on the day and expressed how wrong her actions were. However, she felt she had to do it as all the girls in her clique had shoplifted and it was almost like a badge of honour for the members of the group that they had stolen things.

As the weeks pass, you notice that she becomes more secretive about her phone calls, texts and her whereabouts. She starts to lose weight and changes her style of clothes, looking more and more 'trampy' in your eyes. When you challenge her about her withdrawal from the family and her rapid change of style, she gets angry with you, screaming at you to mind your own business, that she will make up her own mind about her life. It is a far cry from the thoughtful girl who used to love your opinion about how she looked and what she should do. You can still remember that she even used to share confidences about boys she fancied.

In this situation the cogs in the system have started to turn in very different and worrying directions from where they began. It can seem like your daughter has taken on a new personality. But the relative influences of how she thinks, feels and acts become clearer when taken together with her physical well-being and the environment in which she lives.

When we are faced with major changes like this in the mood or behaviour of our teenagers, we inevitably want to help them to change. We want to influence them to return to more social, participative, positive and healthy paths. In the past, when they were smaller and younger, the temptation was always there to influence them by focusing on their behaviour. We spent many years managing their behaviour with the promise of reward or the threat of consequence. Many times these approaches were effective, sometimes not. In adolescence, however, the effects of behaviour-management strategies lose much of their power. Either we can't find the right motivators or our teenagers use their growing sense of self and their own power to directly challenge us. So we might insist that they don't leave the house to meet a friend, and they walk past us brazenly. We demand that they study and apply themselves, and they laugh at us.

So if we have less impact, behaviourally, on our teenagers, how do we influence them? I feel the answer lies in connecting to their emotional world. The more we understand the feelings of our youngsters, the more we can help them to understand their own feelings and, if necessary, change those feelings. With that change we should subsequently see a knock-on, positive effect in their thinking and behaviour because of the inter-relationship of these elements.

Robin: From sporting injury to depression

I never worked with Robin in a formal sense. Rather his mum was the friend of a friend. That mutual friend told me about Robin and he remained, in my mind, a salutary example of just how easily one small change in circumstance can have a big impact in other areas. Through the intercession of our mutual friend I did speak to Robin's mum about his situation, just before things started to improve again.

Robin, aged sixteen, had been training really hard for his club hurling team. The club championship was approaching and he had his heart set on making the team. In fairness to him, he had avoided taking up smoking, was fit and healthy and still loved playing hurling. He was motivated to go to training to impress the coaches and he felt really hopeful of making the team. Despite his high level of involvement with the hurling, his mum had always impressed on him the importance of balance and encouraged him to apply himself to his study. Thankfully he did. Between the schoolwork, his hurling and his social life, he rarely hung around the house. When he was at home he was usually pretty good-natured, although he did sometimes get wound up by his little brother, who idolized him and forever wanted to be by his side.

Then, four weeks before the first match of the campaign, he twisted his knee. Upon further examination by their family doctor he was discovered to have ligament damage that put him out of action for three or four weeks. He had to use crutches, and training and any exercise were curtailed. His mum noticed that in the evenings, as he came back from school, he seemed lethargic, irritable and very negative about everything.

It was at this point that I spoke to his mum. I explained to her my ideas about how our physical selves, our feelings, our behaviour and our thoughts are linked together. I wondered about the impact of his injury on his mood. I encouraged his mum to talk to him about how he was feeling and about how difficult it was for him to be so incapacitated, particularly in advance of the big match.

His mum rang me a few weeks later (when he was off the crutches and back training again). She explained that once she talked to him as I had suggested she got a very clear picture of how his injury had made him feel.

Essentially, he had felt hopeless about his ligaments healing in time to make his place on the team, never mind being fit enough to play the championship matches. This really upset him because he had wanted very badly to play on the team. His mum felt that this hopelessness might have been behind his negativity and pessimism, which was in real contrast to his usual optimism.

He described to his mum that he felt at a loose end because he wasn't going training and therefore didn't have the same access to hanging out with his friends, who were all preparing for the championship. This made him cross and because he was around the house more, he was getting irritated by his little brother, who he felt was plaguing him. He even complained that he couldn't use his normal stress release valve, for when he got cross, of hammering the sliotar against the back wall of the house for about fifteen or twenty minutes to cool down, because he was restricted by the crutches.

His mum noticed, too, that he was complaining of being bored, yet he had stopped studying and spent most evenings slumped in front of the TV. If ever she challenged him about not studying he was really short and grumpy with her, claiming that he had to rest his knee.

All in all, it sounded to me like Robin had developed many features of depression. Those changes to his mood and his behaviour had all come from his relative incapacitation due to his knee injury. Thankfully for Robin and his family his bad mood and lethargy were short-lived and as soon as he was off the crutches and back involved in hurling and his social life he regained his sunnier outlook and active life-style.

My intervention had been relatively small and in fact it was circumstance that had led to the difficulty and resolution for Robin. However, I do believe that because his mum took the time to talk to him, he felt more understood. If his injury had been prolonged then depression may have become lodged. But, even in that situation, his mum's understanding of the impact of his injury would probably have alleviated that bad mood.

EMOTIONAL CONGRUENCE

When we look at and process the feelings that are linked to significant or serious events or experiences in our lives, we are searching for emotional congruence. Emotional congruence is the fit between the experience and our understanding of the feeling that goes with that experience. Most of the time we do have a good and clear fit between what happens to us and how we feel about it, but that is because we are adults and have lots of experience of dealing with the world and the events that occur. Our children, and our teenagers, are unlikely to have the same skill at attaching or associating feelings to events. Sometimes this is due to lack of practice, sometimes it is due to receiving confusing messages from us or others that put feelings at odds with their experience.

Emotional congruence is the fit between the experience and our understanding of the feeling that goes with that experience.

This is best explained by an example. In the first part of the example I am going to describe emotional incongruence, and in the second I will show how to change your child's understanding of what is happening to them to make it emotionally congruent.

I am sure you have had occasions when your small son, perhaps a four-year-old, came in to you with a small graze on his knee after falling in the garden. So imagine the scene is replaying right now. They come into the kitchen, where you are probably hard at work trying to get dinner organized, or you are tidying away the shopping, or loading the dishwasher or any of the other myriad tasks that we have to get through. Your son has been heralding his imminent arrival with loud wailing. You can tell by the increasing volume of the sound that he is on his way to you and so you continue working while you wait to see what his problem is.

As he finally stands there before you, grubby, tear-stained and very upset, you try to get him to tell you what happened, while keeping an eye on the pot on the hob that is reaching boiling point. Through his sobs, he slowly manages to describe how he had been playing in the garden and had been trying to jump the same series of 'show jumps' that his older sister (the prize-winning mare) had built in the 'arena'. Unfortunately, he tripped over the rake on top of the two old paint cans from the garage and in his fall had scraped his knee. 'It hurts,' he tells you.

Throughout the retelling of the story his crying hasn't abated and he keeps holding out his knee for your inspection. The graze isn't particularly big and so, like most of us, your first reaction is to lick your thumb, smear a bit of saliva on the scratch and tell him that he's fine. He tries to protest, and his crying gets louder. Your pot is starting to spill onto the hob. Brusquely, you turn away from him, telling him, 'You'll be grand. That isn't a big cut. Stop being such a baby about a scratch that isn't even bleeding.'

Your son protests some more, but sees that you are no longer giving him any attention and so he limps miserably out of the kitchen, still crying. In this moment your son is experiencing emotional incongruence. He has the feeling that his knee hurts, it is sore, yet he has been told by you that he is fine and that he'll be grand. He doesn't feel fine or grand, and this is the root of his emotional mismatch. He can't really make sense of his feelings now because they don't fit with what he has been told and so the feeling stays with him and he can't deal with it. In practical terms, he will continue to feel sore and hurt and that soreness will continue for longer and be more troublesome for him because he has no way of processing it.

Fifteen minutes later you go to call the children in for their dinner and you see him sitting on the back step, still sniffling and holding his leg. His sister had been encouraging him to join in the game again, but he had sat on the sidelines, occasionally screaming at her to leave him alone. His soreness is prolonged and unsorted.

Now I want you to imagine exactly the same scenario up to the point that your son first stands in front of you. Remember, you are busy and distracted and he is crying. Just like before, you encourage him to tell you what happened. He sobs out the story about tripping up and scraping his knee. 'It hurts,' he tells you and holds up the knee for inspection.

You glance at the scratch and you check your pot on the boil. You look back at his knee and you say to your son, 'Oh you poor thing, that looks really sore.' As soon as you show a bit of caring and as soon as you label the feeling of soreness that he has, he experiences emotional congruence. His real-life experience of his knee hurting has been acknowledged, understood and labelled by you. There is a fit, or a match, between his pain and the feelings that are ascribed to that pain. His first response to such acknowledgement will be to howl louder. It is almost as if, with the empathy you have shown, he has permission to really feel the feeling and of course since the feeling is of physical hurt, he will feel that hurt more intensely.

On the face of it, it may not seem to be a good thing that we have helped our child to feel a feeling more intensely. After all, he is now crying stronger. However, what is actually happening is the appropriate expression of a feeling that matches the child's sense of the reality of the situation. This means that the child can make immediate sense of both the experience and the feeling that he has. By acknowledging and empathizing with your child's feeling, you allow them to bring it all to the surface and out into the open, where he or she can actually deal with it and process it.

In this situation you might then suggest, amidst his sobs, that you will get a plaster for his graze. He just nods miserably. You get a plaster, stick it on his knee and, almost like magic, he happily gets up and runs back out to play, proudly showing off his plaster to his sister. Does his knee hurt less? Probably not. But his hurt has been recognized and understood, so he can let it go and not be bothered by it.

In the first example, where the child experienced emotional incongruence, he couldn't deal with the feelings he had because he may have misunderstood them or been confused by the fact that his true feeling was denied by his parent, an adult whom he trusts. In this situation, the child is most likely to eventually squash that feeling down into his emotional store, to try to make sense of it at a later stage. In the second example, the child has no confusion and after feeling that soreness can let the whole experience go and move on from it.

The experiences that teenagers have in life may lead to more complex feelings but the process to help them make sense of it, and to move on from it, remains the same. If, for example, your teenage daughter feels the hurt of rejection by friends who exclude her from a trip to the cinema you can help her to experience emotional congruence by acknowledging the hurt for her. In contrast, an emotionally incongruent response from you would be to tell her to cop on that there are lots more friends out there and not to mind the one who pushed her away.

REGULATING EMOTIONS

As soon as we can make better sense of the feelings we have, we can regulate them more. This means we are less likely to become unwittingly overwhelmed by them. Practically, this means that when we get irritated or annoyed, we are less likely to have major tantrums and in stressful situations we are less likely to panic. If we are saddened by something, we are less likely to shift into depression. It is not the case that we are preventing ourselves from having feelings, but when we know what they are, they tend to be less intense and more manageable.

> As soon as we can make better sense of the feelings we have, we can regulate them more.

How do teenagers learn to manage their feelings? Ideally, they will have learned those skills from you (and if they haven't yet, they will now!). When babies are small their feelings are nonetheless strong. If a baby is tired or upset, they will experience the feeling throughout their body and will most likely cry out. They cry out because they don't yet have any skills to manage or to regulate their emotions. All of the regulation is done by their parent. When you came in to your teenager as a baby, picked them up, rocked them and soothed them until they stopped crying, you were regulating their emotion for them. When your child grew into toddlerhood and became distressed at the loss of their ball over the fence, you regulated their emotions when you said things like, 'Shhhh, it's okay, we can ask the neighbours to throw it back. It'll be all right, I know it's upsetting but you'll be okay.'

As they get older again, we hope that our constant responding to their feelings is teaching them to recognize and deal with those emotions more effectively. We can't continue to regulate their emotions to the same degree as they get older because they move in wider social circles and we just aren't around them. So we can't manage their feelings in school as they get teased by another child or given out to by the teacher. We can't be in charge of their response to winning or losing on the football pitch. But if, over the years, we have responded to them in an emotionally congruent way, then essentially we have been coaching them in the skill of understanding and dealing with feelings. This is a very natural process that most of us engage in and that leads our children to the point of being able to regulate their own emotions successfully.

Research shows that children and teenagers who have been 'emotionally coached' like this by their parents have better physical health and score higher academically than children whose parents don't offer such emotional guidance. These youngsters get along better with friends, have fewer behaviour problems and generally experience less negative feelings and more positive feelings. Essentially, they have the skills to be more in charge of themselves. And if they feel more in control, they are less likely to be influenced by others and to end up in situations where they follow the crowd unthinkingly.

EMOTIONAL INTELLIGENCE

An awful lot has been written in recent years about emotional intelligence, often measured as an emotional quotient or EQ, and about how it might be even more important than general intelligence, which is measured as an intelligence quotient or IQ. Emotions are an essential tool for having a successful and fulfilling life, but if they run out of control, it can lead to disaster. Our emotions will affect our relationships with other people, our self-identity and self-esteem and our ability to complete a task. We need to stay in charge of our emotions so that they work for us rather than against us.

Emotional intelligence theory – yes, I'm sorry, it's the science bit again! – suggests that there are five main elements to emotional intelligence:

1. Knowing your own emotions. **This means having the self-awareness to be able to recognize your feelings as they are happening. It's really important to be able to read our true emotions because unless we know what they are and when we are feeling them, we can't remain in charge of them.**

2. Managing emotions. **Once we have that awareness of what we are feeling, we need then to be able to manage those feelings. This means not acting out our frustrations, but instead finding ways to comfort ourselves. Managing feelings means dealing with things like anxiety, so that it doesn't prevent us from achieving things. In life we are going to be faced with a range of different emotions in response to the experiences that we have and in order to be able to recover from life's setbacks and upsets, we need to be able to stay in charge of those feelings.**

3. Motivating ourselves. **We need to be able to use our emotions to lead us in the direction of our goals. This sometimes means delaying gratification and holding back from being impulsive. This kind of emotional self-control allows you to stay focused and attentive on what it is that you want to achieve.**

4. Recognizing feelings in others. **Being attuned to the subtle social signals that indicate what others need or want is a really important skill to have. It is essentially the extension of self-awareness to the awareness of others. Being able to put yourself into somebody else's shoes means that you are more likely to tailor your behaviour to outcomes that will work for you and for them. This ability to recognize the feelings of others is called empathy.**

5. Managing relationships. **This is where emotional intelligence can really benefit you in the longer term. Managing relationships is about trying to manage the emotions of other people. It's a skill that great leaders have, to be able to influence, motivate, encourage and support other people. It will also allow you to get on with a wide range of people, even if you don't like them!**

By focusing on the feelings of your teenager, you create a more emotionally intelligent child, and emotionally intelligent children and adults are more resilient. While an emotionally intelligent adolescent will still experience sadness, anger or fear under difficult circumstances, they will be better able to cope with this distress and to comfort themselves and to bounce back.

Let's return to the example of Robin, the injured sixteen-year-old who was missing out on the final preparations for the hurling championship. Being emotionally aware like I am suggesting above is a proven buffer for youngsters against the impact of lots of life's troubles. When faced with the disappointment of his injury, Robin may have been better able to accept that disappointment, and rather than seeing the injury as the end of his playing career, he could have thought more positively and planned for his rehabilitation afterwards. He could have refocused his goals if he believed that this championship wasn't his last chance to succeed in the club. He may well have continued to feel the frustration of his relative immobility, but perhaps he could have taken up an inspirational role with his team-mates and supported them from the sidelines. He could have redefined his injury as an opportunity to work out exactly what he wanted and expected from his hurling and how he could achieve this in the months and years ahead.

Or, to refer back to another earlier example, if your fourteen-year-old daughter had greater emotional intelligence, perhaps she would never have found herself in the position of shoplifting in the first place. She would have been less likely to be influenced by her peers and would have felt more able to stand apart from them and take on board her own values about moral right and wrong. Equally, having made the mistake of stealing, she might have been more able to see it as a wake-up call rather than plunging into guilt and drifting further into her peer group, with the inevitable change in attitude and behaviour that the group supported and encouraged.

THE IMPACT OF NOT SORTING OUT FEELINGS

When we have strong feelings, whatever the source, it is tempting to run from them and to not deal with them. The pressure of our sadness, guilt, anger or fear can easily lead us to stick our head in the sand and hope that the feelings will go away. Indeed, you may have had the sensation yourself of feelings just being unbearable.

One analogy for thinking about how teenagers might be processing (or failing to process) their feelings is to imagine an airing cupboard. That airing cupboard represents the store for your emotions. In the same analogy, your feelings are represented by towels. Every time we have an experience in life, we usually have a feeling that goes alongside it. So, for example, if we manage to achieve something or to excel at a task or in a competition, we might well feel pride or happiness. Similarly, if we feel that we have failed at a task, we might well feel disappointment or upset. A lot of the time we are so focused on the experience itself that we don't necessarily pay attention to the feelings we have. Indeed, it is sometimes only when other people draw our attention to how we might be feeling that we actually become aware of what the emotion is. Nonetheless, we have had the experience and so, equally, we have the feeling that goes with it.

Now, we know that our conscious brain can't hold too much strong emotion at one time for too long. We therefore develop coping mechanisms that allow our brain to have a break from the emotion. One such coping mechanism is to store the feeling away, whether unconsciously or deliberately. If it is the case that we are dealing with difficult feelings, we are actually more likely to store them away rather than to leave them in our conscious mind, where we might have to continue to feel them or to deal with them. In real life this involves moving the feeling to a part of the brain where it doesn't impinge on our daily lives and we essentially forget about it.

Returning to the analogy, the unconscious storage of those feelings is a bit like throwing the towels into the airing cupboard haphazardly and closing the door quickly. For a while this strategy seems to be effective: there is lots of space in the airing cupboard and it is easy to jerk open the door, throw in a towel and close the door again with no great consequence.

What seems to happen after a while, however, is that the build-up of towels in our cupboard grows to the point at which it becomes difficult to open the door without the pile of towels tumbling out. Similarly, it can be hard to close the door afterwards because there is so little space left that the pile of towels barely fits. The idea of going in to search for a particular towel doesn't appeal because, given the messy nature of the airing cupboard, it might be very hard to find that one specific towel without disturbing many others and causing a big upset.

The temptation, then, is to leave the door firmly closed; never to open it unless absolutely necessary and if we must open it, to do so in the knowledge that it might actually cause more hassle and be very difficult for us. The trouble with this is that the towels, representing feelings, never get sorted, never get dealt with, never get tidied and we never really know what kind of towels are in there. The temptation, of course, is to keep building a bigger and bigger airing cupboard or to extend it more and more, even though that means that it takes up more space, becomes more weighty and potentially gets in the way of the rest of the house – where the house represents the rest of your life.

Wouldn't it feel great if we did have the towels sorted, organized, neatly folded and available to us as we need them? In this situation we can quickly scan through the airing cupboard to find a particular towel that we need. In the real world this ability equates to being able to look back at a certain experience and at the feeling that is attached to it in a manner of our own choosing.

In this scenario, the experience of those towels all falling out in an untidy heap around us equates to our experience of our feelings exploding out in an uncontrolled manner. We know that we have a mess of feelings that we can't face dealing with and yet we will be 'tripped up' regularly by those feelings because we end up expressing them in an uncontrolled way and at a much more extreme level than may be warranted by the event that has provoked those feelings. So it is a bit like becoming furious and ranting in anger when in fact somebody has done something that is only mildly irritating. As time passes and our store of unprocessed feelings gets larger, it becomes harder and harder to squeeze them back out of our consciousness. In fact, those feelings just won't go back into the store.

So it's worthwhile trying to organize our airing cupboard. Sometimes that means taking out all of the towels that are in there, even though this seems like a mammoth and messy task. It is probably not one that we would choose to do ordinarily. However, once all the towels are out, it's much easier to sort through them and to realize that, actually, many of the towels are simply replicas of ones that we already have and so we don't need the excess copies. That means that by the time we have sorted through the towels, we might have been able to get rid of a lot of them. This leaves us a much smaller and more manageable pile of towels, which we can then fold and replace in the airing cupboard in more ordered piles. So now when we open the door of the airing cupboard we are not threatened with an overwhelming spillage of towels. We can look in and realize that there are some towels, including ones that we would rather not have, and yet they are important because they are perhaps associated with powerful events in our lives.

We also have more space in the airing cupboard now, which means that when we get new towels we have the space to store them.

Back in the real world, the process of taking out and examining our feelings often involves looking back at experiences we have had in our lives and the emotions that went with them. Looking back in this way usually means that we re-experience the feeling, and it is the re-experiencing that we are often trying to avoid.

I think this has special relevance for teenagers. Nobody particularly likes to experience strong and possibly negative emotions. For example, it does not seem a wise choice to feel the depths of sadness and loss that may have initially impacted us following the death of someone close. It is no wonder that we are unconsciously reluctant to go back into these difficult feelings. But during teenage years the emotional centre of the brain, the limbic system, is under special pressure. That pressure is coming from the onslaught of hormones that are released during adolescence. We all know that at puberty the ovaries and testes begin to pour oestrogen and testosterone into the bloodstream. These hormones are largely responsible for driving the development of the reproductive system and lots of the other bodily changes that we associate with puberty. But there are lesser-known sex hormones, which are testosterone-like, that are released by the adrenal gland, located near the kidney. These adrenal sex hormones are extremely active in the brain and attach to receptors everywhere and exert a direct influence on serotonin and other neurochemicals that regulate mood and excitability within the limbic system.

The effect of this is to create real instability and variability in the moods of teenagers. We are all warned about the mood swings that our teenagers will experience and perhaps it is the influence of these sex hormones that leads to such strong variability. So not only do teenagers reach flashpoints more quickly, they also tend to seek out situations that will stimulate them intensely. It is as if they want experiences that will allow their emotions and passions to run wild. But it also suggests that teenagers may be in even less control of their feelings than the rest of us. And with this level of intensity and unpredictability, it makes particular sense for our teenagers to avoid deliberately stirring up feelings that they had squashed down.

Despite the force of teenage emotions, the brain can still apply strong protective coping mechanisms to prevent those feelings from overwhelming us. And if the feelings are painful, the brain will probably continue to act to keep them bottled up. Indeed, it can seem almost counterintuitive to unbottle those feelings. This is probably the experience your teenager has with a lot of the difficult feelings that he or she may have. However, by unbottling those feelings your teenager actually approaches greater emotional understanding, greater mastery of their feelings and ultimately a stronger sense of self and self-worth. So, it is well worth your while investing in helping them to connect to that emotional world.

THE IMPACT OF STRESS, PRESSURE AND TRAUMA

It should be becoming clear now that every time we experience a stressful or traumatic event, we have a feeling that goes along with that event. The feeling is connected to, almost interwoven with the experience. So much so, in fact, that if we relive the experience we had by remembering it or recalling it out loud, we will often feel that feeling again to the same degree and intensity. This is why survivors of trauma find flashbacks so intrusive – not only are they getting a memory of the traumatic event but they are also flooded with the same feelings of fear and panic, distress or upset.

Nonetheless, as I have described above, the feelings have to go somewhere and so somewhere inside us those feelings are lodged in our inner world. I'd like you to imagine the inner world of your teenager as a prism. If you remember back to your school science lessons, you might recall that a prism is the piece of Perspex that responds to white light being shone on it by casting out all the colours of the rainbow onto a piece of white card. In other words, the prism changes, or alters, the properties of the light to the extent that what goes in seems different from what comes out.

So, too, what goes into the inner world of your teenager is not what seems to come out. Although we might be able to track the particular experiences that our children and teenagers have, we can't always readily predict the feelings that will emerge subsequently. Take, for example, your teenager's experience of the death of a grandparent. We might expect that they will feel sad, upset or even distraught at the death. They might miss their grandparent greatly. But if we ask them to talk about their experience of the death, they may appear nonchalant or withdrawn or even angry. This can catch us by surprise because we don't expect the feeling to have morphed in this way. Somewhere in the inner world of the teenager, feelings get transformed, stored, altered and even lost, at least to our scrutiny.

The one thing we can be almost certain of is that stress and trauma lead to some kind of emotional hurt. Even though our teenagers may not be able to identify exactly what the hurt is and so can't explain to us how they feel, they do know that they don't like to hurt and, as I described above, will often try to block it from their consciousness. However, the feeling that gets stored in the inner world of your child needs to get expressed. At some level it *has* to be expressed. There's a limit to how much feeling we can store away and hope never to re-experience (remember the towels tumbling out!). But the transforming nature of the inner world of the child means that when our teenagers try to express those feelings, it rarely comes out as the pure feeling that might have been associated with the initial traumatic event.

I sometimes think that squashing down the feelings into our inner world leads to a melange, or a mixture, of those feelings. If you remember from that airing cupboard analogy, the release of those feelings, or the expression of them, is often a confused mess. In reality, the confused mixture of feelings seems to come out most often as anger.

To draw a further analogy, the mixing of our feelings in the inner world is much like mixing the primary colours of paint. If you get pots of red, blue and yellow paint and start to mix them together, what you will inevitably get is a muddy brown or black colour. The same will happen if you keep mixing together enough different feelings: what you seem to get is anger. I am never sure why it is anger that gets expressed. Perhaps it is because it is such a powerful feeling, or perhaps it is because the intensity of anger provides a short-term relief from the pressure building up of all those feelings being squashed together.

This is one of the reasons I believe we see so much anger and aggression coming from teenagers. A lot of the time the well of anger that gets expressed does not seem warranted by the stated provocation. So we ask our fifteen-year-old son, 'Have you got all your homework done?' and we get a torrent of curses about the poor quality of education in school and the constant nagging from us, the parent. Do we deserve that litany of curses? No, of course we don't. Is that level of vitriol warranted by the comment we made? No, of course it isn't. Does this happen regularly in families? Absolutely.

The natural reaction of any parent is to get righteously indignant in the face of such unwarranted and unprovoked anger. In this example, our question simply lit the fuse that led to a big explosion of hurt, frustration and annoyance associated with the pressures of school. In the heat of the moment, however, it's very hard to understand and even to recognize that the anger that is directed towards us is more than simply a response to the question we put forward.

Usually this is because it is not the first time that we have had such high levels of anger pointed at us. We may have had to cope with many snide remarks, silences, dismissive gestures, angry outbursts or even threats of violence from our son or daughter.

I recognize that it is very difficult to be empathetic with your teenager when they seem to be doing all in their power to drive you away from them. But what I am encouraging you to do here is to try to look beyond their behaviour and their attitude to the feeling or feelings that lie behind. If it is the case that this anger that gets expressed is actually a mess of other feelings, then these are the feelings that we should be searching for. Those feelings are probably associated with difficult, stressful or even traumatic experiences that your teenager has had. The anger will diminish if they can begin to understand and process the real feelings that are associated with their life experiences.

So we can guess that it is quite likely that your fifteen-year-old son has a feeling of emotional hurt that is triggered by your simple query in relation to his homework. There are two ways we can help to deal with that hurt. On the one hand, we offer some emotional support so that he can begin to process the feelings or, on the other hand, we can let him block the feeling out of his consciousness for a short period.

HEALTHY DISTRACTION

Blocking, or emotional numbing as it is sometimes called, can actually be a useful short-term coping strategy. Even with the best will in the world it is impossible to stay mired in the depths of very strong feelings indefinitely: we either need to sort them or we need to take a break from them. There are healthy ways for your teenager to take a break from their feelings. Healthy forms of distraction include playing sport, hanging out with friends, working, reading, music and so on.

Healthy forms of distraction include playing sport, hanging out with friends, working, reading, music and so on.

The useful thing about all of these distractions is that they engage not just the mind but the body, too. As soon as we engage several modalities, such as our thinking and our physical selves, it has that knock-on to the other areas and so feelings will often change, too. For example, a teenager who does something he loves, like playing guitar, will find it hard to hold onto his anger while he is playing because his mind is so involved in the creation of the music that his fingers go on to produce. Similarly, if your daughter has a passion for tennis and gets out onto the court, she will likely soon forget about her troubles, at least for the duration of the game.

One of the dilemmas facing many parents and teenagers now is the lack of outdoor or sporting opportunities that continue to engage them during their adolescence. I go into more detail in the chapter on peers (Chapter 6) about the withdrawal of many teenagers from sports and other activities. Unfortunately, this seemingly natural pulling back from energetic activity has a very negative side effect when it comes to finding healthy sources of distraction for emotionally struggling teenagers.

Despite my misgivings about the influence of media, I would even include watching TV and playing computer games within this category of healthy forms of distraction. Of course, I would always hold to the principle that too much of anything can become a bad thing and that moderation is the key to any healthy distraction. Many youngsters who are having a tough time may well pursue very solitary activities, like computer gaming. While this does engage the mind and does distract them, it doesn't spark the body in the same way. The temptation to live apart in the fantasy world of the game can be very strong and appealing. Perhaps too strong and too appealing.

So while we might encourage our teenagers to distract themselves, we do also need to ensure that this distraction does not become all-consuming. They need to live in and be connected to the real world.

One of the dangers of failing to offer emotional support, and of our teenagers not finding healthy forms of distraction, is that they can turn to unhealthy forms of distraction as their means of blocking out those unpleasant or troubling feelings.

UNHEALTHY DISTRACTION

One of the dangers of failing to offer emotional support, and of our teenagers not finding healthy forms of distraction, is that they can turn to unhealthy forms of distraction as their means of blocking out those unpleasant or troubling feelings. The most typical things that teenagers will turn to are:

> **anger and aggression**
> **alcohol**
> **drugs**
> **self-harm**
> **sex**
> **eating disorders**

Each of these provides very powerful reinforcement to teenagers. If you feel you have hassles in your life, what better way to block them out than by drinking yourself into a stupor or getting so stoned that the world passes by in a haze. Equally, losing yourself in the powerful physical and emotional maelstrom that comes with sex is a very effective way of forgetting about your troubles for a while. Many teenagers who have tried cutting themselves will talk about the 'release' they feel from the emotional pressure inside. Similarly, exploding in anger and aggression might give temporary relief from a build-up of strong and negative emotions.

It is the effectiveness of all of these outlets at providing that temporary relief that makes them so attractive. If they seem to work to block out or release feelings, then it is only natural that your son or daughter will turn to them time and again. The difficulty emerges, of course, because all of them are ultimately self-destructive. They do more harm than good. Each time your teenager drops into one of these activities they come out the other side a bit more deflated, with lower self-esteem and probably more vulnerable to needing the same outlet again. All of these behaviours have the potential to be highly addictive, both in their own right and because of their effectiveness at providing short-term relief.

I am not suggesting that if your teenager is experimenting with sex or drugs or alcohol that they are necessarily blocking troubling emotions. In the chapter on drugs and alcohol I describe some of the other dynamics that are involved in teenage culture that lead to overuse of these. Similarly, I look in much greater detail at suicide, self-harm and eating disorders, all of which can have quite complex reasons for developing as problems for teenagers. But if your teenager seems to have what you consider to be a problem with any of these behaviours, then it is definitely worth exploring to what extent those behaviours might allow your son or daughter to hide from the real world.

EMOTIONAL SUPPORT

To help them live in the real world, we can offer them emotional support. Essentially, emotional support gives our teenagers a chance to recognize and understand their own feelings. It teaches them the skills that they will need to become emotionally intelligent and also to deal with and manage their strong feelings. The key to emotional support is empathy. Empathy is the ability we have to put ourselves in the place of somebody else and to guess at how they might be experiencing the world. Empathy is not the same as sympathy. When we sympathize with someone we tend to experience the same kind of feeling that they have. So when we sympathize with somebody who is bereaved, we share our own feelings of sadness at the loss of the person who died. When we empathize with somebody who has been bereaved, we share our understanding of how their loss may be leaving them feeling sad (even if we don't feel sad ourselves).

The research on emotional intelligence shows that when you deliberately engage with your child's feelings, it sets them up on a path to be able to cope with many of life's challenges. Here are the steps to engaging in emotional support:

1. **Become aware of your teenager's emotion or feeling.**
2. **Recognize that this feeling is an opportunity for intimacy and learning.**
3. **Listen empathically to your teenager and acknowledge their feelings.**
4. **Help your teenager to find words to label the feeling that they are having.**

It is hard to think about these steps in theory, so let's take a practical conversation that you might find yourself in with your teenager. In the scenario I will present a conversation that doesn't go well and then a second version that might lead to a more successful outcome. In the scenario I will imagine that a dad is negotiating with his fourteen-year-old son about going out to the disco.

> **Dad:** *I don't want you going to that disco. There are kids hanging around, drinking and fighting.*

> **Son:** *But all my friends are going. And you let me go last month. What is your problem now?*

> **Dad:** *I told you my problem. I don't want you getting mixed up in drinking and fighting and the best way to avoid it is to stop you going. And anyway, maybe I've learned better sense since last month and maybe you should cop on a bit too. It's definite; you are not going.*

> **Son:** *But that is so unfair. Fuck you. (Storms off out of the kitchen)*

> **Dad:** *(Following him with his blood boiling) How dare you speak to me like that. Not only are you not going to that disco, now you can take it you are not going anywhere for the rest of this month. You're grounded!*

> **Son:** *I don't care. (Slams the door of his bedroom)*

The outcome of a conversation like this is that both the dad and the son are furious. They probably feel misunderstood by each other, they feel disrespected by each other and they feel alienated from each other. Now they have to try to reconnect and continue to get on. The dad is backed into a corner with the additional major problem now of trying to police his son's grounding. Neither of them was able to stay connected to their own feelings, much less to the other's feelings. I think it is perfectly fine for the dad to set the limit of no disco, but the difficulty he had was that he didn't recognize or understand the feelings that his 'ban' on the disco would instil in his son. So, whatever about the fourteen-year-old losing his temper, it is up to the dad to hold his cool and to try to help his son to cope with the disappointment of not being allowed to go.

Let's have a look at an alternative version of that conversation that includes a little more empathy and emotional support from the dad.

> **Dad:** *I don't want you going out to that disco. It is nothing but trouble. There are loads of kids hanging around, drinking and fighting.*

> **Son:** *But all my friends are going. And you let me go last month. What is your problem now?*

> **Dad:** *I told you my problem, I don't want you getting mixed up in drinking and fighting and the best way to avoid it is to stop you going. And anyway maybe I've learned better sense since last month. It was only when I picked you up that I realized how dangerous it was and how little supervision there is of you all. That worried me and then I got worried for you.*

> **Son:** *But that is so unfair. I can handle myself and I don't drink – you know that you didn't smell anything off my breath and I could tell you were sniffing when I got in the car. And all my friends are there, too, so nobody would mess with us because they know we stand up for each other.*

> **Dad:** *True, I didn't smell it off you. But it doesn't take away from the fact that it is dangerous and I don't want you going. Maybe in a few months, when you turn fifteen, but not now.*

> **Son:** *That's not a good enough reason. I'm going anyway – you can't stop me.*

> **Dad:** *You sound really disappointed that I've decided you can't go. And I am sorry to have taken a decision like this, but I am doing it because I think it is best and safest for you.*

> **Son:** *You don't care about me; you're just trying to wreck my life. I don't need your protection.*

> **Dad:** *I can hear your frustration. I'm guessing you'd love to go because all your mates will be there. And whether you like it or not it is still my job to protect you until you are a bit older. I remember the excitement and craic of discos, so I know what you feel you are missing out on.*

> **Son:** *No you don't; you're so past it.*

> **Dad:** *Take it easy with the tone. We don't talk nastily to each other in this house.*

> **Son:** *Sorry, but I really want to go. It's really important to me.*

> **Dad:** *What is so important about going? There'll be lots more discos.*

> **Son:** *Yeah, maybe, but not too many more chances with Grainne from my class. She asked would I be there. That makes it a practical certainty.*

> **Dad:** *Ahh, it is all coming clearer to me. I was worried about drinking and fighting, maybe I should be more worried about sex.*

> **Son:** *Jesus, dad, stop.*

> **Dad:** *Only messing with you. Well, maybe it's more unfortunate if you miss on a chance with Grainne, but I still won't let you go this month. But I hear you saying you are getting more mature. I guess if you can deal well with this disappointment then that'll be another marker for me and maybe we can look sooner at you going another time.*

> **Son:** *Whatever …*

> **Dad:** *Okay, I'm not sure we are going any further with this now, because you sound like you are getting fed up and I don't want a row, so let's take a break and we can always come back to it.*

In this version of the conversation the dad and the son still arrive at somewhat of a stalemate, but the process was much calmer and healthier and the door is very much left open for further discussion. So even though the dad is prepared to keep talking, he did restate the limit several times and didn't budge (or 'give in', as some parents fear). This was a dad remaining firm, but understanding. His son was no less disappointed or cross about the ultimate decision, but he was better able to cope with those feelings because at least his dad was clearly aware that this was not an easy thing for him to accept. Importantly, because the door is still open, the son can also see that by managing his feelings on this occasion there might be benefit in being able to show greater maturity and then being allowed to go to the disco in the nearer future.

The key moments of emotional support were when the dad said, 'You sound really disappointed that I've decided you can't go,' and later when he said, 'I can hear your frustration. I'm guessing you'd love to go because all your mates will be there,' and then finally when he said, 'Well maybe it's more unfortunate if you miss on a chance with Grainne, but I still won't let you go this month.' Each time he guessed at both the feelings his son might be having and even at the reasons his son is having those feelings. Let us be in no doubt that we still have to make tough and unpopular decisions on our teenagers' behalf, but by showing emotional understanding and by offering the emotional support to your son, you can make those decisions and still maintain a working relationship.

IN CASE OF EMERGENCY . . . KEY POINTS TO REMEMBER

→ Emotions are an essential tool for having a successful and fulfilling life, but if our feelings and emotions run out of control, it can lead to disaster.

→ Your aim is to help your teenager to be able to recognize their feelings and to be attuned to them so that they can respond with feeling as opposed to responding because of feeling.

→ There is a strong inter-relationship between feelings, behaviour, thinking and our physical well-being. In many ways they operate like interconnected cogs in a system, such that when one changes, it has a knock-on effect on the others.

→ The more we understand the feelings of our youngsters, the more we can help them to understand their own feelings and, if necessary, change those feelings.

→ Emotional congruence is the fit between the experience and our understanding of the feeling that goes with that experience. When we have congruent experiences we can deal with the feelings more completely.

→ By acknowledging and empathizing with your teenager's feeling, you allow them to bring it all to the surface and out into the open, where he or she can actually deal with it and process it.

→ An emotionally intelligent adolescent will still experience sadness, anger or fear under difficult circumstances, but they will be better able to cope with this distress and to bounce back.

→ The pressure of our sadness, guilt, anger or fear can easily lead us to stick our heads in the sand and hope that the feelings will go away. What actually happens is that the feelings can become 'stuck'.

→ Youngsters who have intense feelings that are trapped and unprocessed or unresolved tend to blow off the emotional pressure in their behaviour.

→ Not only do teenagers reach flashpoints more quickly, they also tend to seek out situations that will stimulate them intensely. It is as if they want experiences that will allow their emotions and passions to run wild.

→ Somewhere in the inner emotional world of the teenager, feelings get transformed, stored, altered and even lost. What seems to emerge most easily, from the mix of all of their feelings, is anger.

→ The key to emotionally supporting our teenagers is empathy. Empathy is the ability we have to put ourselves in the place of somebody else and to guess at how they might be experiencing the world.

→ By showing emotional understanding and by offering emotional support to your teenager, you can help them to be attuned to their own feelings and so they may have less need to show you their distress through difficult behaviour.

4. CONFLICT, DECISION-MAKING AND THE DYNAMICS OF POWER

turning a tug-o-war into a successful negotiation

Our teenagers are growing to a point of being fully responsible for their behaviour, their money, their looks, their friends and their goals in life. Reaching that point of independence is a gradual process. Along the way we may have been fully responsible for any or all of those issues on behalf of our child. As we begin to let teenagers take greater responsibility, we must negotiate with them. In an ideal world we will already be using some kind of shared decision-making process that gives us an involvement in all of these important areas. Not being able to negotiate any of this with our teenagers puts us at a significant disadvantage because they will make decisions with regard to all of these things whether our voice is heard or not.

No doubt you will find that despite your best intentions of shared decision-making, sometimes the 'talks' break down. What you are left with in those situations can be hardened attitudes and polarized opinions. So what do you do when you find yourself on the other side of a void from your teenager? The answer is that you bring in the similar but different skills of conflict resolution.

Bridging the gap is usually the responsibility of the adult in the relationship between child and parent. No matter who breaks the trust (usually it is our youngsters who don't live up to their side of the agreed decision), it'll still be up to us, the parents, to try to regain and rebuild it.

Coming back from the edge of hurt isn't easy, however. Many of us can have our own very powerful feelings of injustice and betrayal based on the actions or comments of our teenage children. As we become intuitively aware that their thought processes are more complex and their understanding of the world and relationships is developing, their words and actions have more power to hurt us. We no longer dismiss statements as the angry utterances within the tantrums of children. Now they can seem to take on a more personally attacking nature and we take it to heart more.

What is probably happening, in fact, is that the rows are more adult, plus our teenagers may have greater skill in an argument. Nonetheless, there remains an onus on us to hold on to our feelings, to keep a cooler head in the row and to try to use new skills derived from conflict resolution to diffuse the situation rather than to inflame it.

The kinds of skills we use in resolving conflicts (or solving problems) are very similar to the skills of making good decisions. I spoke in the introduction about my belief that the job of a parent is to be totally in charge of our children when they are small and then slowly, as they grow, develop and mature, to increase their responsibility and let them take increasing amounts of control on the way to being fully independent of us. In reality, allowing them to take greater responsibility is very difficult. Part of our reluctance to relinquish control comes from our worry that our teenagers will make bad choices if left to their own devices. I have addressed both the skills for effective decision-making and how we can understand teenage risk-taking behaviour in an effort to help you quell that anxiety.

Indeed, the conflict and anxiety we experience with our teenagers can often reflect our fears about the shifting balance of power and control in our relationship with them. Rather than reach a stage of feeling powerless, manipulated and controlled by your teenager, you will want to share power and combine your power with theirs in the same collaborative manner that I am suggesting for resolving conflicts. To that end I will explore in greater detail the dynamics of power within parent-teenager relationships.

CONFLICT

Conflict within families is inevitable. There is always going to be a struggle between opposing interests, principles, values, feelings or standards – and that might be just between the parents! For the same reason, conflict is natural. Because it is natural, it has the potential to be healthy also. Unfortunately, our usual experience with conflict is that it is negative. We often assume that all conflict is bad and should be avoided. It is true that conflict that is not resolved, or at the very least acknowledged, can be very destructive, but that isn't the case for all conflict.

Sometimes, when we have fights with someone in the family we can feel like we are going around in circles. We know that the rowing is taking up huge amounts of time and energy, but it never reaches a resolution. Regular conflict can sometimes alienate and polarize you from your son or daughter to the point that you don't even want to try because you are anticipating a bigger row. As teenagers get bigger and stronger physically, that too can add a new dimension to conflict and sometimes parents can end up afraid of their 'child' who is now bigger, stronger and has the potential to be physically threatening. Below I have identified various styles of dealing with conflict. When two power-based styles collide, it can be vicious and destructive of the very fabric of a family.

The good news is that conflict doesn't have to be like that. Not everyone approaches conflict with an aggressive or dominant attitude. There are ways that you and your teenager can learn to work together to resolve disputes and I detail them in this chapter. If you work in this kind of way, you will find that you might be stimulated to be creative, to consider alternatives, to find better ideas and end up with a better course of action for the family. Conflict usually results in change. Somebody, or everybody, does something differently in the aftermath of resolving the conflict. Part of our reluctance to see conflict positively is that we can also be reluctant to introduce change because it can be anxiety-provoking.

If you chose D, your style could be characterized as a 'turtle'. Turtles withdraw to avoid the conflict situation entirely. If you are turtle-like in your approach, then it is quite likely that you are making little attempt to satisfy either your own personal needs or the needs of your teenager. However, ignoring it means that it won't go away. In fact, if a point of conflict is ignored, it tends to grow larger. Ultimately, if you keep avoiding conflict, it will eventually become unmanageable.

If you chose E, your style could be characterized as an 'owl'. Wise owls use problem-solving behaviour in which both sides meet their needs at a level sufficient to avoid feelings of losing. This is a style that promotes collaboration. Everyone wins and conflict is reduced or eliminated. It usually occurs most effectively when there is a sense of working towards some common good. In practical terms, you and your teenager have to feel that, for example, the needs of the family outweigh your own personal needs. In other words, you will both seek to reach an agreement to make family life better rather than focusing on trying to defend your personal position. If this is your style, then you will probably notice that you always go into a conflict situation expecting to have to change or modify your original viewpoint. You will also have an expectation that by working together you will actually reach a better solution than if either of you were to try to come up with a solution independently. Critically, in your relationship with your teenager this means that you must see both their opinion and their contribution as valid and valuable. For it to work, they too must reciprocate and see your opinion and contribution as valuable. In the next section I am going to focus on how you can best achieve this style of conflict resolution.

In the figure below I have drawn each of these styles (represented by its animal) according to how the style combines the two potentially competing agendas of being assertive and meeting one's own needs (I win) and being cooperative and meeting the needs of someone else (you win). So, for example, the owl scores high for cooperation and high for assertiveness, but the teddy bear scores high for cooperation and low for assertiveness.

Most people have characteristics of more than one style, and may even behave differently depending on the person with whom they are in conflict. So when you are with your husband or partner, for example, you may be able to take an owl-like approach because you feel equally invested in the family. With your son, on the other hand, you might adopt more of a shark approach because you don't believe that he shares your desire to get what is best for the family. Generally, however, one category emerges.

I would always recommend that if you want a more effective style, you should work towards the owl, or problem-solving, approach. With this approach, you are always aiming to collaborate in solving the conflict.

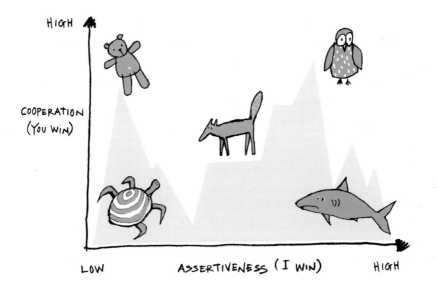

HIGH

COOPERATION
(YOU WIN)

LOW   ASSERTIVENESS (I WIN)   HIGH

Styles of resolving conflict and their relationship to cooperativeness and assertiveness.

WORKING TOGETHER TO RESOLVE CONFLICT

Collaboration promotes an understanding of everyone's perspective. It increases communication, cooperation and interdependence and instils a feeling of integrity, trust and mutual support. With that list of impressive outcomes, who wouldn't want to work collaboratively! Listed below are some things to consider, specifically when involving your teenager in sorting out problems.

> Pick the right time to talk. **Don't try to discuss a serious issue as your teenager runs out the door to school. On the other hand, a more formal sit-down talk might be over the top with smaller decisions. Remember that your teenager may not have a great attention span, or that they might genuinely have other things to do. Car journeys are often the best of times for these kinds of conversations. Make sure, though, that there will be enough time to discuss the issue fully, even if final agreement isn't reached in that time.**

> Be ready to listen. **Go into each conversation with an open mind and really listen to what your teenager says. Remember that part of what you are hoping to achieve is a creative exploration of possible solutions to the issue. Your teenager is likely to have lots of ideas, but they need to be expressed and you have to encourage them in the way in which you listen. Review my strategies on active listening from Chapter 2, which may really improve your sense of connection to what your teenager says.**

> Identify common ground. It may seem intuitive, but recognizing that there are already some points of agreement is very encouraging and it is good to be explicit about the commonality that is there. Sometimes the common ground will be ideological (i.e. you share a common belief or set of principles). Sometimes the common ground will be practical (e.g. you agree that there isn't enough money for a family holiday abroad, but you need a break from the house). Sometimes there will be commonality of feeling (e.g. everyone is upset that no agreement has yet been reached and everyone has a desire to find a solution to the problem).

> Be clear about your intentions. Your son or daughter will want to know how you plan to use the information or the opinions that they give you. For example, will they be helping you choose between a small number of ideas to solve the problem, or are you open to completely new suggestions? Is the final agreement that you reach binding, or will you withhold an 'opt out' clause if things don't go the way you expect?

> Set a good example. Demonstrate to your teenager how to listen actively and how to manage difficult feelings. Your own anger and frustration are probably the two key feelings to be in charge of. Practically, you might do deep breathing or take short 'cooling-off' breaks. Show that you have an understanding of their feelings (empathize) and that you can see things from their perspective, even if you don't agree with them. The whole previous chapter on understanding your teenager's feelings is worth reading in this context. If you are trying to make a decision about an issue that is in dispute, then try to go through the decision-making process that I suggest later in the chapter in a transparent and obvious manner. By talking through each of the steps that you are following, your teenager can watch and learn how they too can follow a similar process.

> Encourage your teenager's skill development. Make a point to notice when your teenager exercises good judgement or when they show good communication skills. For example, they may list the pros and cons of a decision or suggest a good solution to a family problem. Another example might be when they calmly state their idea without trying to shout down your idea. It's quite likely that your teenager is trying out new ways of thinking and solving problems and that your positive feedback will encourage them to use the effective strategies in other situations.

> Continue to be 'the parent'. Do remember that no matter how much you involve your teenager, collaboratively, in sorting out problems or making decisions, you are ultimately responsible for their health and safety. So it's okay to put your foot down and be a 'shark' when you need to, but be sure to explain why you are doing this. Remember that any decision made by an authority figure is easier to accept when we understand the reason behind it.

STUMBLING BLOCKS TO COLLABORATIVE WORKING

There are a few behaviours that will definitely get in the way of working together. The first of these is aggression. Sometimes we can be confused between aggression and assertiveness. Assertiveness is about stating your opinion clearly. Aggression is about trying to frighten or overpower somebody else. As soon as you or your teenager start to get aggressive, then the likelihood of reaching resolution to an issue decreases. Your best bet, in fact, is to leave things be and take a 'cooling-off' break. It may be that you can't come back to the issue until the following day – so be it.

Another set of blocking behaviours falls under the umbrella of 'irritators'. These are the kinds of things that annoy or frustrate other people. Sometimes these can be habits, like snuffling, chewing fingernails or sighing audibly. Other times the behaviours are the antithesis to active listening, such as refusing to make eye contact, constant use of sarcasm or dismissive tones of voice, pacing around the room and talking over someone or shouting them down.

It is also unhelpful to label any disagreements that you have with your son or daughter, particularly when those disagreements are historical. I'll be willing to guess that you have gone into some kind of conflict with your teenager and reminded them of previous incidents where they failed. In some incidents you were probably able to identify where you had a difference of opinion with them and where you were proven right because by choosing their own path, things didn't turn out well. Similarly, our intention in reminding them of the disagreement or of their failing is to punish them further or to prove that we make better choices than they do. In many ways it is immaterial if you make better choices. What this process of collaboration is all about is showing them how they can make better choices and reach more agreement in the future.

What this process of collaboration is all about is showing them how they can make better choices and reach more agreement in the future.

DECISION-MAKING

We want our teenagers to be wise decision-makers. If they make bad choices (as they will from time to time), we need to know that they have the skill to learn from their mistakes in order to make better decisions in the future. Part of your goal, as a parent, should be to try to withdraw from the decision-making role as much as possible or as much as is safe, with the confidence to know that your teenager will still make good choices. But it is unrealistic to expect your teenager to make good decisions when they haven't had the opportunity to practise. If you make a habit of talking through both small and big decisions amongst all family members, you will not only be helping your teenager to stay involved in the family but you'll also be helping them to develop critical skills. The practice of sharing decisions may also avoid a lot of unnecessary family conflict.

> We want our teenagers to be wise decision-makers. If they make bad choices (as they will from time to time), we need to know that they have the skill to learn from their mistakes in order to make better decisions in the future.

You'll probably find that making decisions with your teenager can be challenging. Just when you figured out how much freedom to give them and where to draw the line, they change. Their continuous physical and psychological development means that they grow into the capacity for greater responsibility and their ability to make decisions also improves.

You may remember in the first chapter I looked at the development of teenagers in five key areas: their movements towards independence; their cognitive development; their sexuality; their physical growth; and their moral and ethical development. It's important to remember that their development is complex. So while they might be mature physically, their cognitive and sexual attitude may not have matured to the same extent. In other words, your daughter might look like a young woman but she doesn't actually have the readiness for the complexities of sexual relationships. This means that boys might put her under pressure to make decisions that she will struggle with.

You may also find that your teenager doesn't show the same level of maturity from day to day, or in all decisions. This may be one reason why teenagers sometimes make 'good' choices and other times make 'bad' choices. For example, some days your fourteen-year-old daughter may be patient with her eleven-year-old sister, remembering what it was like to want to hang out with her own older sister. On other days, she can be selfish and impatient and won't empathize with her sister at all.

TYPICAL DECISION-MAKING PROCESS

I usually consider six steps to be involved in making a decision. In practice, we will often carry out the first five in a number of seconds, depending on the issue and our sense of how long we can afford to deliberate. But even though the process might seem instantaneous, it will still follow the same basic structure:

1. Define the problem or the issue
2. Brainstorm possible options or solutions
3. Consider the consequences of those options
4. Decide on the favoured option
5. Implement the decision
6. Review and evaluate the outcome

When you are with your teenager, try to be explicit about which of the six steps you're working on at a given time. To make the process clearer for you, we will work through an example.

Let's imagine that your thirteen-year-old son has forgotten to do a school project that is due in two days' time. There is at least one full evening's work in it and he could probably do with devoting both nights to it. He also wants to play in the first under-sixteen (u-16) league match with his local rugby club tonight and then has a first cup match with his regular under-fourteen (u-14) team tomorrow night. He considers it a big honour (as do you) that he was selected for the u-16 team as he is passionate about rugby, as well as being very good at it. He is really keen to play in both matches because he wants to establish himself in the club. However, you are also concerned that he won't get his school project done if he plays and you don't want him to start letting his schoolwork slip for the sake of sport.

1. Define the problem

The first thing to consider in defining the problem is giving yourself a bit of space and time to react, emotionally, to the issue. A lot of the time, strong feelings will have a big impact on how we might go on to address the issue. It's really helpful, therefore, to be aware of how you feel about the problem. Then you need to think through what the problem is and try to describe it precisely. In our example, you are probably trying to balance your feelings of pride at your son's sporting achievements and your concern about his education. So, a clear definition of this problem is that your son has two competing priorities, sport and education, and not enough time to achieve both of them fully.

2. Brainstorm possible solutions

Your aim is to try to come up with as many creative solutions as you can. It's more important that ideas are generated than that they are evaluated. So even if a proposed solution seems outlandish, don't reject it straight away. Look to see if there are any new or hidden bits of information that might also be relevant for the problem. For example, have other students ever managed to get an extension on a project? If your son doesn't play for the u-16 team, will this be his last opportunity for a trial with them? Weigh up the accuracy and the credibility of the different sources of information. For example, your son might tell you that lots of other pupils get extensions on projects, but you might choose to have that verified by a teacher. In this instance, your solutions might include:

> **Miss out on the u-16 game and work hard to get the project completed so that your son is free to play the u-14 game**

> **Focus only on the project and don't play any rugby**

> **Seek an extension of the project and play both games of rugby**

> **You do the project for your son so that he can play both games of rugby**

> **Let him stay up late to work on the project both nights and hope that he isn't too tired to focus on the work**

> **He doesn't do the project, but plays both games of rugby and faces whatever consequences the school sets for not doing his work**

3. Consider the consequences

This is the time to talk about the advantages and disadvantages of each option. Sometimes, it can be helpful to write out the pros and cons in a table. When I do this, I don't just compare the number of pros against the number of cons because sometimes each can have a specific relevance or importance that outweighs another. So, for each pro and each con, you can assign a weighting from 0 to 10, where a higher number denotes greater relevance or importance. I have done this for the first option that I suggested above and you can see that even though there are three reasons for and three reasons against the option, you would still favour choosing it above not choosing it because the reasons for are essentially more important.

> Miss out on the u-16 game and work hard to ensure the project is completed so that he is free to play in the u-14 game

PROs

	Score
1. Gets project done	8
2. Plays u-14 cup game	10
3. Shows commitment to both sport and education	8
	TOTAL 26

CONs

	Score
1. Misses chance to trial for u-16	10
2. May resent schoolwork	6
3. May not get project fully done	5
	TOTAL 21

Example of weighting pros and cons.

4. Decide on an option

This is the key moment. For parents working with their teenagers, it is also the hardest bit because it may be that the agreed decision is not the solution they would first choose. But it is really important that your son is committed to whatever is the decision, which might mean that you have to be willing to let him go with a less-than-ideal solution. In this case I would certainly be opting for the first solution that we did our pros and cons for. Your son may, however, manage to give a strong enough push to being allowed to work late on the project at night and play both matches. From his point of view, the added benefit of getting to try out for the u-16s might be enough motivation to give him the enthusiasm and the energy to work on the project.

5. Implement the decision

Once you have agreed your decision, you can plan how to implement it. If it is your son's favoured solution, you might agree a late-night cut-off of midnight or 1am, beyond which he is not allowed to work, even if the project doesn't get completed. The real strength of including your son in this decision-making process has been that he now owns the decision in a manner that would not have been possible if you had imposed a solution on him. This means you can make him accountable for what happens. This increases his responsibility and it is good learning for him.

6. Review the outcome

This is the time, after the event, when you try to evaluate the decision. It is a post-mortem, of sorts, in which you go back and compare the actual outcome with the other possible outcomes. If you went with your son's favoured option, did he manage to get the project done by working the late hours or did he find that he neither got the academic work done nor had the right rest and energy levels to play good rugby? A good question to pose is whether, in similar circumstances, you would make the same decision again. If so, why? If not, why not? What has your son learned from the process?

RISK-TAKING AND DECISION-MAKING

We all know that there are many risks facing teenagers today. This is part of the reason why we want them to have good decision-making skills. Later in the book I look at things like alcohol, drugs, sexual behaviour and suicide, amongst other things. Each of these issues will force your teenager to make a choice at some stage. Unfortunately, bad choices about these risks can have terrible consequences for your son or daughter and, by extension, for you and the rest of the family.

We all know that there are many risks facing teenagers today.

As teenagers do make bad choices in any or all of these areas, we will often try to frighten them to highlight the risk involved. The reality is that teenagers do know the risks involved. Research conducted in the US shows that teenagers will overestimate their risks for negative outcomes like contracting HIV and other STIs, getting lung cancer and suffering adverse consequences of drinking alcohol. This certainly suggests that teenagers are well aware of their vulnerability. It also challenges the myth that teenagers believe themselves to be immortal and invulnerable to harm.

One factor that does seem to be important in teenage decision-making is the role of their peers. When it comes to risk-taking, it seems that simply being in the presence of other teenagers leads young people to take greater risks. In one study, teenagers and adults were asked to drive in a car simulator. In the simulation a traffic light suddenly changes from amber to red and participants have to make a split-second decision about whether to stop safely or drive through the junction as the light turns red. When teenagers and adults were alone in the mock-up car, there was no difference between the two groups in terms of how many people preferred to stop or chose to run the light. It seems that the decision to cross the junction is very much based on each individual's risk-tolerance. In other words, some people seem more comfortable with taking a higher level of risk than others.

It was only in the second part of the experiment that differences between teenagers and adults became apparent. All the participants were again asked to drive in the simulator and faced with the same scenario. The only difference was that on the second journey, they were accompanied in the mock-up car by a group of peers. On this occasion, many more teenagers ran the risk of crossing the junction than they had when they were alone in the car. In contrast, the majority of adults maintained the same level of risk and either stopped or drove on at much the same levels as they had when they were on their own. This suggests that the simple presence of other peers raises your teenager's risk-tolerance and might influence your teenager to take more risks than they would on their own.

The key to understanding teenage risk-taking is in their brain. Magnetic resonance imaging (MRI) scans of adult brains and teenage brains show that areas of the frontal lobe of the brain of teenagers are still maturing. The frontal lobe of the brain is that bit just behind your forehead, above your eyes. The frontal lobe has many tasks, but two important ones when it comes to risks are their jobs of mediating impulsivity and regulating judgements. Generally speaking, teenagers are more impulsive and are less likely to consider long-term dangers associated with a particular activity. Also, generally speaking, teenagers may not grasp the overall gist of the situation and may only focus on discrete parts of it. Let me explain both these concepts with an example.

Your teenage son has an opportunity to have sex with a girl that he fancies. The only decision he has to make is whether to use a condom or not. He may be well aware of the risks of catching a disease or of making her pregnant. Nonetheless he might choose to have unprotected sex on the basis that the likelihood of disease or pregnancy is very low from a single encounter. The perceived short-term benefit of greater pleasure and a more real experience may seem to outweigh those risks.

An adult in a similar situation is less likely to even deliberate. Adults will go straight to the gist of the situation, which is that when it comes to the risk of disease or pregnancy, nothing is worth risking one's longer-term health or future happiness. As a result, adults are more likely to make a categorical decision 'no' than a thought-through-and-deliberated-upon 'no'. It is almost as if when adults make risk decisions, the whole decision is greater than the sums of its parts. We don't just rely on measuring the pros and cons, we also have a general sense, or a gut-feeling, about a situation.

It would seem, then, that if we want teenagers to make better judgements about risk, we need to teach them to think categorically as well as rationally – we need to teach them to get the gist of a situation. The decision-making process that I outlined above very much suits teenagers' methods of deliberating between risk and reward. The only thing it doesn't do is to give them a sense that sometimes no possible benefit is worth a particular risk. So while it will teach them good rationalization when it comes to decisions, it doesn't help them to rely on their gut instinct. You might find it helpful to use analogies to explain this concept to your teenager. One such analogy is, for example, the question: 'Would you play Russian roulette for €1 million?' This forces them to think in more categorical ways.

However, as we know that teenagers' brains are still maturing and developing, we also know that they will find this skill hard to master. Importantly, we also need to manage their exposure to risks. We still need to limit them as much as is reasonable from being in risky situations or having to make risky choices while their brains mature and their decision-making skill improves.

UNDERSTANDING POWER

I was tempted to title this section 'power and control', but actually my understanding of power is that it is really all about influence. Many of us are reluctant to talk about power. We see power as a bad thing. We sometimes assume that because one person has power, then other people don't have it. We think power means dominating and controlling others without care. We even see power, sometimes, as corrupting. But power is not a bad thing. If I am powerful, it doesn't actually take from your power. Let me use an analogy to explain.

Imagine that you and I are batteries that are used to power two torches. I am a big battery and you are a little battery. Obviously I hold my power internally and so do you. Just because I am a bigger battery with more power, it doesn't diminish your size or your power. If we want to compete, then we can compare our power levels and decide that I have more and so maybe it is me that should supply the power to both torches. But if we don't want to compete, then we could hook ourselves up in tandem and use our combined power to supply both torches and maybe even a third torch. This is the use of our combined power in a collaborative manner.

As parents we need to be powerful because we need to be able to influence our children and our teenagers. But we don't have to use our power to compete with them all the time. When teenagers disrespect us, ignore us and do their own thing, irrespective of our wishes, it can seem like we have lost the ability to influence them. In terms of the power competition, we seem to be losing. I would suggest, however, that we might in fact be trying to use the wrong kind of power to influence our teenagers or using it in the wrong way. First, then, let me describe the various sources of power that I perceive within families.

ROLE POWER

We are probably more used to having role power associated with our working lives. For example, we may be a manager, or chairperson of a meeting, or the head of a division or a project team leader. Each of these roles comes with a certain level of power, such as supervising other people's work or other people needing our approval before they act. It may be up to us to dictate what other people do and when they do it. If we apply role power to the position of parent, then maybe it was most recognizable when your children were younger and you expected them to do things simply because you told them to. So whenever you found yourself saying, 'because I am the parent and because I say so,' as the justification for your child or teenager to do as you asked, you were relying on your own role power. It is our job to make decisions on behalf of our small children and so it is a good thing to have role power in those instances. We need to be able to tell our child to stop when they are about to run out into a roadway and have them respond instantly because it has come from us.

RESOURCE POWER

Resource power refers to the power we have to control things with rewards and sanctions. Certainly, we rely heavily on resource power as a means of influencing our children's behaviour. Most of us will have used the promise of rewards or the threat of consequences as behaviour-management strategies for encouraging compliance with our wishes. These are tried-and-tested strategies that we know will work. The difficulty is that they should not be the only strategies upon which we rely to influence our children because by their teenage years, we may not be able to find the right kinds of rewards to motivate them or we may find that they dismiss, reject or ignore the consequences that we set.

PERSONAL POWER

The power that derives from who we are as a person is sometimes more intangible and harder to define. But often it can be thought of in terms of things like our charisma, our expertise, our willpower and our confidence. Personal power tends to motivate and influence people because they believe in us and want to please us. People with a lot of personal power generally have a good ability to communicate, they build relationships and they can attract other people by instilling a sense of self-belief about how

5. SELF-ESTEEM

promoting it, cherishing it and building on it

I get regular requests to talk to parents about self-esteem. They worry about how their sons and daughters are making their way in the world and often attribute many of the obstacles and hassles that their teenagers face to issues with their self-esteem.

They worry that their teenagers are not confident. They worry that they don't stand up for themselves. They worry about a son's negative view of his ability, or a daughter's severe criticism of how she looks. When teenagers are withdrawn, self-absorbed or preoccupied with how they fit (or not) within their immediate social circle, parents will typically question the strength of their self-esteem. Many times that questioning is valid, and it is usually valid because self-esteem is one of those social and emotional constructions that is so bound into many of the ways in which we think, feel, act and experience our bodies. Our environment and the things that happen to us in life also greatly influence self-esteem, often mediated by our thinking and feeling. Self-esteem is hugely influential in how we interact with others and how we perceive the messages we get from them.

Research shows that having low self-esteem is associated with lots of risk factors for teenagers. For example, youngsters with low self-esteem are much more likely to be dependent, conforming and susceptible to peer pressure. So teenagers with low self-esteem are much more likely to follow a crowd and end up doing what everyone else is doing rather than standing up for themselves. In contrast, the research also shows that high self-esteem is related to emotional maturity, stability, realism and a high frustration tolerance. So we tend to cope better in the world when we have high self-worth or self-esteem.

Our perceptions of the judgements we receive from others form the basis for our beliefs and understandings of ourselves. The biggest single influence on our teenager's self-esteem is us, their parents. How we treat, respond to and judge our children and teenagers will have a big impact on the strength of their self-esteem. Again, researchers can shine a light on this for us: it has been shown that the more conflict there is in a family, the lower the self-esteem of the children and teenagers living in that family.

Self-esteem is one of those issues that can seem a bit 'chicken-and-egg'-like. For example, do our teenagers have low self-esteem and therefore think and act in negative ways? Or, alternatively, do they receive constant criticism from us or their peers that eventually leads them to think badly about themselves and develop low self-esteem?

The reality is that it is probably a mixture of both. On the one hand, children and teenagers do frequently get judged on their behaviour. If that judgement is predominantly negative, then they will almost certainly begin to judge themselves negatively and so develop low self-esteem or self-worth. On the other hand, there are some children who do believe that they are not worthy, that they are at their core unlovable, and they do go on to create self-fulfilling prophecies whereby they behave in ways that make it very difficult for anyone to accept them or at times to love them.

By the time they are hitting their teenage years, those children will certainly feel like they have nothing to lose when it comes to acting badly. If their own, and other's, expectation of them is low, then they won't be surprising anyone by acting as ne'er-do-wells at home, at school or out on the street. They will be equally unlikely to feel motivated to achieve for themselves because in their heads, what is the point? If I never do well, why bother trying? If I have never been able to succeed academically, never been able to read or write as well as my peers, why should moving to secondary school be an exciting challenge? It is more likely to be a further nail in my coffin of self-belief.

In effect, self-esteem can be part of an ongoing negative cycle for some teenagers. Feeling useless and believing that you are not worth having good things happen to you will almost certainly lead you into activities and pastimes that underline that uselessness or lack of self-worth. As the adults around you perceive those activities to be negative or bad, you get lots of negative feedback from them about how bad, bold, disrespectful, lazy, selfish and even delinquent you are. With that kind of feedback coming your way regularly, it is easy to continue to believe that you are, in fact, bad.

So, the evidence is there that self-esteem is one of those things worth investing in. My plan in this chapter is to give you the understanding about self-esteem and the tools needed to build it in your teenager.

THIS CHAPTER LOOKS AT . . .

→ **What is self-esteem?**

→ **The importance of parents' own self-esteem**

→ **Things that can be bad for self-esteem**
- ✳ *Unreasonable expectations and attitudes*
- ✳ *Self-depracation*
- ✳ *Not minding your body*
- ✳ *Rejecting positive feedback*

→ **Strategies for building self-esteem**
- ✳ *Identify strengths and abilities*
- ✳ *Give opportunities to contribute*
- ✳ *Treat mistakes as learning opportunities*
- ✳ *Let your teenager solve problems and make choices*
- ✳ *Encourage effort rather than success*
- ✳ *Give undivided attention*
- ✳ *Accept your teenager for who he/she is*
- ✳ *Communicate with respect*

that you are proud of his achievement at sport. So you might say something like, 'You did great scoring that goal, son, I'm really proud of you!' This will undoubtedly be of benefit to him. But if you were to say, 'You did great scoring that goal, son, you must feel really proud of yourself!', then the impact is even greater. In the latter case you are encouraging your son to be proud of himself, never mind whether or not you are proud of him.

Our own self-esteem plays a very significant part in our ability to positively affect our teenagers' self-esteem. If, deep in your heart, you don't believe that you are a worthy person, it is very hard to pass on a sense of worth to your children and subsequently teenagers. We will probably have developed our self-esteem from the sense we made of a lot of our own experiences as a child. Depending on whether our interactions with our own parents, relatives and teachers were generally positive and affirming or negative and dismissive, we will probably have come to develop either a belief that we have a clear place in the world or, at the other extreme, a deep self-hatred and a belief that we will be rejected in the world.

There comes a point at which we can no longer simply blame our experiences in childhood, but must come to accept that we actually continue to maintain our level of self-esteem in adulthood. While the early development of your self-esteem may have been heavily influenced by your parents and others close to you, as an adult you must now take responsibility for how that self-esteem either develops or continues to remain low. It is possible to change your self-esteem and to begin to feel more positively about yourself. But first you will need to challenge certain kinds of behaviour that you engage in that actually serve to keep your self-esteem low. I explain several types of this behaviour in the next section. I have also suggested ways of challenging those behaviours and thoughts. Indeed, as you think about these behaviours with regard to yourself, it is also possible to identify whether they might apply to your teenager.

→ Paula: Perpetuating low self-esteem

Paula was a mum who came to see me about her thirteen-year-old daughter, Ellen. Ellen was being bullied in her new secondary school by a group of girls who consistently excluded her from their games and said mean things to her. Paula herself was terribly upset that Ellen was being treated in this fashion. Very quickly in our first session she described how Ellen's experiences had triggered memories for her of being bullied in her own primary school.

As she talked about Ellen's difficulties fitting in to the group in school I could see Ellen sinking further into her chair as her eyes remained firmly downcast. I suggested to Paula that she and I might meet separately and that I would meet with Ellen on her own for a short while that first day. Ellen stayed very shy throughout our first meeting and while I empathized with her situation I didn't make any suggestions to her about how to change things. First I wanted to talk to her mum in greater detail.

The next session I held with just Paula. I explored further her childhood experiences of bullying. It turned out that she too was criticized by other girls and told that she wasn't good enough to be part of their clique. Those experiences had been mirrored in her workplace, where she got consistent negative feedback from her boss for her performance, and which she left as soon as she got married to Ellen's dad. In fact, Paula felt that she had been put down by other people all her life. She kept repeating to me that 'I know I should be able to stand up to those people, but I just don't feel able.' She also confided that some of the criticisms of her were probably warranted as she may not be the most efficient worker. When I questioned her about this she explained that she never seemed to have enough time to do anything and always felt that projects were backing up on her. She extended this difficulty to her current home life where she felt that she was constantly rushing around and never seemed to be able to complete any tasks that she set for herself.

When I asked her about her relationship with her husband she described him as 'really very good to me . . . considering . . . ' I invited her to finish this statement and she went on to say, 'well, considering, that I make such a mess of being a mother'. It seems that her husband was also critical of her parenting ability and her capacity to keep the house and home functioning. She described that she 'ought' to be able to keep it spotless since she had all day that Ellen was in school to work at it. She explained that her husband had exacting standards in relation to many aspects of their home life, which she approved of, and which she felt obliged to uphold.

Towards the end of the session I suggested to Paula that she didn't seem very happy with her life. She simply shrugged and replied that 'everyone has crosses to bear'. Rather than accept her view I challenged her by suggesting that she'd enjoy life more if she felt valued and useful, rather than feeling like a failure as she did much of the time. She looked at me, not quite sure what I meant, then wondered out loud, was the therapy not supposed to be for Ellen rather than for her.

Since she had raised the point, albeit facetiously, I went on to give her my opinion that sometimes the most effective therapy with children and teenagers is carried out by their parents. All their parents might need is a little guidance and direction from someone like me to point them in a helpful direction. I explained that if Paula were the one to help Ellen to build her self-esteem and give her specific strategies for dealing with the bullies she was encountering, that it would strengthen their relationship and would feel more normal for Ellen than having to 'attend a psychologist' and perhaps believe that there was something wrong with her.

What I didn't explain to Paula that day was another opinion I had that sometimes parents who have very low self-esteem can role model, negatively, poor coping strategies. I hoped that by ostensibly focusing on strategies for Ellen to build her self-esteem and deal with the bullies then Paula, too, might gain insight into how her own self-esteem was low and how she might benefit from feeling more capable and more valued in her life. I was sure that if Paula started to feel better about herself this would transfer, positively, to Ellen, who then might begin to value herself.

I felt very pleased with myself for both my clinical insights and my plan to help build Paula's self-esteem so that she could in turn build Ellen's self-esteem. The only glitch was that Paula and Ellen never came back. Perhaps Paula didn't appreciate my insinuation that she might need help herself, perhaps she felt that I wasn't focusing directly enough on helping Ellen or perhaps her husband pulled the plug on their attendance. Who knows the reason, but I do wonder now how things turned out for them.

UNREASONABLE EXPECTATIONS AND ATTITUDES

Sometimes we can get stuck when we have rigid and inflexible attitudes. Those attitudes might be about us, they might be about other people or they might be about the future. Typically, when we think in ways that include the words 'should', 'must', 'have to', 'ought to' and so on, we are adopting this kind of thinking. 'Having to' do something leaves little room for manoeuvre! Think about phrases like 'I must keep the house clean,' 'My son should obey me,' 'Things will never change,' 'I ought to help out at the school fair.' In each of these situations you are putting unreasonably high expectations and demands upon yourself. Usually we justify these demands and beliefs by telling ourselves that nobody else is in a position to influence the particular situation, only ourselves. If we don't do it, then nobody will. There is a high likelihood that those expectations can never be met, with the result that you will continuously feel like you are failing if you don't achieve the standard you have set.

Part of the antidote to this kind of thinking is to look around and spread the responsibility. You need to realize that there are other people, close to you, who can share the burden. You might also want to re-evaluate some of your expectations of yourself and lower them to make them more reasonable and more achievable.

I am not suggesting that you shy away from challenges altogether. Even though introducing change might provoke anxiety, try to feel that fear and do it anyway. One of the big blocks to accepting challenge when you have low self-esteem is this fear of failure. But failure is actually a relative term. If the only measure of success and failure is the final outcome, then trying something new could indeed be a risky occupation. After all, who can predict with certainty that you will reach the goal? But the simple act of trying something new can be viewed as a success in itself. Investing effort, taking risks and learning new things about your abilities are also measures of success, irrespective of whether your final goal is achieved.

THINGS THAT CAN BE BAD FOR SELF-ESTEEM

SELF-DEPRECATION

Another common thing you will do if you have low self-esteem is to talk about yourself in a self-deprecating way, a way that puts yourself down. 'I was terrible at school so I am no use to you now with your homework,' 'I never get anything right,' 'Everyone else seems so confident.' These statements are all examples of self-deprecation. They all reflect either dissatisfaction with or dislike of your current situation, yourself or indeed a rejection of yourself and your ability. In this way they might simply be an extension of the feelings of rejection and dismissal you had when you were a child.

You can challenge this kind of negative thinking. The first step is to notice that you put yourself down. If you think negatively about yourself and your abilities, then you must bring your awareness to that. Once you realize the ways in which you talk yourself down, you can engage in positive self-talk. So for every time that you think you can't do something, you turn it around and tell yourself, 'if I work hard, I can make progress.' Or you might find it helpful to affirm yourself in a number of ways, for example, by repeating phrases like 'I am a unique being,' 'I deserve respect,' 'I am useful,' 'I am worthy of being valued and loved because I am good.' Repeating these statements on a regular basis, allowing them to reverberate and to become true for you may help to combat some of the negative attributes that you currently assign to yourself.

NOT MINDING YOUR BODY

How we look after ourselves physically is another way in which we can run down our self-esteem. Be wary if you find: that you are constantly rushing and racing; that you have little family time; that you have to do everything perfectly; that you suffer from sleeplessness and are overtired; that you rarely say 'no' to the demands that are made of you; that you're fretful; that you are under- or overeating; or that you become dependent upon alcohol or drugs. These are all signs that you're not minding yourself and it is likely that you are not minding yourself because you don't feel that you're worthy of being minded.

You can show caring towards yourself by slowing down your lifestyle, by eating healthily, by taking regular exercise, by socializing with friends, by taking time for leisure, by treating yourself and by acting in a calm and relaxed way.

In your heart, you need to accept that you are worth caring for. You can show caring towards yourself by slowing down your lifestyle, by eating healthily, by taking regular exercise, by socializing with friends, by taking time for leisure, by treating yourself and by acting in a calm and relaxed way.

REJECTING POSITIVE FEEDBACK

If you have low self-esteem, you probably find it very hard to accept a compliment, affection or positive feedback from other people. While you may be very aware of criticism and negative feedback, you are probably more likely to discount and ignore the positive feedback. I think back to the feedback sheets I used to get following my public talks and how I would always pick out the few negative comments and quickly skim over the many positive comments. Another way in which we do this is to see praise as specific to the one situation (and so not generally applicable to us), whereas we will view criticism as a general comment on our state of being, a comment that applies to all aspects of ourselves. Sometimes this is because we are predisposed to focusing on the negative. To challenge this tendency you might want to start recording the good things that happen in your life. I am forever suggesting to parents that they catch their child being good instead of catching them being bad. In order to get into this habit, I get them to write down three good things their child did each day. It is amazing how much positivity occurs in life that we just don't pay attention to.

Another thing to try is slowing down in those situations where do you get positive feedback from others and attend to it. Notice what is being said and allow it to fit with what you know about yourself, or allow it to become learning for what you can know about yourself. Similarly, if somebody is critical of you or your behaviour, then recognize that this is their judgement and don't automatically assume it to be correct. Try to keep the criticism specific to your action on that occasion and challenge any belief that this reflects a general problem for you.

STRATEGIES FOR BUILDING SELF-ESTEEM

As in many situations of parenting, the first step to minding our children and our teenagers is to start minding ourselves. We have to look at our own self-esteem and try to avoid both modelling behaviours and reacting from our low self-esteem in our interactions with our teenagers. We need to feel good about ourselves so that we can help our teenagers to feel good about themselves. With all this in mind, you won't be surprised to learn that the strategies for helping your teenager to build their self-esteem follow similar lines. The strategies are designed to either help them feel good about their abilities and their capability or to help them feel loved, accepted and valued in their own right.

IDENTIFY STRENGTHS AND ABILITIES

We usually assume that our children, and certainly our teenagers, know what they are good at. Most of us have praised them along the way for their performances at sport, or music, in drama or academically. Yet many youngsters doubt their ability in a range of areas. Many of them might have a sense of skill in one particular field, such as a sport, but see it as a specific talent. This means that they then can discount its importance as a general indicator of their capability. So when, for example, your seventeen-year-old daughter struggles to study for her Leaving Certificate and complains of being a terrible student who will amount to nothing in life, you might remind her of the athletic talent she has demonstrated in regional and national championships. Her typical response will be, 'Yeah, well, that's true, but running won't get me a job and I can't run through the exams.' It is hard then to counter that logic.

In fact, it is tempting to let her dismiss her athletic ability because it doesn't seem to be related to her studying capacity. But I would suggest that you can try to challenge her negative outlook by identifying what it is about her running that is both positive and transferable to other situations. So, you might explain about the racing strategy she uses, like determining when to push harder or when to hold back a little. Or describe the judgements she makes about her comfort and physical reserves during a race. Acknowledge her determination and dedication to train hard and how she stays fighting in a race even when the going gets tough. These broader aspects of her personality and thinking style can certainly help her with her attitude to studying and can also give her a strong reminder of how accomplished and effective she can be.

A harder dilemma for some parents is finding strengths and abilities in a son or daughter who has dropped out of sport or other activities and is lethargic and unmotivated to do anything. Where do you begin to draw out anything positive about this kind of child?

If we look at the comments just above and try to rephrase them in ways that show acceptance of who your teenager is but that still acknowledge how you feel, they might look like this: 'I don't understand piercing, it seems to me like a mutilation of your body,' 'The music you listen to just wrecks my head. Have you thought about using headphones?', 'I worry about the messages you send out when you wear those clothes. I worry that people will only view you as a sexual object and not a whole person,' 'I feel angry when I see you lying around the house all day because I get no help and I worry that you get unhealthy,' 'It upsets me to think that if you keep following the example of your friends, it's only a matter of time before you start getting into the same kind of trouble that they are in.'

If you look closely at the rephrasing of the comments, you will notice that the most important change is that now you are talking about how you feel and about what you observe, you're not making judgements about your teenager. Look, for example, at all the 'I' statements that are used in the rephrased comments. There is a greater sense of respect visible in the second set of phrasing.

COMMUNICATE WITH RESPECT

As I have just shown, it is all too easy to dismiss, mock or denigrate your teenager. You may have heard the phrase, 'praise in public; punish in private'. When other people are around the idea is to build your teenager up, to try to help them feel good about themselves. When you do have grounds to be critical of their behaviour or of how they are speaking, then choose a private moment to talk about it. Avoid being dismissive of your teenager's opinion just because you don't agree with it.

Look back at the chapter on communication and think again about the ways in which you speak to your teenager. Think about whether you open up conversations to allow them to explore their own ideas and beliefs, or whether you close down conversations to try to ensure that it is your word and only your word that ever gets heard in your house. Think about the way in which you talk to your teenager, including the non-verbal behaviour that you use and the tone of your voice, and try to work out whether your teenager is going to feel uplifted by your communication with them or just put down. Remember that if you don't lift them up, they may not have the energy, skill or motivation to lift themselves up.

IN CASE OF EMERGENCY . . . KEY POINTS TO REMEMBER

→ Self-esteem is essentially the extent to which we value ourselves and see ourselves as worthy individuals.

→ Self-esteem is concerned with two main areas: our sense of being lovable and our sense of being capable.

→ Self-esteem is hugely influential in how we interact with others and how we perceive the messages we get from them.

→ Our perceptions of the judgements we receive from others form the basis for our beliefs and understandings of ourselves.

→ The biggest single influence on our teenager's self-esteem is us, their parents. How we treat, respond to and judge our children and teenagers will have a big impact on the strength of their self-esteem.

→ Identifying the strengths and abilities of our teenagers will help to build their self-esteem by giving them reminders of their accomplishments and their effectiveness.

→ Giving our teenagers opportunities to contribute to the family gives them a feeling of usefulness that also bolsters self-esteem.

→ Feeling blamed for making mistakes will make teenagers feel worse about themselves, whereas if we treat mistakes as learning opportunities then they get more sense of personal growth.

→ The more chances that teenagers have to make choices and solve problems the more responsible they feel and it too builds self-esteem.

→ Acknowledging effort (rather than just success) is a means of combating a feeling of failure that will have a huge impact on your teenager's development of internal motivation.

→ When your teenager feels acknowledged and noticed, particularly for positive things, then they will feel better about themselves.

→ Teenagers have their own thoughts, feelings and beliefs, which matter to them. Accepting your teenager for who they are gives recognition to the heart and soul that may not be visible.

→ Try to be respectful in talking with your teenager, avoiding the temptation to dismiss, ridicule or denigrate them. Your job is to build them up, not break them down.

6. PEER PRESSURE

'but *everyone* else is doing it, so why can't I?' Why, indeed!

During adolescence peers (i.e. their friends of a similar age) play a large part in a young person's life and typically replace family as the centre of a teenager's social and leisure activities. Teenagers have various peer relationships and they interact with many peer groups. Parents, naturally, worry about the 'herd' mentality that might exist in such groups. One strong leading voice might require all in the group to follow the behaviour and opinions that he/she voices. Teenagers who are 'easily led' become vulnerable in such situations to the will of another or a group of others. Some youngsters give in to peer pressure because they want to be liked, to fit in, or because they worry that other youngsters may make fun of them if they don't go along with the group. Others may go along because they are curious to try something new that others are doing. The idea that 'everyone's doing it' may influence some youngsters to leave their better judgement, or their common sense, behind.

As children grow, develop and move into early adolescence, involvement with peers and the attraction of peer identification increases. As pre-adolescents begin rapid physical, emotional and social changes, they begin to question adult standards and the need for parental guidance. They find it reassuring to turn for advice to friends who understand and sympathize, friends who are in the same position themselves. The perception of many teenagers is that even if they wanted to have the support or advice of their parents, their parents 'don't listen'. When we parents do make ourselves available to talk and listen to our teenage children we get told, 'You don't understand.'

By trying new things and testing their ideas with their peers, there is less fear of being ridiculed or 'shot down'. It is within the safety of such a group that they can experiment with their newly developing identity. Working out who you are and what you believe in is a tricky and at times risky business. So it makes sense to surround yourself with others that you think believe in the same kind of things that you do.

Like many other adults, I can often feel nervous when I see a group of teenagers whom I don't know. I anticipate that they will perceive safety in numbers and use their collective psychological strength to challenge me in some way. Of course, this view reflects some of my own vulnerabilities, but it also, I believe, reflects the energy that teenagers derive from engaging with and feeling part of a defined peer group. A group of teenagers will often appear greater than the sum of its parts. You may have found that your son's or daughter's friends are lovely on a one-to-one basis, but as soon as they are together they appear more aloof and even condescending. Whatever it is, there is definitely something going on with teenagers and their peers!

My intention in this chapter is to give you insight into that powerful draw of friends during the teenage years. That draw can be an incredibly positive thing for your teenager, but it can also be difficult for them and challenging for you as a parent. So we'll look at all the dynamics of peer friendships and the pressures they put on our youngsters and on us. For example, how do you respond when your teenager wants to do something because all their friends are doing it, like going to the disco? Where can teenagers hang out? What kind of social spaces are created that can allow teenagers to congregate safely? What do you do when friendships turn sour or when bullying begins? Are there other kinds of relationships that you can nurture that might help you to counteract some of the negative effects of peer pressure? I also want to examine the ways in which teenagers seem to socialize now, looking at the influence of mobile phones, instant messaging and social networking online.

HOW PEER PRESSURE WORKS

Usually we think peer pressure is an attempt to get someone to do something dangerous or unhealthy by the use of heavy-handed (and at times threatening) taunts, pleadings or demands. It is rarely that obvious, however. Occasionally, there may be attempts by a group of 'bad kids' to convince a 'good kid' to try a drug, change a relationship or break the rules of school or society. But when you look closer at how the majority of teenagers are interacting, you see that this form of peer pressure makes up only a small proportion of the many ways that peers become direct or indirect influences on each other. Peer pressure is usually not so overt, threatening and relentless. In fact, most of us willingly choose groups of people with whom we feel comfortable. Once we feel part of that group and identify with the norms of the group in terms of attitudes or behaviour, we allow those norms to influence and even override our personal habits, our individual moral inhibitions or our own desires. We willingly go along with the group. There is a wonderful slogan T-shirt that says: 'The Goth Society – individuality through conformity'. That's a fairly concise rendering of teenagers' willingness to submerge into peer group mores while establishing themselves as separate from their parents and some other teenagers.

It seems that peer pressure is so influential partly because it is often quite subtle and difficult to detect. A teenager going to a party and simply observing behaviour such as drinking, smoking or other drug use amongst all their friends could feel enough pressure to conform and engage in those behaviours themselves. The role-modelling of their friends is a powerful influencer for them. This is especially the case if their closest friends are the ones drinking. The primary influence in any teenager's life is their closest friends (just when you thought it might be you!). Although acquaintances, and even strangers, could exert some amount of peer pressure, it is usually the close friends who are most influential.

This also catches us parents by surprise. We expect to have to deal with large group pressures from systems like school or sports clubs. This is not surprising given that it is the general social or cultural pressures on teenagers that receive most attention in places like the media. The large group exerts a general pressure on its members. It directs the trends in clothing, music, habits and behaviours, entertainment and 'political correctness'. The pressure to conform varies; it is not usually a spoken or written guideline, it's just what 'everyone' is doing. In these situations peer pressure can actually be avoided by keeping quiet or by putting on the appearance of conformity.

It is when you look at the close relationship your son has with one, or several, best friends that you see real pressure. This is the setting that is sometimes overlooked. The pressure that takes place among close friends is not so easy to escape. You can't fake it with them: they know what you stand for and what you really believe. The nature of close friendship is that you care more about them and their opinions than those of anybody else. What your best friend approves of or disapproves of exerts great pressure on you. This pressure is personal and forceful.

In my work with parents and teenagers I regularly find that it is friendships that have been freshly formed in teenage years that become one of the biggest areas of conflict. So many parents describe how their son was easy-going, relaxed and reasonably focused in his primary school years, but as he made the transition to secondary school it seemed to his parents that everything changed. Parents then attribute this change to the new friends that were made in secondary school. And it is true that if your son's or daughter's new best friend happens to be independently into alcohol, drugs, mitching from school, getting into fights or getting into trouble with the law, then there is a greater likelihood that your child will get drawn into this too.

It is also completely understandable that teenagers give in to peer pressure because they need that companionship and they need to be accepted. This is human nature; there is nothing we can do about it. So, perhaps our role as parents is to try to influence our teenagers who are so caught up in this companionship that they are willing to sacrifice who they are (or who they think they are) just to receive it.

TEENAGE CONGREGATIONS

We all know, intuitively, that teenagers need to hang out. We know that it's good for them, socially and developmentally, to be with their peers. But when you look around most villages, towns and cities it seems there are very few natural places for teens to go to hang out with each other. This is why street corners, parks and young children's playgrounds become teen zones. But usually these become places for teenagers to congregate by default and mostly teenagers are not welcome in these places. I have already described my anxiety when I come across a group of teenagers and if I feel it, I'm sure that others do too. Sometimes, then, there is an automatic assumption that groups of teenagers are a threat and a menace.

In continental Europe there are specially designated public areas that were created for teenagers. These are usually places that provide some kind of shelter from the elements and therefore become a natural place to come to be together. Some of the arguments against creating such social spaces are that once teenagers get together, there will be an increase in littering, an increase in antisocial behaviour and consequently a greater threat to the local community. Thankfully, what these communities have actually found is that by creating spaces for teenagers to go and to congregate in more open and public areas, it leads to less socializing on street corners and in playgrounds designated for young children. Those who worried about the potential threat found that the streets, parks and playgrounds get reclaimed for other groups in society to use freely. Because the areas are open and public there is less antisocial behaviour, and while there is more litter generated by having groups together it tends to be localized and therefore easier for the local authorities to clean it up.

We have very few designated social teenage spaces in Ireland. Sports clubs, drama groups and most importantly schools are probably the biggest of our venues for teenagers to congregate in. The great thing about these places is that, in theory, the activities should be having a positive influence on your teenager.

I know also from talking to many parents that they really worry about what's happening once their teenager is gone out of the house. Automatically, parents are left with less control and greater anxiety about the potential dangers and temptations that are out there for their teenagers. For many parents this anxiety is offset by their knowledge that their son or daughter is reasonably responsible and mature and so they can place greater faith in them. Some parents try to counteract the desire to be out and about by inviting their teenager's friends to come to their house. Aside from the obvious problem of an increase in smelly feet, this can also put pressures on parents because as the host of a gathering of teenagers, most parents feel responsible for what those teenagers are doing. Another part of the developmental process for teenagers is that they do need to have space that is private and separate from their parents. So even when teenagers are in your house, you're not going to be interacting with them all the time and so similarly you are still not always in a position to influence their behaviour (although there is the hope of at least some supervision!).

Irrespective of the venue, lots of parents are left with the dilemma about how much social freedom to give their teenager. And it is a big dilemma, especially as there is a limit to how much parents can enforce a decision not to allow their teenager to go out. And with so few places to go, I think this is why venues like discos have an additional relevance for teenagers. In fact, making a decision about whether or not your daughter or your son is going to go to their local disco is one of the typical trigger points of conflict in many homes.

GOING TO THE DISCO, OR NOT?

There are always risks for young teenagers, especially when going out unsupervised to a disco. However, there are also benefits for them, socially and developmentally, from going out with their friends. Sooner or later you need to be able to let your teenager take increasing responsibility for their behaviour and that includes letting them go to discos. Developmentally, it is important for them to be trusted by you, even if they make a mess of that trust on occasion. They also need to practise mixing with, negotiating with and being self-assured with the opposite sex. Discos provide all those things, as well as being good fun.

Most of us worry about our youngsters getting drunk, getting stoned or getting laid. We know from our own experience and from all of the media reporting that discos are magnets for all of these kinds of behaviours and so our danger antennae are very much on high alert. But we need to remember that alcohol, drugs and sexual experiences are available to lots of youngsters, irrespective of whether they go to the local disco. We are right to be protective of our children and teenagers, but we need to recognize that there are limits to how much we can achieve this.

When it comes to deciding about letting your child out to the disco, here are some of those factors that I think you should consider in making your decision.

MATURITY AND RESPONSIBILITY OF YOUR TEENAGER

One of the first judgements you need to make is about how mature and responsible your teenager is. You need to think about how your teenager interacts with their peers. Does your son seem confident and assured when he's with his mates? Have you ever had examples where you know he's gone against the group plan? While it is not the only indicator of responsibility, it is certainly encouraging for parents to see this kind of self-aware behaviour. Of course, just because he can stand up for himself in one situation is no guarantee that he will continue to stand up for himself in all situations, but it does nonetheless provide a little bit of comfort for you. You can at least hope that if he finds himself in a situation where he doesn't agree with what is being suggested, he might stick to his own beliefs.

It's also worth looking for evidence that your daughter has been responsible and trustworthy in other situations. So, for example, if you've gone out and left her on her own in the house and she has stuck to her word that she won't have friends in, that's a good sign. Another example might be if your son is able to manage his money such that he never really seems to go short and isn't constantly haranguing you for extra cash. If your son or daughter works a part-time job, then what is the opinion of their employer about their responsibility and trustworthiness? You may find, also, that your own sisters and brothers who will have interacted with your son or daughter will have an opinion about how responsible they are.

Nonetheless, even the most mature and responsible of teenagers will make mistakes. So there are bound to be times when they get themselves into trouble and what you need to be confident about is what they do when trouble strikes. Ideally, what you want is for your son to come to tell you that he is in trouble. The more you know, the more you can help. In contrast, if your son is secretive and blocks you from everything going on in his life, then you can be pretty sure that if problems emerge at the disco you won't hear about them.

WHAT YOU NEED TO KNOW ABOUT THE DISCO

You can be pretty sure that whatever information you receive from your teenager about the disco is probably only half the story. They may tell you that it's an under-fifteens disco, there is no alcohol served and that everybody goes. When you begin to explore a bit more, probably by checking with other parents, you will discover that not everybody goes and that there is plenty of alcohol available around the venue. In your exploration, try to find out who is organizing the disco. Then, check

You can be pretty sure that whatever information you receive from your teenager about the disco is probably only half the story.

MOBILE PHONES AND ONLINE SOCIAL NETWORKING

I think it is fair to say that teenagers get addicted to their phones. There is almost instant feedback to be had from using your phone. It can seem that texting and teenagers are synonymous. A text sent always invites a response and even that anticipation is reinforcing as the sense of expectation slightly heightens our adrenalin levels. Research backs up this view with reports that teenagers feel that texting beats talking because it allows for greater multi-tasking capacity, speed, control and privacy. A US study published in October 2008 found that 42 per cent of teenagers can text with their eyes closed!

Indeed, I was once counselling a fifteen-year-old lad who had been talking on and off about his relationship with his new girlfriend over a few weeks. One week when he didn't mention her I enquired after her. He explained that they had discussed the state of their relationship and decided that actually they didn't really fit well together and that they should split up. I empathized, but reinforced the apparent maturity of their communication and decision-making. He nodded and then told me, 'In her last text she said that if anyone asked I was to say she dumped me.' It turns out the whole 'discussion' about breaking up had simply been two or three texts in each direction.

Teenagers, just like the rest of us, become dependent on their phones for the simplest of social arrangements. I've had the experience of coming up to Dublin for a two-day trip and leaving my mobile behind, and I felt like I was missing a limb. I felt my life was more complicated because it made changing any aspect of my pre-planned schedule more difficult. I was so desperate that I made an appeal on the radio for anyone passing my house to bring it up to me, but then realized that without my phone I couldn't coordinate a drop-off in case anything changed in my plans so that I might miss the delivery.

There is also the fear of missing out that drives many of us, teens included, to want to stay connected. This can be especially important for teenagers who definitely want to stay in the loop with their friends. This is backed up by other findings of that US study, which showed that over half of the teenagers surveyed see their mobile phone as the key to their social life. Interestingly, the same US teenagers also use the mobile phone as an indicator of social status and popularity.

Teenagers, just like the rest of us, become dependent on their phones for the simplest of social arrangements.

WHY THE CONNECTIVITY IS A GOOD THING

Both the ease of communication and the wide extent of communication are good things. It's good that teenagers can be in contact. Just before I was writing about teenagers socializing in a physical sense and I spoke about teenagers needing safe, adult-free zones where they can be, and interact, with other teenagers. A mobile world allows for that. In fact, I would extend this to include social networking sites like Bebo or MySpace. In both social networking sites and a social phone network, teenagers create a digital space to interact with one another without parents and other adults.

Although, as all our parents would have told us, 'too much of anything is a bad thing'. Moderation is the name of the game. For some parents it is the 24/7 nature of their teenager's use of the mobile that creates the problem. Their mobile phone use needs to be balanced with real-life networking; hanging out with friends and involvement in school and activities inside and outside your house.

SOME OF THE DANGERS INVOLVED

There are dangers involved in both overuse of the phone and in social networking. A 2008 study in Sweden on youngsters aged between fourteen and twenty showed that teenagers who excessively use their mobile phone are more prone to disrupted sleep, restlessness, stress and fatigue. These findings are as a result of their daytime use of the phone. But some teenagers are connected around the clock. One of my teenage clients explained that she regularly gets texts coming in at 1.00, 2.00 and 3.00 in the morning and will always sleep with an ear to the phone and will always respond to any contact, no matter what the time. Overuse of a phone, therefore, has clear health dangers.

Bullying by phone and online is also easier and more faceless and, as I discuss in the next chapter, you'll often see hurtful comments being passed by text or online, profiles being altered online, or humiliating photos being taken and shared. A survey conducted by the National Centre for Technology in Education in Ireland in 2008 found that over half of teenagers who use social networking sites had suffered or witnessed cyber-bullying, such as hate messages, unsolicited pornography, threats or abusive solicitations.

Also, many of us forget that anything we upload to a website will have the potential to be there forever because even if we subsequently remove it, someone else may have downloaded it to later upload again. Even when you restrict access to just 'friends', your information, photos and such can get forwarded on to people you don't know. Teenagers are not known for their foresight and planning, so it is quite likely that they could impulsively upload some embarrassing photos for a laugh. It has already happened that some employers are now paying companies to trawl the internet, looking for any information about prospective candidates for employment. Would you want a future employer to be looking at piccies of your son puking his guts up or mooning with his mates?

The same Irish study found that 40 per cent of teenagers had met someone face-to-face that they had first gotten to know online. Everyone talks about the potential dangers of this, yet its prevalence suggests we really need to educate teenagers about this.

GUIDELINES FOR MOBILE PHONE AND INTERNET MONITORING

In an ideal world you will have agreed rules from day one of your child's first mobile phone or when teaching them to use the internet.

In an ideal world you will have agreed rules from day one of your child's first mobile phone or when teaching them to use the internet. Always remember that as a parent you are trying to minimize the risks that might be involved for your child. You have probably noticed that every family makes their own choice about the age at which children/teenagers are allowed their first phone or are allowed to access the internet unsupervised. With phones, as a rule of thumb, I believe that age should be when they have some independent means of paying for the phone credit! For other things like unsupervised computer time, watching age-restricted movies and so on, you must be guided by your own instinct. If you don't believe that something is good for your child or younger teenager then don't be afraid to say 'no'. Like with other areas of potential conflict, be prepared to explain your decision and also be prepared to negotiate it if your child or teenager has valid reasons why you should change your mind.

Once they have a phone, or permission to use the computer, the more talking you do about your expectations for both mobiles and internet use, the easier it will be later, as your teenager will accept that you have a role in how they use these social tools.

In order to ensure that there are clear 'family times', you need to create certain times of the day, like mealtimes, as mobile-free zones. Similarly, just like in school, the time set aside for homework should be phone-free, although restricting internet use can be harder as it is sometimes a study tool. You may have to negotiate separate time for homework-related access and social access.

If you are finding that your teenager is one of those who receives texts through the night, then it might be worth creating a mobile phone curfew of 11.00pm (or whatever you agree with them) and physically take the phone from them at that point.

For now, most of us can still monitor our teenager's use of the internet by having the computer in a public place in the house and again creating the understanding that you will randomly monitor their usage. However, with the rapid expansion of internet-enabled phones and reducing tariffs for data use, you will probably find that your son or daughter will have the capacity for far greater and less controllable access in the future.

If you want to educate yourself and your teenager further, there is a very helpful Irish website – www. webwise.ie – that has been developed by the National Centre for Technology in Education. It has information for us parents about the technology involved, the benefits and the risks and how to keep safe online. There is similar, but separate, information for children and teenagers. It is well worth a little surfing.

CREATING COMMUNITIES

This chapter has been focused on your teenager's social groupings and the relative impact of the pressure that they put on them. Yes, they may be influenced negatively and they may be influenced positively by their peers, but at a wider, macro level your teenager is also being influenced by society at large. The voice-pieces of society are the various forms of media, including TV, radio, newspapers, magazines, music and the internet. These social and cultural media now insinuate messages from around the globe about what is good, what is bad, what is to be valued, what is to be ignored, what is to be wanted and what is to be desired. One of the great difficulties for parents is that the value and moral messages coming through the media are often at odds with their own views, beliefs and morals.

In the past the influence of media was much less and their own personal influence and the influence of their community were much stronger. In Ireland there was a sense that we all belonged to a homogenous society that was largely structured around a Christian faith and the Catholic Church, in particular. To a greater or lesser extent people held to the beliefs of the Catholic Church and these beliefs were clearly known and supported throughout entire communities. As has been shown, no more than any large system the Catholic Church had its failings, but when it came to supporting parents to raise children and teenagers, in particular, there was a reassuring simplicity attached to a strong set of common beliefs and morals being espoused by the whole community. It meant that what you said as a parent was supported by others that your teenager came across in their day-to-day lives. Their school teachers, the shopkeepers, the Gardaí, your neighbours, even the national TV and radio stations all gave very similar messages.

As a result, if your son was loitering in the town, for example, and had the potential to get up to mischief (as teenagers do!), there were many people who would have been quite happy to tell him to cop on and move on. More importantly, he would have listened. He may have grumbled, but he wouldn't have challenged because he knew that whatever he said or did would be reported back to you and that you would agree with the assessment of whoever had spoken to him. Similarly, your neighbour who met him downtown would have felt confident to guide and direct your son, knowing that you and they held similar opinions and that you would be grateful to them for helping to keep your son 'on the straight and narrow'.

This kind of an interaction can only happen when people know each other and know each other better than a simple salute of recognition. In our current society there are very few people who would either have the courage or the motivation to approach a group of teenagers who are loitering. I spoke earlier about my own anxiety about coming into contact with a group of teenagers. I know that I would be reluctant to approach them, never mind to try to redirect them. Most people, because they don't know the teenagers and don't know the teenagers' parents, would feel too afraid to tell them to move on and stop causing a nuisance.

How can we create communities where people can know each other at a slightly deeper level? And, more importantly, how do we identify common values, morals and even common goals with other people? Of course, there will be differences and there will be points upon which we don't agree with other people, but really the task is to identify broad themes of similarity and also a sense of common purpose and commonality in approach. I made reference earlier to sleepovers and to teenagers taking advantage of having a 'free house'. Free houses get created when teenagers can lie to their parents in the knowledge that their parents have no way of properly checking whether the details of the night away are as described. Feeling unable or unwilling to establish the plans for the sleepover is exactly the situation that can and will occur when you have no connection to your teenager's friends and their friends' parents.

When children are small we tend to accompany them if they go to play in a friend's house. Often, in those situations, we get invited in for a cup of tea or a short chat. If the friendship continues, we will probably get to know that friend's parents. It may even be that through the contact of our children with their friends we actually come to establish some long-term friends of our own. But because teenagers tend to exclude us from aspects of their life and quite likely will exclude us from their developing friendships in their teenage years, we don't have the same opportunity to get to know other parents. But if we really wanted to we could create the opportunities to meet those other parents, and perhaps we should. Even if the meeting doesn't lead to long-term friendships for us with those parents, it's much better that we have a face to associate with the name, and that we've had at least one or two conversations that might give us some sense of whether there is any commonality or shared values.

Equally, when children are small we accompany them down to the hurling field, the soccer pitch, the basketball courts, a drama class, a ballet class and whatever other activities they happen to be doing. Here again, there are opportunities to meet like-minded parents and, as you wait and chat, you will probably come to know some of them. Many of us, at different stages, may even have volunteered to help out as an assistant to the coach or a parent volunteer with the scouts. By getting involved at this level we become even more connected to the community that is associated with the particular activity. But once children are old enough to make their own way to the sports field or the local hall, we tend to leave them off. In practice, this means that we tend to withdraw from those communities, we become less involved, we know less about what is happening and we know fewer of the adults who are actively involved.

Parents' associations in schools regularly complain about the difficulty in motivating parents to come out and attend functions. So much of the time the functions that are arranged have the added benefit of providing a social forum for parents to meet and to talk about issues that are common to all. Wouldn't it be great if parents' association meetings, talks, fund-raising events and so on were so well attended that you could almost guarantee you get to meet the parents of those friends that your teenager had just established? Wouldn't it be great if, in those moments, you could share your views about how potentially dangerous it is for them all to be out and about in the town at 1.00am? You could, perhaps, agree as a group that you will all insist on your respective teenagers coming home at midnight. In my view one of the most important functions of the parents' association in any school is to be that social link between parents who might have no other reason to come into contact with each other.

In the past I used to run parenting groups where six to ten parents would come together every week, over a five- to six-week period. Even though those six people did not know each other on the first night, the one thing they had in common was that they had a child (or children) that they wanted to be dealing with differently. As the weeks progressed, those six parents shared vast amounts of information about themselves and their families, about the things that worked well and the things that didn't work well. Usually there would be many laughs, a few tears and a great sense of 'being in this together'. Consequently, the most consistent response in the feedback forms at the end of every course I ran was that the most influential part of the course was the support they received from other parents. Simply knowing that other parents had the same kinds of issues and troubles as they did made a big difference to their attitude and perception of how they could cope.

We are all aware that the world has been caught in the grip of a massive recession and that one of the few positive aspects to emerge from this has been people's sense that they now have to rely more upon each other than upon themselves as an individual. There is, genuinely, a greater sense of the collective good rather than of individual greed. Most of the time when we work together with other people we achieve far more than when we attempt the same task alone. It's human nature to want to be connected to other people and I believe that the greater the connection between us and the other people in our geographical community and in the wider parenting communities, the greater the chance of our messages to teenagers being echoed and supported by other people.

As I have shown above, there are many natural social opportunities to meet other parents. So the best way to rebuild communities is to get involved. Go back to showing a practical interest in the sports clubs, drama clubs, scouts, parents' associations, local tidy towns groups, parish councils or any other social grouping in your neighbourhood. The more that you and your teenager are known in your community, the more support you will have if the going gets tough.

CHOOSING MENTORS

I have a colleague whom I was talking to about the difficulty teenagers face in communicating with their parents and also the struggle that parents have in communicating with and influencing their teenager. I was explaining to my colleague about my opinion that parents should try to enlist the help of other people who might be able to influence their teenager. The people I had in mind were those adults that their youngster held in some level of esteem and respect, such as teachers, sports coaches, aunts, uncles and grandparents and even friends of the family. The key element that this person must bring to the relationship with your teenager is a sense of mutual respect. These are the kind of people that I would consider could be a mentor for your teenager. I am assuming that the person is somebody whom you respect and who you believe shares many of the same values that you hold to.

The difference between that person and you is that they still have a connection to your teenager when it seems that your own has broken down. So when they talk, your teenager listens; when your teenager has a problem, perhaps this is the person that they will go to for advice. Sometimes, it is in our interest to actively promote and encourage a relationship between another trusted adult and our sons and daughters because that way the really important messages that we would like to transmit to our teenagers, but are blocked from doing, can be passed on by these people instead.

> Sometimes, it is in our interest to actively promote and encourage a relationship between another trusted adult and our sons and daughters because that way the really important messages that we would like to transmit to our teenagers, but are blocked from doing, can be passed on by these people instead.

As I spoke about this concept my colleague was nodding enthusiastically. She agreed that it is vitally important that teenagers have a relationship with some adult who they can trust and whose opinion they still respect. She also felt that while these relationships can sometimes form naturally, at other times they need to be developed, encouraged and cultivated. She also went on to describe her own view that teenagers need 'legends' to look up to.

She described a 'legend' as a person, either in the immediate community or in a wider national or even international community, who can inspire, motivate and role model positively for young people.

She felt that there can be a crossover between the person I describe as a mentor and the person she describes as a legend. It may be, for example, that one of the senior players in the local GAA club has also represented the county in the national championships and their stories of the commitment and effort that they have had to invest, as well as some of the things that they had to forgo to achieve that goal, will inspire and motivate your teenager to reach for something similar.

Even though I was complaining about the potentially negative role of the global media, she pointed out that there are actually some really strong positive role models who are in the public eye. The difficulty, which she also pointed out, is that sometimes these people don't realize the influence and impact that they have on developing adolescents. In fairness, it is unrealistic to expect them to think about how their actions are going to impact on people they don't even know. Yet because teenagers, and others, view them with such a sense of respect and status, their actions are hugely influential.

In other cultures where communities may appear stronger and less fractured, there is also a strong cultural sense of the 'elder'. Similar to my ideas about mentors and my colleague's about legends, elders also share in, and in fact are the custodians of the collective wisdom of a community, based on their experience and their knowledge of the world. Elders tend to be the older members of the community, who have lived through life and have had an opportunity to process and to learn from the experiences they have had. Who explains to your teenage son how to grow up to be a man? What information does your daughter use to learn what it is to be a woman? In other cultures it will be the elders who tell stories, give advice, pass judgement on disputes and give guidance and direction to the young people in that community. I don't think we have great respect for elders. In our society old age is a sign of weakness, not of wisdom. There is a stronger culture of youth and vitality, drive and ambition, which shuns the learning of those who have gone before us.

So yes, peer pressure is hugely influential during adolescence. Your teenager is intimately bound in with their friends and the views, values and trends that their peers are experimenting with. A lot of the time those peer influences are hugely positive for your son or daughter. Some of the time, the influences are very negative. But we know that these are not the only influences on teenagers. It is not fair to teenagers to simply abandon them to peer pressures, with a helpless sense that we have lost our influence, and then to complain if we don't like their friends. By connecting ourselves more closely to the communities in which we live and by surrounding ourselves and our teenagers with strong positive role models, we can still hope to offer a strong alternative to any of the negative influences of their friends.

IN CASE OF EMERGENCY . . . KEY POINTS TO REMEMBER

→ During adolescence peers play a large part in a young person's life and typically replace family as the centre of a teenager's social and leisure activities.

→ It makes sense to surround yourself with others that you think believe in the same kind of things that you do. It is within the safety of such a group that teenagers can experiment with their newly developing identity.

→ Most of us willingly choose groups of people with whom we feel comfortable and we then allow their norms to influence and even override our personal habits, our individual moral inhibitions or our own desires.

→ The primary influence in any teenager's life is their closest friends.

→ What a best friend approves of or disapproves of exerts great pressure on teenagers.

→ Part of the developmental process for teenagers is that they do need to have space that is private and separate from you, so they will naturally congregate in places where adults are absent.

→ Most of us worry about our youngsters getting drunk, getting stoned or getting laid and so fears of letting them off to the disco can be based on a reality of these risks.

→ Younger teenagers are especially vulnerable, due to their comparative immaturity, to being overwhelmed by the highly charged physical and emotional energies associated with all that is on offer at discos.

→ While you might be prepared to negotiate about going to the disco, it is also okay to hold firm on not letting them go if you can explain your decision to them.

→ You can be sure that if your child is of an age to experiment with drugs or alcohol, they will use unsupervised sleepovers as the ideal vehicle for that experimentation.

→ Mobile phones and online communication do provide an adult-free zone that teenagers need, but like everything we need to ensure that they are using phones and computers in moderation.

→ You have to use your own judgement entirely to decide what age to allow your son or daughter to have unfettered use of a phone and the computer.

→ Being connected to strong communities offers social support for parents and teenagers alike.

→ Sometimes your ability to influence your teenager is limited by their temporary rejection of you, or your beliefs. In such situations you might be able to enlist the help of a mentor for your teenager.

→ Mentors have experience and credibility that is valued by your teenager and so can serve as powerful role models or influencers.

7. RELATIONSHIPS AND SEX

a parent's guide to the birds, the bees . . . and the blushing

To be honest, by the time most of our children hit their teenage years they have amassed a significant amount of information about sex. Oftentimes the Relationship and Sexuality Education (RSE) module in the primary school curriculum will have imparted a lot of the physiological information that children need. If they haven't learned it in school, it is highly likely that they will have been told about it by their friends. However, we should never assume that our children have all of the information that they require, nor should we assume that the information they do have is accurate. It remains an important task for parents to share their knowledge with their children about sex and sexual relations.

Also, and possibly more significantly, the physiological information about sex is only the tip of the iceberg. In fact, we all know, and our children and teenagers need to know, so much more about sex, sexuality and relationships. It is in the sphere of sexuality and relationships that we parents have the biggest responsibility to share not just our knowledge but also our views, opinions, beliefs and moral standpoints. Clarity on these issues gives our children a compass that they can use to steer their own course in developing their sexuality and forming healthy relationships.

You can be amazed by how much knowledge you will have gathered about sex, sexuality and relationships, but it is only when you start discussing it with your teenager that you will realize the breadth of what you will want to share with them. This chapter will contain my views, beliefs and opinions to give you a starting point in order to clarify your own. It will also give you my best guess at the really important information to cover and suggested ways of discussing it.

THIS CHAPTER LOOKS AT . . .

The trouble with talking about sex
  * *Parents' reasons for avoiding 'the chat'*
  * *Teenagers' reasons for not talking to you*
  * *My guess as to the real reason*

When to start talking about sex

Preparing to talk about sex

Other sources of information

What you actually have to talk about (yes, every detail and area!)
  * *The changes of puberty*
  * *The biology of sex*
  * *Relationships and emotions*
  * *Sexual feelings*
  * *Gender roles*
  * *Sexuality and sexual preferences*
  * *Sexually transmitted diseases*
  * *Contraception and pregnancy*
  * *Boundaries in relation to physical intimacy*
  * *The role of alcohol and sex*

The likely outcome of effective sex and relationship education

THE TROUBLE WITH TALKING ABOUT SEX

Our teenagers are happy, indeed prurient at times, to find out the intricacies of their friends' sexual exploits. Once they have some level of comfort with their own sexuality and how they express it, they rarely feel any embarrassment with their peers. We too can be happy, amongst our adult peers, to talk about sex and sexuality. So why does the gulf appear when we have to talk sex with our teenagers?

The Irish Study of Sexual Health and Relationships (ISSHR) was carried out with over 7,000 Irish adults and reported on in 2006. One of its findings was that, overall, for most people either sexual matters never came up with parents or, when they did, discussion was 'difficult'. So if it is the case that we adults either never talked to our own parents or found it a difficult conversation, perhaps it is no surprise that we then go on to struggle to talk to our children and teenagers.

So, here we are in the heart of our adulthood and yet the topic of sex, relationships and our teenager has the power to stress and embarrass us to the point of inaction. In theory, we know we should talk to our children and teenagers about sex, sexual development, sexuality, relationships, intimacy and love. In reality, we often avoid the subject like the plague.

PARENTS' REASONS FOR AVOIDING 'THE CHAT'

Perhaps our difficulty occurs because sex remains a taboo subject. Certainly in years gone by sex was rarely talked about and even more rarely featured in any media. Religious beliefs, too, were hugely influential blocks to discussing sex. There seemed to be no permission for adults to discuss sexual matters amongst themselves, never mind with their sons and daughters.

But surely things have changed? A quick glance at the TV listings for any day would suggest that there are no restrictions on how matters of sex and sexuality can be broached. Between TV, the internet, magazines and books there are innumerable sources of information, discussion, innuendo and explicit images of all things sexual. But in the context of talking to teenagers about this stuff, none of it seems to matter. Despite the massively increased visibility of sex in today's media, it remains a sensitive subject for parents and their children to discuss.

Some parents fear that by telling their child about sex they are likely to encourage sexual experimentation. Perhaps the concern is that we are implicitly giving permission for our youngsters to try out stuff. This can be balanced, however, by giving clear guidelines about how sex should fit into their lives.

Another reason is that many parents think that their teenager is more informed about sex than they actually are. Such parents are probably relying on the RSE programme that runs in schools. Some parents may even think that their son or daughter knows more about sex than they do!

TEENAGERS' REASONS FOR NOT TALKING TO YOU

Many teenagers will give off signals that they know all about sex. They are hoping that if they appear knowledgeable, then their parents will believe they really do know it all. In reality, however, although they tend to feel confident in what they know, when tested their actual knowledge is low.

We know that many adolescents want to be treated as adults. When the subject of sex comes up, some of them may feel talked down to by their parents or other adults. Indeed, you may hear some complaining of being lectured to. Other teenagers may not talk about sex with their parents because they see parents as close-minded, uncompassionate or not clued in to the problems today's teenagers face. Which may be true, of course!

MY GUESS AS TO THE REAL REASON

Perhaps closest to the heart of the reluctance to talk about sex is you and your teenager's own cringing embarrassment at the thought of facing each other while the words sex, penis, ovulation and condom float from your lips. The trouble is that talking about sex in an open way explodes the myth that you are asexual and forces your son or daughter to accept the reality that you are a sexual being. I wonder if the core of the difficulty is that your son or daughter can't bear the thought of you, the parent, 'doing it'.

Another factor we might allude to is how we struggle to broach the topic because we fear to destroy their innocence. We wonder whether we push them to adulthood too early by talking about changes to their body and how their developing sexuality may be expressed in the future. We can use this anxiety as a strong reason to avoid talking sex with them.

I believe that 'destroying their innocence' is actually a euphemism for our recognition that our children are growing into sexual beings and that they too will be (if they are not already) 'doing it'. By talking to them we must also acknowledge that our teenagers are sexual beings. This seems to be the crux of the difficulty. It just doesn't seem 'right' for parents and their children to reciprocally accept that human beings, and consequently each other, are sexual. In reality, though, it is right and proper for parents to guide their children through the complexities of relationships and developing sexuality.

WHEN TO START TALKING ABOUT SEX

In an ideal world, telling your teenager about sex and relationships would be a process that began at age ten or eleven. Catching them before puberty actually hits not only prepares them for what is ahead but allows them greater freedom to take the information on board. From that age onwards, conversations could happen every so often. Perhaps they would occur in line with specific developmental milestones, like your daughter's first period, your son's first shave or their first girlfriend or boyfriend.

Oftentimes, the easiest opportunities to have conversations arise when sex or relationships turn up on the TV. Such occasions might lead to questions (probably only from a younger teen) that you can respond to. Alternatively, you might use the chance to raise or further discuss the issue that was being broadcast, even if your son or daughter didn't ask a question.

It goes without saying that some teenagers experiment sexually. This in itself will pose a huge challenge for some of us as it could reach the point that we need to decide whether or not our teenager's sexual activity will be allowed in the family home. Imagine having to talk about the reality of their sexual behaviour without any prior grounding or discussion about sex and relationships. So if you are able to have an open and honest discussion about sex, then you can set ground rules about exactly these kinds of situations.

There is no quick fix for the shyness, embarrassment or stress that comes with 'the chat'. This is a good reason to think about it less as 'the chat' and more as 'the series of chats'. The more you talk about it, the easier it gets.

Dealing with facts and issues in smaller chunks, over time, takes the pressure off having to talk about everything all at once. Instead, you create a process that gives your child a stronger sense that sex, sexuality and relationships are very much a part of growing up and that the significance of the issues can change over time. Consequently, they are just as valid a topic for conversation as anger, schoolwork, timeliness, dress sense, friends, sports, hobbies and pastimes.

> There is no quick fix for the shyness, embarrassment or stress that comes with 'the chat'. This is a good reason to think about it less as 'the chat' and more as 'the series of chats'. The more you talk about it, the easier it gets.
>
> Dealing with facts and issues in smaller chunks, over time, takes the pressure off having to talk about everything all at once.

PREPARING TO TALK ABOUT SEX

Mothers are usually the ones who talk about sex with their teenagers and they tend to be 'in charge' of these conversations and to direct them. This is especially the case if they are talking with their sons. In contrast, the most interactive conversations take place between mothers and daughters.

I mentioned earlier that teenagers are more likely to be turned off the subject if they feel lectured to. They are likely to disconnect in this way when a parent or adult dominates the conversation because then they feel overpowered. If this kind of disconnection happens in an early conversation, they may withdraw from further discussions with you about sex. Such a communication gap would reduce the number of conversations you are likely to have about sex and that may have a knock-on effect on your son's or daughter's knowledge about critical sexual health issues or about healthy emotional relationships.

The fact that more mothers do the talking also raises the issue of why we dads don't get in on the act more. We all know that we are significant role models for our youngsters and so it is important that we show guidance and interest in the sexual and emotional development of our sons and our daughters.

To get into the swing of talking to your son, it might be helpful to first talk about the issue(s) with your partner or other carers. You might think of it as a rehearsal. The first time you utter a phrase like 'and the man's penis, which is hard and stands upright, goes into the woman's vagina' can be quite traumatic! So it helps to have said it to someone other than your teenager first.

Talking about sex and relationships with your partner also helps you to clarify the kinds of values and messages that you want to deliver to your teenager. Clearly there is so much more to it than the biology of sex and it is crucial that you are clear about the moral and value beliefs that you have. Indeed, passing on your values is more important than simply passing on information about biology.

> Clearly there is so much more to it than the biology of sex and it is crucial that you are clear about the moral and value beliefs that you have. Indeed, passing on your values is more important than simply passing on information about biology.

It might also be helpful for you to read relevant books or magazines about sex and sex education, so that you are knowledgeable about the 'facts of life'. Having greater or clearer knowledge can help to raise your confidence. If your child asks you a question that you can't answer, there is no harm. You can always find out later and come back to fill in the blanks for your child. Or you and your teenager might go and find out together on the internet or in a book.

I dedicated a whole chapter earlier to communication, so in terms of the manner of your conversation, do use the strategies from that chapter. Really it is about holding to the premise of having two-way conversations. The more included and listened to your teenager feels, the more helpful the conversation will be.

One way to do this is to use examples from your observations of your own child to demonstrate where you stand on moral issues. This will give them a strong sense of being noticed and attended to. Also, if you are trying to find out what your son or daughter believes, then make sure to ask your questions in an open-ended way. Here is a typical example of one such brief conversation about values between a parent and their fourteen-year-old daughter.

> **Parent:** *I overheard you talking to your friend yesterday about the goings-on at the disco.*

> **Teenager:** *What? What exactly did you hear?*

> **Parent:** *Well, I heard you talking about her boyfriend and how he cheated on her by 'meeting' another girl that night.*

> **Teenager:** *I can't believe you were listening in on my private conversation!*

> **Parent:** *I am sorry about that, it was unintentional at first and then I became genuinely interested in what you were saying. I was particularly interested with your advice to her not just to dump her boyfriend, but to tell him first how hurtful his cheating was.*

> **Teenager:** *Yeah . . . well . . . she was really hurt, you know.*

> **Parent:** *I am sure she was. Trust is so important in relationships. We all need to be able to trust someone that we are close to. Imagine if you told a boyfriend something in private and then couldn't trust them to keep it in confidence.*

> **Teenager:** *I wouldn't ever do that.*

> **Parent:** *Which? Tell them a confidence or have a boyfriend?*

> **Teenager:** *(laughing) Tell them a confidence!*

> **Parent:** *I wonder . . . because when we are intimate with someone else, we do share private things. What about that thing you told your friend about your plan to 'meet' the other boy?*

> **Teenager:** *Oh God! You did hear everything. I can't believe you!*

> **Parent:** *I am sorry for listening in. But the point I am making is that you shared that private information with your friend about wanting to 'meet' the other boy and so you trusted her. I am sure that if you get on as well with a boyfriend, you will share similar confidences with him.*

> **Teenager:** *Yeah, but boys are different – you don't tell them important things.*

> **Parent:** *Of course they are different, but some things are the same in friendships between girls and girls and between girlfriends and boyfriends. As relationships deepen, being willing to trust them and expecting them to trust you is really important and you probably will tell them important or private things.*

> **Teenager:** *Okay, whatever.*

> **Parent:** *Is that my signal to shut up? Information overload!*

> **Teenager:** *No, I'm still mad with you for eavesdropping. (but said with a bit of twinkle in her eye)*

> **Parent:** *Fair enough, and I am genuinely sorry, but I am also glad that it gave us this chance to talk about important things about trust. (smiling) And don't go kissing anyone till you're twenty!*

> **Teenager:** *Oh you are so gross! (laughing too)*

This conversation ended relatively innocuously. The parent could have used it as a further opportunity to talk about the daughter's plans to 'meet' a boy and about how she needs to respect herself and her body. But in this instance the parent judged that they had said enough and that to keep going might alienate them from their daughter. The parent may also have been trying to avoid passing judgements on the plans to go kissing (and possibly more) a boy because this was even more likely to alienate the daughter. Throughout this conversation the parent just focused on the positive values the daughter had expressed and reaffirmed their own views about trust. The more you can show empathy and reduce judgements, the more helpful it will be when it comes to discussing the sexual mores that you want to encourage them to live by. Hopefully, like in this example, this leaves the door open for future conversations, including ones about kissing and such like!

OTHER SOURCES OF INFORMATION

The main alternative source of sexual education is provided in schools. It is never meant to be a substitute for parents educating their own child. In Ireland, sex education through the Relationships and Sexuality Education (RSE) programme begins in primary school and is returned to at stages during secondary school.

Never assume that your child has learned what they need to know from this programme. Lots of factors, such as their mood, the level of giddiness and acceptance of the programme amongst the class and the manner in which the programme is delivered, can affect the degree to which your son or daughter will take in the information.

The RSE programme will address certain values, but they are not necessarily tailored to your own family values. So here again is an area where you will need to be clear about your own position.

Another source of information for teenagers is the media, primarily TV, internet and magazines. In all cases the images and messages can be contradictory to what you believe in and confusing or overwhelming for your child. We are flooded with sexual images from the media every day of our lives. A teenager's perception of sex and sexuality can be skewed by incorrect or misleading information from all of these sources. The only way to determine if you are comfortable with what your teenager is exposed to is to be aware of what they are seeing and hearing as much as possible. Don't be afraid to limit what they see either. Anything to do with sex can be titillating and fascinating for your teenager, but that doesn't mean that they should be watching it.

Similarly, when you do know that they are watching programmes or reading magazines that give strong sexual messages, then use this as an opportunity to share your views, and encourage theirs, in relation to the understanding of sex that they are developing from what they are witnessing.

A further source of information is their peers. Usually, this is the least reliable of all the information your child receives. Especially at the start of adolescence, the level of accurate information in your child's peer group will be limited. So, even though they might trust the word of their mates, you definitely shouldn't.

Numerous studies have shown that the most influential role models for a child are their parents or carers. By keeping silent, you allow your teenager to act on unreliable information. This can put them at considerable risk. Remember that you know your teenager best and that means that you can tailor the information according to your son or daughter's stage of development, life experience, personality and knowledge level.

THE BIOLOGY OF SEX

Babies get created when the genetic information of a Mam and a Dad gets merged. Half of the information comes from the Dad and is stored in each sperm that he creates. The other half comes from the Mam and is stored in each egg that she creates.

Men produce sperm in their testes (also called testicles), which hang in a bag of skin called the scrotum behind the penis. Towards the end of having sex the sperm get sent out of the testes, down special tubes (called the Vas Deferens) and get mixed into another liquid before coming out through the penis. Sperm mixed into the liquid is called semen and is generally creamy-white coloured. We call the moment of the sperm coming out of the penis ejaculation. Millions of sperm are contained in each ejaculation of semen.

Women create one egg each month in their ovaries, which are located inside them. Each egg travels down a special tube called the fallopian tube towards the woman's uterus (also called her womb). If a sperm reaches the egg and penetrates it (called fertilization), that is the moment the genetic information gets merged and we call that moment conception, as from then on a baby starts to grow and form. That growth happens inside the woman's womb. It takes about forty weeks from the moment of conception for a baby to grow inside the Mam before it is ready to come out and be born.

In order for a man to put sperm inside a woman so that it can reach her egg he must put his penis inside her and ejaculate (squirt) his semen into her vagina. This is called sexual intercourse or, more usually, just sex. A man gets an erection (remember, this is when his penis fills with blood and it goes hard and stands up) to make it easier to put his penis into a woman's vagina. The woman's vagina also becomes moistened to let the man's penis slide in easier. The physical sensation of sex should feel good for both the man and the woman.

Once inside, the man's semen travels up into the woman's uterus and her fallopian tubes (hoping to meet an egg!). Every time a man and woman have sex there is the possibility that they may create a baby. The only way to be sure that you won't make a baby if you have sex is to use some kind of contraception. The most common kinds are condoms (which the man wears over his penis to catch all the semen and so stop the sperm ever going into the woman) and the contraceptive pill. The Pill could actually be any one of a number of different hormone tablets that stop girls and women from producing an egg.

Otherwise, an egg is released each month and the woman's body prepares her womb in case a fertilized egg needs to grow into a baby. A special lining covers the womb that is full of nutrients to help a fertilized egg to grow. If the egg doesn't meet a sperm, then it can't grow into a baby and so it and the special lining get flushed out by the woman through her vagina. It comes out as blood and is called menstruation. Another name for it is having a period. It happens once a month unless a baby is growing in her womb.

If a man doesn't ejaculate his sperm as semen, the sperm simply get absorbed into his body and fresh sperm are made.

The reason everyone gets so hyped up about sex is that it is usually mixed with incredibly powerful feelings and emotions and the physical sensation of having sex is also usually great. Sometimes the sexual feelings we can have seem to take over our minds and it is all we can think about. The powerful nature of the feelings is really important, as sometimes we can make bad choices because we are so overwhelmed by our feelings we don't think through to the consequences of what we are doing. Mostly, you only want to have sex when you are in love with the person you are going to have sex with and so the sexual feelings are mixed with a wonderful desire to be intimate and close to the person.

The physical sensations of sex feel really good for most people, so sometimes people will try to recreate lots of those sensations without the intercourse part of sex (the 'putting the penis into the vagina' bit). Kissing is regularly part of sex as it is a real signal of intimacy and closeness. Sometimes people will touch each other on their sexual parts, so that might mean holding or stroking a man's penis or touching the opening part of the woman's vagina. It might mean touching, holding or stroking a woman's breasts, a man's nipples or each other's bottoms. Oral sex is where a man kisses (or uses his tongue to touch) the opening to a woman's vagina and where a woman kisses or takes into her mouth a man's penis.

It can also feel good to touch your own body sexually. Touching, rubbing, squeezing or stroking yourself on your genitals is called masturbation. Masturbation is not a bad thing. It is, however, something that most people keep private and do at a time and in a place where they will not be disturbed.

All the sexual parts of your body are private and nobody should ever touch you there unless you are welcoming that touch. It is really important that you never feel under pressure to either touch someone else sexually or to allow yourself to be touched sexually when you don't want it. The same is true of sex. You should always come and talk to us if you feel that you are being put under pressure, by anybody, to do something sexual that you don't like.

RELATIONSHIPS AND EMOTIONS

Relationships are great. Most of us get stressed that we aren't in one and then as soon as we are in one, we get stressed that it might end. Right at the start is a time when we are often willing to ignore any negatives about the other person and also we might try to hide or cover up anything we believe to be negative about ourselves. One of the dangers is that early in a relationship we can be so keen to make it work that we are willing to say or do things that we don't really believe in, but do them simply to impress the other person. Staying true to yourself and what you value is a crucial part of having a successful relationship.

There is usually a strong physical attraction between you and the person you want to go out with or have a relationship with. This means that the start of any relationship is madly exciting, fun and filled with anticipation and expectation. This physical attraction is often tied up in lots of strong sexual feelings. So if you don't pay enough attention this can sometimes overwhelm the emotional part of building a good, strong and healthy relationship with someone. So even in the whirling tingle of a new relationship you need to think about how well you connect with someone, not just physically but emotionally and psychologically too.

Humans need to be able to build strong and sustaining relationships with other people. We know that we can usually achieve more with the support, love and help of others. Instinctively, we are also on the lookout for that one other person whom we will commit to sticking with in a long-term relationship for life. That is usually the person we will want to create a family with. This always works best when there is a strongly built emotional, psychological and physical connection between us and that other person.

It is only as you get to know someone better that you might be able to work out whether this is going to be a good or bad relationship.

The basis of good relationships

Good relationships are based on trust. That means that you can rely on the other person to do what they say they will and to follow through. Trust takes real jealousy out of the equation as you can know that the other person is committed to you even if they chat with other people.

Good relationships are fair. That means one person doesn't make all the decisions. Fairness means that your voice is just as important as the other person's. You should get to give a little and take a little in a relationship.

Good relationships encourage communication. That means that you are both interested in talking about things that are important to you. It also means that you know how to resolve problems by listening and negotiating rather than just rowing. Equally, you should feel comfortable talking about some of the trickier things or things that may embarrass you slightly; what you do or don't want to do sexually would be an important thing, for example.

Texting, instant messaging and online social networking are great tools of communication, but they all rely just on words and words alone sometimes can be misunderstood. Being able to use a special tone of voice or smiling as you talk are ways, for example, of letting the other person know you are just joking, even though the words alone might otherwise be understood to be hurtful. So remember to talk.

Good relationships are based on mutual respect. This means that each of you should be willing to not push the other into doing stuff that you aren't comfortable with. You need to value who the other person is and understand that they have boundaries, and those boundaries shouldn't be challenged. Like if you don't want to drink alcohol, then your boyfriend or girlfriend shouldn't put you under pressure to drink. Similarly, if you don't want to have sex yet, then that's okay and you need to be respected for that decision.

You can still be your own separate person in a good and healthy relationship. Good relationships don't exclude friends or family who were there before the relationship began. Never feel obliged to drop your friends and even though you will naturally spend less time with other friends, don't forget about them as they can be a great source of support and advice in the days to come.

People who have long-lasting relationships are honest with each other. Lying is the surest way to break trust and without trust it's only a matter of time before you'll split up.

Some common problems that arise in relationships

It is very hard to love someone else when you don't love yourself. A really common problem with relationships arises when you rely on someone else to make you happy. Dependence on someone else won't last; you need to be able to feel good about yourself all on your own.

Another common problem is that sometimes we can get too caught up in our own feelings, worries and needs and so we run out of emotional space to think about someone else and what they might need.

Similarly, you can feel that your other half wants too much from you and the whole relationship can feel like a burden. Being in a relationship is supposed to be good fun and if it doesn't feel like that often enough, then it might be time to move on.

People's changing expectations and interests are another common source of difficulty. Especially during your teenage years, but even at any time in life, as you grow and develop your priorities can change and then you can find you don't have that much in common after all.

Dealing with hurt and rejection

The two most effective ways to deal with hurt and rejection are to experience a bit of emotional support and to take an 'emotional break' from the pain of the hurt that you might feel. Your friends and us, your parents, are the ones who can best support you if you feel hurt or rejected. We can offer a listening ear and a shoulder to cry on. We will make you feel loved and cared about anyway.

Taking an emotional break or dissociating is an okay thing to do as well. Healthy distractions include hanging out with your friends, playing sports, watching TV, playing PlayStation, or getting stuck into your hobbies like reading and so on. The key to taking a break is to remember moderation in all things. Too much of anything becomes a bad thing, so don't withdraw completely into the world of online gaming, for example. Some more dangerous ways of dissociating that are best avoided are drinking, drug-taking, self-harming, promiscuity or aggression. Unfortunately, these are all effective ways of avoiding the pain of hurt or rejection, but they are all extremely self-destructive and potentially very dangerous.

Getting good at relationships

You can get better at relationships by practising. I don't mean practising sex, but practising all of the skills of give and take, mutual respect, trust, fairness and so on. By making friendships and losing friendships you'll come to know who you are and who you like and then you will make better choices about more serious relationships too. Three good habits for life are:

> **Know what you want and don't be afraid to ask for it**
> **Never agree to anything that you don't feel will be good for you**
> **Learn from your experiences, especially the difficult ones, and don't make the same mistake twice**

SEXUAL FEELINGS

At any time in life sexual feelings can be very powerful. While you are this age your hormones are especially active and so sexual feelings can often be present even if you aren't thinking sexually about anyone at that moment. You might find that you daydream a lot about sex. There is nothing wrong with strong sexual feelings. Part of what you need to learn, however, is to interpret them correctly. There is more to relationships than just sexual feeling.

Sexual attraction is a wonderfully powerful experience, but it can also blind us at times to the reality of who the other person is. You can let the thrill of your sexual feelings rule your head and then you can end up in a relationship with someone that you discover you don't particularly like. So think about the qualities of those people you are already friendly with and use them as a guide for the kind of qualities you want in a boyfriend or girlfriend.

VALUES

We all have values. Values are the core things that we believe in, like 'all life is sacred' or 'honesty is the best policy'. Sometimes you develop your values through experience and trial and error, but usually you learn your values from watching those around you and how they express their values.

That means that the values expressed by us, by teachers, by religions and by your friends will all be part of who you are. It's okay to take advantage of the years of wisdom that those values embody. Listen and watch those people that you respect, see how they live their lives and copy what they do.

I have my own core values about respect for other people. That means I choose not to take advantage of them. It means that I listen to them. It means that I look to see what positive role they might play in my life or in the life of my family. It means I choose not to put people down or deliberately make them feel bad about themselves.

I have always tried to treat you with respect. I'm sure there are times when you may not have felt that, but it was certainly my intention that you would know that I cared about and respected you.

I also value honesty and truth. I like to think that if I make a commitment to someone, I always follow through. It is important to me that people know that I tell the truth. This makes it so much easier for people to trust me and on the same basis I always want to reach out and trust other people.

I know I can't assume that you want to share my values. But what is important is that you see from the way I've lived my life that good things come of treating other people well. So never be afraid to be true to what you believe in or to speak the truth. But if you have an issue with someone, you need to be able to raise that issue with them directly. Never say anything about someone behind their back that you are not prepared to say to their face.

Never assume that you're better than anybody else, or believe that you have no power to influence someone whom you view to be more powerful than you are.

It will always be easier for you to make choices if you ask yourself, 'Is this good for me and is it good for other people?' If the choice you are about to make in a relationship, or about what you do sexually, is not good for you and may not be good for someone else, then think long and hard about it. If you want you can always come and ask my advice or talk to someone else that you trust.

GENDER ROLES

Knowing how to be a man or a woman is not a lesson you can learn. In reality, by now you probably have a clear idea about manhood and womanhood, even if you can't put it into words. This is because you will have watched me and other men. You will have seen how we interact with and how we treat others. Similarly, by watching your mother you have picked up a sense of how women can be in society.

There are other influences as well. Typically the various different kinds of media give many views of how men and women should be and should interact. The portrayal of men and women in magazines and films, for example, can be very powerful influencers for you about how you should be and act as you grow up.

Teachers, sports coaches and others have also been shaping your expectations of what boys and girls and men and women can and should achieve. Often the messages are subtle, for example, the way boys and girls can be guided into certain gender-typical subject choices.

By definition, 'gender roles' refers to the behaviours and attitudes expected of male and female members of a society by that society. What is important for you to remember is that while your gender does influence certain things, it does not have to slavishly trap you into acting in only one kind of way. The key for you is to try to be as open as you can, and to hold onto your values because they will guide you better in how to treat people than the messages you get from society about what is expected of you as a man or as a woman.

SEXUALITY AND SEXUAL PREFERENCES

Generally, our gender is bound into our physical selves. By dint of having a penis we are men; because you have a uterus you are a woman. The roles we take on as men and women do get strongly influenced by society and the expectations that are there about how men and women should act. Sexuality comes from within, however, and is not bound by our physical make-up. Our sexuality describes the kind of person we are sexually attracted to. Heterosexual men and women (sometimes referred to as 'straight') are attracted to the opposite sex. Homosexual men and women (sometimes referred to as 'gay' or 'lesbian') are attracted to the same sex. Bisexual men and women are attracted to both men and women.

There is no right and wrong way for your sexuality to develop. You may find that over the years your sexuality seems to shift and it can be confusing sometimes to know exactly how you feel. Lots of people experience the same kind of uncertainty. You've probably already noticed a strong pressure to be straight. Most people do develop into heterosexuality. Experimentation, sexually, is okay as long as you are able to make sense of the feelings you have. Never make global assumptions on the basis of one, or limited, experience. So don't assume that you are gay just because you have tried things sexually with someone of the same sex.

As sexuality and having sex is one of the most powerful ways of expressing emotional intimacy, this is what you should be focusing on when it comes to understanding your sexuality. You can ask yourself: with whom do you consistently connect at an emotionally intimate level? Does your sexual expression of that intimacy also seem to fit comfortably?

The preferences you express can be determined in part by your experience and also, hopefully, by your own sense of what feels right and comfortable for you. Even the extent to which you welcome sexual contact from someone else describes preferences. In that sense it is good to be choosy. It is good to know what you like and sometimes you will only learn the difference between what feels right and wrong to you by trying things out. However, this requires you to be thinking consciously in order to best make sense of what is happening to you.

SEXUALLY TRANSMITTED INFECTIONS

As their name suggests, sexually transmitted infections (STIs) are infections that are passed from one person to another during sexual contact. The most common ways to get an STI are from having sex (either intercourse, oral or anal sex) or from touching each other's genitals (like mutual masturbation, for example). So the infection passes from skin to skin or through bodily fluids. So, even if you are just 'meeting' people without having sex, it is still possible to get STIs. HIV infection, the precursor to AIDS, can be passed through the exchange of bodily fluids (but not from skin to skin contact). HIV is not solely an STI as it can also be transferred through infected blood, so an infected drug user who shares needles, for example, can pass on the infection even without sexual contact.

The most common STIs in Ireland are genital warts, non-specific urethritis (like a kidney infection) and chlamydia. On top of these there are at least twenty other types of STI. About 3 per cent of Irish men and 2 per cent of women are diagnosed with STIs. While some of these common STIs are not curable (so they won't ever go away and you can pass them onto other people), they are all treatable (so the symptoms won't be bothersome for you). It is really important that you go to a doctor or a clinic to have a check up and get whatever treatment might be necessary.

It is possible to reduce the likelihood of catching an STI by physically protecting yourself during sex by wearing a condom. But it is impossible to guarantee that you won't catch anything. By having unprotected sex (vaginal, anal or oral sex) you massively increase the risk of getting an STI, including HIV/AIDS.

You can't tell by looking at someone if they have an STI. Similarly, they can't tell if you have one. So if you ever do catch an STI, it is crucial that you tell your sexual partner as they will need to get tested too. The kind of symptoms to look out for are:

> **An unusual discharge/liquid or smell from your vagina, penis or bum**
> **Blisters, boils, lumps, swelling or itching in or around your vagina, penis or bum**
> **A burning or painful feeling when you pee**
> **Pain during sex.**

The symptoms are different for every STI and you might have one of these symptoms without suffering from an STI. Other STIs have no obvious symptoms at all. If you have any worry at all that you might be infected, then come and talk to me so that you can get tested, or even just go straight to the doctor.

CONTRACEPTION AND PREGNANCY

I have mentioned this before, but I want to explain it in more detail. Depending on the kind of contraception, it may have one or two functions. All contraception is designed to stop pregnancies occurring. The other functions are to reduce the risk of STIs and to regulate menstrual cycles. The most common forms of contraception are the condom (worn by the man) and the Pill (taken by the woman).

Condoms are rubber sheaths that cover the length of the man's penis and prevent sperm that is ejaculated from entering the woman's cervix and onwards. So by keeping the sperm separate, they prevent it from ever getting close to an egg and so conception can't occur. They also have a secondary function as a protection against STIs as they reduce the likelihood of genital-to-genital skin contact and so prevent the infection from passing from one person to the other.

Condoms are only successful if they are used correctly. So make sure you follow the directions that are included in the packet. Drinking or taking drugs can really reduce your likelihood of either remembering to use a condom or putting it on correctly.

There are several forms of contraceptive pill and they must be prescribed by a doctor. They work by releasing a synthetic version of your hormones, either oestrogen and progesterone or just progesterone, into your body. This regulates your menstrual cycle and prevents the release of eggs. If there are no eggs, they can't be fertilized and you can't get pregnant.

Sometimes doctors prescribe the Pill when a girl or woman has irregular or very heavy periods, and this is a secondary role that they have. If they are used correctly, they can be great forms of contraception but offer no protection against STIs. They must also be taken according to the directions given and missing a day can mean that you are not covered and could become pregnant, so always read the pack instructions carefully.

Other forms of contraception, such as the cap, like condoms, provide a barrier to prevent sperm reaching the womb and fallopian tubes. Your best bet is to go to a family planning clinic or your GP for advice on other forms of contraception.

Sometimes teenagers don't use contraception because they aren't sure of what it is (which is why I am explaining it to you) or because they are afraid of their parents finding out. I would much rather know, and have a chance to discuss it with you, if you are thinking about contraception and sex.

Even though it requires some planning and thinking ahead, it doesn't ruin the spontaneity of sex (although I'd rather you weren't too spontaneous anyway!). Preparing to be safer by carrying condoms, for example, doesn't imply that you are promiscuous, just wise.

BOUNDARIES IN RELATION TO PHYSICAL INTIMACY

Having boundaries in relation to physical intimacy is the way in which we protect ourselves and what we value. Ultimately, it is about your self-respect. Do you see yourself as someone who is worthy of being treated well? You don't expect to be hit by someone who cares about you and so neither does anyone have the right to touch you sexually where you don't want to be touched.

Sexual intimacy, while it can be a wonderful thing, places us in situations of real vulnerability. Letting someone close enough, emotionally and physically, means that they have the potential to hurt us more. If you have sex with someone that you care about and then he or she tells everyone about it behind your back, you could feel betrayed. Sexual intimacy comes back to being able to trust someone.

Betrayal can be such a painful experience because it rocks our faith in others and may prevent us from trusting again in the future. So before putting yourself in a position of real vulnerability by being sexually intimate, you need to know that you can trust the other person and that they love you and respect you.

The difficulty sometimes arises though when our own powerful sexual feelings (a pretty primitive emotion) overwhelm us and we can forget or push aside that self-respect. But I can almost guarantee you that if you don't respect yourself and your body, nobody else will either.

Part of the reason why the age of consent for sex in Ireland is seventeen for both boys and girls, and for both heterosexual and homosexual sex, is that the older you are, the better developed your skills at negotiating the complexity of sexual relationships. All of the advice from adults who have passed through adolescence is that waiting to have sex makes you feel better in the long run. The earlier you have sex, the more likely you are to regret it later.

Having boundaries in relation to physical intimacy is the way in which we protect ourselves and what we value. Ultimately, it is about your self-respect.

Alcohol reduces inhibitions and so when you are drinking you don't apply the same restrictions to your behaviour.

THE ROLE OF ALCOHOL AND SEX

Alcohol reduces inhibitions and so when you are drinking you don't apply the same restrictions to your behaviour. You might say or do things when you are drunk (or are even a little tipsy) that you would normally never say or do. This is very important when it comes to sexual behaviour because if you are drinking you might take more risks sexually.

I remember reading a newspaper article that reported on a survey about teenagers and sex. One of the things that I strongly recall was that the teenage boys said that if a girl was drunk, that was her way of saying that she wanted sex. The boys believed that girls were more shy about having sex and so when a girl got drunk that was her non-verbal message to the boy that she wanted sex. This is not true! In fact, the girl may have no such desire and so if the boy tried to have sex with her he would be doing it against her will. If the girl is indeed drunk then she may not have the capacity to be clear about saying 'no' or being able to get out of the situation. Anybody who takes sexual advantage of someone else who is drunk is committing a crime. The trouble is that when alcohol is involved neither of them may be making good choices.

Even if you agree that you want to have sex, if you are drinking you may not make a good choice about using contraception and that, too, could have really serious consequences. Drinking, and thinking about having sex, can be very dangerous. You must be so careful to mind yourself. I believe you shouldn't ever drink at your age. By being patient and waiting until you are older you will probably learn to make better choices.

THE LIKELY OUTCOME OF EFFECTIVE
SEX AND RELATIONSHIP EDUCATION

Okay, this is me back talking to you, the parent! As a final encouragement for you to talk to your teenager about all of this stuff, I have included below the findings of several pieces of research about the effects of parents talking openly and over time with their teenager about sex.

> **Teenagers will feel more comfortable and will act in a more comfortable way when discussing sensitive sexual matters with parents and others.**

> **Teenagers will seek out contraception, if they decide to be sexually active.**

> **Teenagers will wait longer before first having sex.**

> **Teenagers will be more confident and able to refuse to engage in high-risk sexual behaviour.**

That's a pretty convincing list, I think. So don't put it off any longer – get talking!

IN CASE OF EMERGENCY . . . KEY POINTS TO REMEMBER

→ The physiological information about sex is only the tip of the iceberg. In fact, we all know, and our teenagers need to know, so much more about sex, sexuality and relationships.

→ Despite the massively increased visibility of sex in today's media, it remains a sensitive subject for parents and their teenagers to discuss.

→ Perhaps the heart of the reluctance to talk about sex is your and your teenager's own cringing embarrassment at the thought of facing each other while the words sex, penis, ovulation and condom float from your lips.

→ In an ideal world telling your teenager about sex and relationships would be a process that begins at age ten or eleven.

→ To get into the swing of talking to your teenager, it might be helpful to first talk about the issue(s) with your partner or other carers. You might think of it as a rehearsal.

→ Use examples from TV shows or events in their lives as sparks to begin conversations about sex and relationships.

→ Try to be clear not just about the information that you pass on (I have listed it below) but also be clear about your values and beliefs in terms of sex and relationships.

→ The more you can show empathy and reduce judgements, the more helpful it will be when it comes to discussing the sexual mores that you want to encourage them to live by.

→ Never assume that they do know this stuff, even if they try to block you by claiming to know it all. Teenagers are notorious for having and spreading misinformation about sex.

→ The core information that your teenager needs to know includes:

✳ *the changes of puberty*	✳ *sexuality and sexual preferences*
✳ *the biology of sex*	✳ *sexually transmitted infections (STIs)*
✳ *relationships and emotions*	✳ *contraception and pregnancy*
✳ *sexual feelings*	✳ *boundaries in relation to physical intimacy*
✳ *values*	✳ *the role of alcohol and sex*
✳ *gender roles*	

8. SCHOOL

surviving the demands of learning, exams, bullying and more

The transition from primary to secondary school is a very significant one for many children. The structure of secondary school is very different, with different teachers for each subject lesson and movement between classrooms several times in a day. Some children love this new-found freedom, they love the greater independence they are accorded and they settle into the new system easily and well. But not every child finds it so easy. Some youngsters find the greater movement and change over-stimulating and under-controlled. They struggle to regulate themselves without the constant presence of a single teacher to help them control their behaviour. They find it harder to settle into classes and concentration can suffer.

Similarly, the start of secondary school is usually a chaotic social melting-pot in which all of the pupils are trying to make sense of the social order in their new peer group. Some children will act up, or act out of character, to try to place themselves in a particular grouping or to receive or avoid recognition from particular peers.

The impact of both the academic and social changes can be stressful on children. Children quickly get characterized by their behaviour, their attitude and their performance and those characterizations, for better or worse, can endure throughout a child's subsequent secondary school career.

For those children, therefore, who earn a negative reputation early on, school can quickly become a progressively more punitive and demotivating environment. Of course, youngsters' school experience must be seen in the context of their whole life experience. So how they cope with the attention they receive or don't receive in school will be mitigated by those other experiences.

You may find yourself reliving some of your own school experiences, vicariously, through your teenager. For many of us dealing with headteachers and teachers can be a frustrating experience, too, particularly when you feel you constantly have to take responsibility for your teenager's irresponsibility.

So this chapter will look at the ways in which some school-related problems can emerge, what factors influence school performance and how you can support your child if they are struggling within the system. It also looks particularly at the issue of bullying, which can often emerge most strongly in school. Finally, I have looked at how to help your teenager to prepare for and to cope with the exams that become a central part of the teenage school experience.

THIS CHAPTER LOOKS AT . . .

- Putting school in context
- Moving from primary to secondary school
- Common learning difficulties
- Attention deficit hyperactivity disorder (ADHD)
- Your support for your teenager's education
- School support for your teenager's education
- Bullying
  - *Forms of bullying*
  - *Why teenagers keep bullying to themselves*

- *How you might spot if they are being bullied*
- *How to respond to your bullied teenager*
- *Strategies for dealing with bullying*
- *If your teenager is the bully*
- Exams
  - *Benefits of stress*
  - *How exam stress develops*
  - *How stress impacts on teenagers*
  - *Dealing with exam stress (study-related)*
  - *Typical study plans for teenagers*
  - *Dealing with exam stress (body-related)*

PUTTING SCHOOL IN CONTEXT

When we think of our teenagers (and our children before that) and their education, we often think of school separately. However, this entire book has been looking at the wide range of issues that affect and impact on teenagers. So, if it is the case that your teenager is struggling in school, then it may not be helpful to think only about their school problems in isolation from the rest of their lives. Bear in mind that any (or several) of the following issues may be seriously affecting their schoolwork and their ability to settle into the social mix of school:

> **Eating disorders**
> **Cutting, piercing or other forms of self-harm**
> **Depression**
> **Smoking, drinking and drug use (marijuana, ecstasy, etc.)**
> **Suicidal ideation (thinking about suicide)**
> **Anxiety disorders**
> **Grief and loss**
> **Divorce or parental separation complications, custody battles**
> **Early sexual experimentation**
> **Physical, emotional and sexual abuse**
> **Bullying at school and in their neighbourhood**
> **Low self-esteem**
> **Sexuality**
> **Social phobia**
> **Learning difficulties**
> **Poverty**
> **Homelessness**

Moving to secondary school can be an easy transition for some. However, it is definitely a transition and so the change involved can be stressful and difficult to cope with for others.

MOVING FROM PRIMARY TO SECONDARY SCHOOL

Moving to secondary school can be an easy transition for some. However, it is definitely a transition and so the change involved can be stressful and difficult to cope with for others.

Lots of parents who have gone through the process will tell you that whatever difficulties their child may have experienced in primary school, it is nothing to the struggles that they subsequently faced in secondary school. It may have been clear to you during primary school that your son or daughter had difficulties with learning, with their behaviour, with both or with neither. Your child may have been one of the lucky ones who managed to progress through primary school within that average category, coping well enough academically, socially and behaviourally. However, many parents will have had regular contact with the school in relation to things like attention deficit hyperactivity disorder (ADHD), autistic spectrum disorders (ASD), intellectual disability, specific learning difficulties (for example, dyslexia), general problems with attention or concentration, difficulties fitting in with other children and sometimes aggression or other behavioural problems.

With luck, you have been supported by your child's school to both identify and resolve some of the difficulties that were present. Hopefully, you have been able to access the appropriate assessments either within the educational system or within the health services. Depending upon the outcome of those assessments you may have had dealings with the school principal and the special educational needs officer (SENO) to determine what, if any, additional support might be needed for your child to cope better in school. Over the last number of years significant additional resources have been made available to support children who are struggling emotionally, academically, behaviourally or physically in school. Most notably, resource teaching, which is one-to-one teaching, and special needs assistants (SNAs) have really helped those children who struggle in a full class to make better use of the education that is on offer.

Of course, there is huge variability in the quality of schools, the quality of teachers and the individual needs of each pupil. Nonetheless, broadly speaking, primary schools have been quite successful over the last number of years in increasing the availability of additional supports for their students.

Over the last number of years significant additional resources have been made available to support children who are struggling emotionally, academically, behaviourally or physically in school.

The fact that our primary school system is based on having a single teacher with each class for at least one academic year also gives the teachers a chance to get to know the individual pupils in their class and to tailor the work more closely to their ability. In my experience, primary schools tend to manage the additional resources that they receive to try to maximize the benefit not just to the individual pupil but also to other pupils who may not fully meet the criteria for additional resources, but who can really be helped by sharing the time of, for example, an SNA. In most situations it therefore feels like there is a good support network for pupils and their parents.

Shifting to secondary school can feel like that support network, which has been carefully constructed and developed, gets demolished. It may not always be apparent to the parents, but if your child has been identified as having particular needs and has been allocated resources on the basis of those needs, then those resources are intended to follow your child from class to class and also from primary to secondary school. So it is really very important for parents who are already aware that their child has a difficulty to speak with the principal or vice-principal of the secondary school in which they are enrolling their child to see how many of those resources will continue to be available to their son or daughter. As the structures are different in secondary schools, it is not guaranteed that the resources will be available. But unless you go to ask, you may never know and the school might equally never be aware of what your son or daughter is entitled to.

I think it's easier for parents to have this meeting when the difficulties relate to learning capacity or physical disability. In contrast, many parents whose child has been displaying emotional or behavioural difficulties in school will choose not to draw these to the attention of the secondary school for fear of stigmatizing their child and also setting them up to be identified as a 'behavioural problem' from day one.

Unfortunately, while the intention may be to avoid stigmatizing your child, the real effect of not alerting the school can be quite different. Without understanding and support from the principal, vice-principal and teachers, your son or daughter may actually struggle more with their behaviour than they would otherwise have done. I believe it is worthwhile to be clear from the outset about the difficulties that your child has been experiencing and also to be explicit about the fact that you're looking to work cooperatively with the school to manage those difficulties.

Of course, not only do you have to worry about the transition of support and resources from primary to secondary school, you also have to worry about the individual and personal impact on your child of that transition to secondary school. Many students transfer from a primary school to a secondary school within the same catchment area and so they go with many of their friends and just have to cope with getting used to the new environment. Other youngsters move to secondary schools outside of their catchment area and have to come to terms with a whole new social mix, as well as a new physical environment.

The first couple of years of secondary school are often the most challenging as young teenagers come to terms with the physical tumult of puberty and the emotional and psychological shift into adolescence. It is a time, as I have earlier described, when it can be very difficult to feel comfortable in your body and in yourself. Your son or daughter will have to work out their place in the social groupings of the class, the year and even the school. Bullying tends to be at its peak in the twelve to fifteen-year age groups and the jockeying for position, socially, can be very hard to navigate. (In a later section of this chapter I am going to deal more completely with the topic of bullying.)

Also, within that first two years your young teenager is trying to get used to the comparative freedom of the school system. The movement between classes and the fact that students may be allowed out during breaktimes all mean that teenagers are not subjected to the same level of supervision that they probably were in primary school. Also, they are under greater pressure to organize their own time to be ready for each class, including making sure that they have the right books and are in the right place. They have to cope with possibly more study, more homework and a longer school day. Alongside this, they have a series of different teachers with whom they may find it hard to make a connection. It can be more difficult for them to really get to know teachers in the way that they did when they had the same teacher all day, every day, for the year.

That settling-in period, then, certainly in the first year, is a time when parents need to be vigilant and to be checking in with their son or daughter and the year-head or other authorities within the school. Never assume that just because your son says nothing about his day in school that he is coping okay. Talk to him about the complexities that you can understand in terms of making or adjusting friendships, accommodating to a new and challenging environment and the need to practically organize and orient himself each day.

COMMON LEARNING DIFFICULTIES

A lot of the time poor school performance is clearly linked to learning problems. But sometimes underlying difficulties are not clearly identifiable at a young age, or the right kind of assessments may never have been sourced. So, just in case your teenager has made it through primary school without identification of an underlying learning difficulty, I have included below some information about the different signs you might look out for and the impact it may be having on their school performance.

Learning disabilities can affect how children listen, think, store, retrieve, write, read and communicate information or perform mathematical calculations. Sometimes, behavioural difficulties emerge as a child tries to mask their inability to perform academic tasks, or as a result of feeling like a failure in comparison to other children in the class. As they get labelled as a 'messer' early on, teachers or parents may not put in the same effort to try to understand if something other than behaviour is the issue.

Among the ways that a learning disability can affect the way your child learns is by interfering with the input of information to the brain. This can be a visual perception disability, causing your child to reverse or rotate letters and numbers or to not be able to focus on specific letters and words on a page, or it can be an auditory perception disability, so that similar words sound alike and cause confusion or your child may not be able to process words as fast as people are speaking them.

Learning disabilities can also cause problems with the integration of sensory information, or how the brain processes and makes sense of the sensory data that is sent to it. This can affect the information received from vision, touch and balance and can affect your child's gross and fine motor skills. Gross motor skills refer to things like walking or using something like a racquet to hit a ball. Fine motor skills refer to things like dexterity with your fingers for holding a pencil. Specific integration disabilities include sequencing disabilities, in which your child confuses the sequence of words, letters or numbers in maths problems. They can also have organizational difficulties and find it hard to plan ahead, so for example run out of space on a page, or fail to have the right books ready for a subject lesson.

Children with learning disabilities can also have problems with the way that they output information. This means that they have difficulty expressing themselves either through speech or through the way they write or draw.

Most children with learning disabilities have one or more of the above problems affecting the way that they input, integrate or output information. Some children with learning disabilities have always had trouble learning new things, while others do well in school at first but then start to have problems as school gets more difficult or the challenges get more advanced. In an ideal world they will have been recognized and hopefully helped during the primary school years, but if not then you need to request that the secondary school seeks a psychological assessment to try to determine the nature of the difficulty.

As you can imagine, when learning difficulties are not recognized it has a huge impact on how a youngster is perceived. Oftentimes the youngster is being blamed for poor performance over which they have little control. Once teachers, and even other pupils, realize that there are explanations for why a youngster is struggling academically or socially, then they tend to be more tolerant of certain kinds of behaviours or mannerisms. They might also be more accepting of a different standard of work or interaction.

ATTENTION DEFICIT HYPERACTIVITY DISORDER (ADHD)

I have highlighted ADHD not because I believe it to be a panacea explanation for many school-based difficulties but because I know it is a term that is bandied around and a label that is assigned regularly to young people. For this reason it is useful to look more closely at what exactly ADHD is. In particular, one of my concerns is that ADHD is often posited as *the* diagnosis for any young person who is distractible or challenging in a classroom. While there are a small proportion of teenagers who do have ADHD, I believe there are many more who are mislabelled. In this section I have identified those behaviours that are signs of ADHD so that you can be better informed if your teenager is being suggested as having ADHD. I have also set out some things to consider if, in fact, it is the case that your teenager has ADHD.

Inattention, hyperactivity and impulsivity are the key behaviours of ADHD. It is normal for all children to be inattentive, hyperactive or impulsive sometimes, but for teenagers with ADHD these behaviours are more severe and occur more often. To be diagnosed with the disorder, a youngster must have symptoms for six or more months and to a degree that is greater than other teenagers of the same age. The symptoms must have been present from before the teenager was seven years of age and they must have been evident in two or more social settings (typically, home and school). Be careful when you are reading through the list of symptoms below that you don't just look for symptoms that seem to fit your teenager. Do pay attention to those that don't seem to fit them and also be wary of jumping to conclusions if just a small few of the symptoms seem to match.

Teenagers who have symptoms of *inattention* may:

> **Be easily distracted, miss details, forget things, and frequently switch from one activity to another**
> **Have difficulty focusing on one thing**

> Become bored with a task after only a few minutes, unless they are doing something enjoyable

> Have difficulty focusing attention on organizing and completing a task or learning something new

> Have trouble completing or turning in homework assignments, often losing things (e.g. pencils, copies, books) needed to complete tasks or activities

> Not seem to listen when spoken to

> Daydream, become easily confused, and move slowly

> Have difficulty processing information as quickly and accurately as others

> Struggle to follow instructions

Teenagers who have symptoms of *hyperactivity* may:

> Fidget and squirm in their seats

> Talk nonstop

> Dash around, touching anything and everything in sight

> Have trouble sitting still during dinner, school and any 'down' time

> Be constantly in motion

> Have difficulty doing quiet tasks or activities

Teenagers who have symptoms of *impulsivity* may:

> Be very impatient

> Blurt out inappropriate comments, show their emotions without restraint and act without regard for consequences

> Have difficulty waiting for things they want or waiting their turn, even to speak

> Often interrupt conversations or others' activities

If it is the case that ADHD has been identified earlier in childhood, then it is most likely that the symptoms of ADHD will continue as your child enters adolescence. Some children, however, are not diagnosed with ADHD until they reach adolescence. This is more common among children with predominantly inattentive symptoms because they are not necessarily disruptive at home or in school. In these children, ADHD (or just attention deficit disorder – ADD without the hyperactivity) becomes more apparent as academic demands increase and responsibilities mount.

Although hyperactivity tends to decrease as a child ages, teens who continue to be hyperactive may feel restless and try to do too many things at once. They may choose tasks or activities that have a quick payoff rather than those that take more effort but provide bigger, delayed rewards. So, for example, they might choose to drop to ordinary level in all their subjects because the classes seem easier rather than sticking with higher level in those classes where they do well. Teenagers with primarily attention deficits struggle with school and other activities in which they are expected to be more self-reliant.

INTERVENING WITH ADHD

To help them stay healthy and provide needed structure, teenagers with ADHD should be given rules that are clear and easy to understand. Helping them stay focused and organized – such as posting a chart listing household chores and responsibilities with spaces to check off completed items – may also help. Teenagers with ADHD often have trouble controlling their impulsivity and tempers can seem to flare up more easily. In these kinds of situations getting stuck into a power battle will definitely be less effective than giving them some time and space to calm down before trying again to resolve whatever issue led to the outburst.

Medication is often suggested to help with the symptoms (noticeably the inattentiveness). I am not qualified to comment on the benefits or otherwise of the medications. What I would suggest is that you ensure that medication is prescribed by a child psychiatrist and that you get regular monitoring while your teenager is using it. If medication is successful, the benefits in school can be great as it can lead to a shift in distractible and distracting behaviour and so your teenager can experience more positive interactions with teachers and peers. This can have a knock-on effect on their self-esteem and they can start to feel better about their school performance and ultimately about themselves.

YOUR SUPPORT FOR YOUR TEENAGER'S EDUCATION

There are a number of teenagers who experience a drop-off in school performance and motivation in secondary school irrespective of learning difficulties or issues like ADHD. For these youngsters it may be that some other emotional issues (such as those I listed earlier in the chapter) block their ability to attend and concentrate. Sometimes your teenager will view things such that, in the overall scheme of what is going on in their lives, school becomes less important. You may notice that your teen is starting to skip classes, not do homework, get to school late or do worse in class tests. In these situations it is vital that you form some allies in school. Get to know your child's year-head and some of the subject teachers. Generally, most youngsters form good relationships with at least one teacher, if not them all. Find out who your child seems to connect with best and show yourself to be willing to work cooperatively with those allies in the school.

In very extreme situations you may well get called in to a larger team meeting where the principal or vice-principal might be present with several teachers or guidance counsellors, or the home–school liaison teacher. In these situations the common theme is usually that everyone is concerned about what is happening with your child. So, whether it may be a drop-off in performance or an increase in challenging behaviour, everyone around the table will want to try to get things back on track.

The outcome of such a meeting might be that you have some things to do and the school will have some things to do. Your tasks may be to become actively involved in your teenager's schoolwork, by regularly talking with teachers, reviewing homework and helping with study strategies. You might also have to help your child develop a daily study routine for after school, during which he can study and do his homework. Also, you might try to prepare a quiet environment for your child to do his homework, without the distraction of a TV, iPod or siblings.

Avoid creating a power struggle over homework and school performance. If there is already a power struggle and your teenager's academic performance is worsening as he is becoming more defiant about schoolwork, you can try and withdraw yourself from the conflict by making your child responsible for his performance. Make time available for schoolwork and homework by limiting television, video-game use, extracurricular activities or an after-school job. You may also want to provide incentives or rewards for improved school performance and removing other privileges, such as phone, iPod or the right to go out with friends if things continue to worsen.

Punishments and consequences may lead to major stand-offs with your teenager because when they reach the age, the size and the cognitive awareness that they can resist the punishment or you can't enforce the punishment, suddenly you can become powerless. (I have dealt with the dynamics of power in Chapter 4.) It may be that by using such strategies you actually create a greater power struggle than you had been hoping to avoid. This is one of those situations where you need to make a judgement about whether your intervention will improve or inflame the situation.

Usually reinforcement is more successful with younger children and by the time adolescence rolls around, teenagers are beginning to be more internally motivated to achieve in their own right. But this is a process, not an event. Until your son or daughter shows a clear intention and self-directed goal, you may have to continue to provide the external motivations to encourage and discourage the respective behaviours you want to see more of and less of.

If you are aware that there have been very significant and possibly traumatic experiences that are affecting your teenager, then it is worth getting outside help from professional therapists (like psychologists, psychiatrists, psychotherapists or counsellors). Resolving the source of distress will usually lead to a huge reduction in either the acting-out behaviour (rows, fighting, delinquency, etc.) or the internalizing behaviour (like depression, anxiety, social withdrawal, etc.). In both situations your teen becomes freed up, emotionally, to resume a focus on school.

SCHOOL SUPPORT FOR YOUR TEENAGER'S EDUCATION

I have already alluded to some of the resource-based supports that schools can make available to students. These include one-to-one teaching and SNA support to help your teenager with their attention and organization. Some schools will have guidance counsellors who can assist with other emotional issues that are affecting your teenager. The kind of issues that schools will be hoping to help generally fall into the following categories:

> Improving memory and attention span: **this might include seating your child so as not to be distracted, making instructions clear and unambiguous, repeating instructions, using visual aids to support what is being said or having special cues to remind your child to get back on task.**

> Improving organizational skills: **the school could establish a daily checklist of tasks or assignments for your child, or help him or her to create a notebook to record homework, project deadlines or test schedules. This is especially helpful for youngsters with ADHD.**

> Improving productivity: **this refers to breaking down the tasks into more manageable chunks or sometimes reducing the overall amount to be achieved to boost a sense of completion. It can also involve varying the type of work to be done or the way that material is presented. This is also where one-to-one teaching can be really beneficial.**

> Improving performance: **this can be achieved by giving your child additional time to complete work or tests. Perhaps oral testing instead of, or in addition to, written testing might be fairer. Similarly, continuous assessment places more emphasis on overall effort and work completed and less on the outcome of a test.**

> Improving behaviour and impulse control: **having a warning system to alert your child to times when his or her behaviour begins to step out of line. Many schools operate a card or points system (usually negatively based), where the collection of points for misbehaviour leads to detentions, suspensions or other sanctions.**

It is good for you and your teenager to be fully informed about how the school will be trying to support them in class. It is more helpful if you are in agreement with the school policies and processes as you can then demonstrate a united front with the teachers and principal to encourage your teenager. You can be sure that if you are in conflict with the school, for whatever reason, it will transfer onto your son or daughter and they too will lose faith in the school.

BULLYING

Bullying is one form of very negative peer pressure and, despite the efforts of schools, tends to be a feature of everyone's experience of the education system. It tends to be very tied up in the desire of the bully to exert power and control. Interestingly, both bullies and those that they bully tend to have low self-esteem. The bully uses their threatening behaviour as a mask to hide the fact that they feel vulnerable and bad about themselves. A bullied child, on the other hand, feels the hurt of the taunts or the blows and feels confirmed in beliefs like they are weak or stupid or unpopular. If the taunting relates to any aspect of their physical self, like their weight, height, looks, mannerisms or sexuality, it just serves to underline whatever negative attribution the bullied teenager has already given to those physical characteristics. There are several different forms of bullying and I have listed them next.

Bullying is one form of very negative peer pressure and, despite the efforts of schools, tends to be a feature of everyone's experience of the education system.

FORMS OF BULLYING

> **Verbal:** examples of verbal bullying include name-calling, sarcastic remarks and put-downs. It also now includes written forms, such as comments on a Bebo page or texts on a phone.

> **Physical:** as the name suggests, this kind of bullying usually involves hitting, kicking or pushing. Physical bullying tends to happen more amongst boys, who use their physicality as a frightening means of exerting power.

> **Psychological:** examples of psychological bullying are deliberately excluding someone from a group or spreading malicious stories or photos of someone against their wishes. Again it is very prevalent on social networking sites where youngsters can be deliberately removed as a 'friend' or embarrassing photos or confidences get shared with a group.

> **Threatening:** threatening forms of bullying include demands for money or property, such as i-Pod or mobile phone.

WHY TEENAGERS KEEP BULLYING TO THEMSELVES

It is an awful experience to discover that your teenager is being bullied. Part of that distress often arises because we only hear about the bullying by accident or if someone else tells us. Most youngsters fear that the bullying will get worse if they tell. Sometimes this can be part of the threat of the bully; sometimes it is just the belief that exists while in the state of powerlessness that many teenagers who are bullied feel.

Teenagers may also try to avoid upsetting you, believing it is better to try to cope with this on their own. This is another good reason to really work hard at keeping communication open with your son or daughter. It is good if they have had the experience in the past of coming to you with an issue about which they may have felt some level of shame, distress or embarrassment. If, in such situations, they have found you to be understanding, caring and supportive, then it is much more likely that they would come to you with an issue like bullying. Sometimes the reluctance of a youngster to talk to their parents is exacerbated if they believe that you too might be scornful of their inability to protect themselves.

HOW YOU MIGHT SPOT IF THEY ARE BEING BULLIED

Given that despite your best efforts your teenager may not feel confident enough to talk to you about being bullied, you need to have other strategies for identifying if bullying may be happening. There are a few signs to look out for and I have listed them below. Usually it is not simply a case of one of these reasons, rather it is when several of them occur together.

> Expressions of fear or anxiety about going to a particular venue or about meeting with a particular group. **This may be more noticeable if your teenager had previously been relatively confident about going to school or going down to the local youth club or being part of a local sports club.**

> Prolonged bad mood or unhappiness can also be a warning sign for bullying. **It is important to remember, though, that this can also occur for lots of other reasons. To identify that bullying may be the issue, you would probably be looking for additional information about the broader context in which the bad mood or unhappiness seems to be developing.**

> Dropping activities or friends that they previously had been very connected to might be another indicator that something is wrong. **Again, sometimes teenagers will withdraw from activities for other reasons, such as disinterest or to fit in with peers. However, classically, if your teenager starts to make excuses why they don't want to go to school or why they no longer want to meet up with certain friends, then it is worth checking with them if something else is behind their reluctance.**

> Unexplained bruises or cuts or regular requests to replace 'lost' items could be suggestive of physical or threatening bullying. **Do remember, however, that lots of teenagers are forgetful and careless and so sometimes there is a genuine reason why things go missing.**

HOW TO RESPOND TO YOUR BULLIED TEENAGER

The most important thing is to think about how you can support your son or daughter. You have two main tasks: help them to understand their feelings about being bullied and give them strategies to help avoid being bullied in the future, or at least to come and seek help sooner if it does happen.

The first step is to open up a dialogue with your teen about the bullying. Talk to them about what was happening to them and how they felt about that. Bear in mind that teenagers are not always fully able to express their feelings. You may need to suggest feelings that they might have had and then let them agree or disagree. Essentially you are trying to empathize with them about the experience. Read back over Chapter 3, especially the section on how to emotionally support your teenager. Empathetic statements such as I have described in Chapter 3 may be the best way to connect now with your son or daughter.

You may have found that your teenager has learned that they actually do get their own way by being pushy or threatening. This may, in fact, be their method of interacting with you and with others that you know. If this is the case, then you probably feel much as if you're being bullied yourself and it can be hard to think about standing up to your own son or daughter and you may feel unable to do it. However, somebody needs to stand up to them and if you feel unable to do it, then look into your wider social network of extended family or friends to see if there's somebody there who can challenge this kind of behaviour from your own child. It would be ideal if you or that friend could teach your teenager how to negotiate. If you look back at Chapters 2 and 4, you will see many strategies for communicating and resolving conflicts that don't involve bullying. These are the kind of skills that your teenager needs to learn.

EXAMS

The state exams are often much-hyped affairs. The significance placed on performance in the final exam is, at times, terrifying. The irony is that, irrespective of the hype surrounding the exams and their stated importance, I believe that the majority of teenagers would take them seriously anyway. Once your son or daughter sees the exams as relevant and important, then they will probably feel anxious in the build-up, irrespective of how you or anyone else is defining those exams. Exam anxiety is really common. Indeed, many of us feel worry, stress or fear before any test. I know you may be long moved on from your own exam experiences, but think of your own driving test as an example, or your most recent job interview.

Mind you, most parents I have ever spoken to with regard to their teenager studying for exams have described that the build-up to the exams was more stressful for the parents than for their sons and daughters. Indeed, the pressure that exists impacts on whole families sometimes, where the student is stressed, grumpy and short-tempered and everyone else is treading on eggshells to avoid further upsetting him or her in the lead up to the exams.

BENEFITS OF STRESS

While we usually think of stress as a bad thing, it's important to feel some level of stress. A little bit of stress acts as a motivator and without it we may end up being too laidback, to the point where we wouldn't bother doing anything. So a small amount of stress is helpful. The key is not to let it get too great because too much stress becomes counterproductive. In fact, I have included a graph opposite that shows the relationship between stress and performance in any task. You can see that as stress increases, so too does your performance of the task. Critically, though, there is a point at which the stress can become too great and then it starts to interfere with performance and performance drops off. The key is to keep optimum levels of stress so that you stay in the area of best performance.

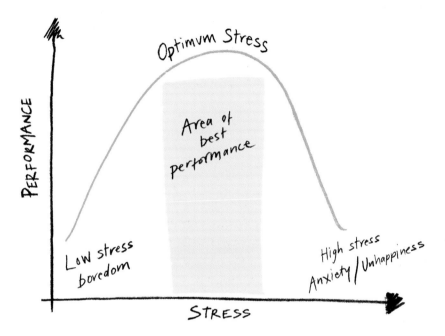

The relationship between stress and performance

HOW EXAM STRESS DEVELOPS

I think there are three main reasons why exams are stressful for teenagers. The first reason is an anticipatory anxiety, the second is a fear of failure and the third is stress about the amount of work to be done. Any or all of these reasons might be involved for your teenager, so we shall look at each one in turn.

Anticipatory anxiety, as the name suggests, is a worry about something that is unknown. When we don't know what to expect, we can create ideas, expectations and anticipations in our minds. These may be accurate and based on what has been explained to us, or they may be completely of our own creation. Lots of students sitting the Junior Certificate may experience anticipatory anxiety about what sitting in the exam hall will be like since none of them will ever have sat there for a state exam. This is one of the reasons that many schools run 'mock' exams in February/March.

Sometimes it is a fear of failure that piles on the stress. This is often mediated by the child's own expectations or the expectations of others. Undoubtedly, parents and teachers will have expressed opinions about both the importance of the exams and how well they expect the youngster to achieve (or not, occasionally!). If your expectations, or those of others, are very high, then this can really pressure your son or daughter, who will probably not want to disappoint you. By the time of the Leaving Certificate many students have a clearer idea of what they want to do after school and so they are probably aiming to achieve a certain result for themselves to give them those college choices. This means that they might be putting undue pressure on themselves, particularly if the results required are high.

Sometimes it is stress related to the volume of work to be covered. The curriculum can be vast and depending on how methodical students are in their preparation, they can reach a point of feeling overwhelmed and under-prepared. Panic at not getting the course covered or revised can set in.

HOW STRESS IMPACTS ON TEENAGERS

No matter what the source of the stress and anxiety, the experience of it will be the same. Essentially, stress is a very physical experience. Adrenalin gets released when we get stressed and this increases our heartrate and the rate of our breathing and leads to muscle tension, or that feeling of a knotted-up stomach. Once our bodies start feeling stressed, it impacts on our mood and our thinking and the whole experience becomes a bit circular. You might remember back in Chapter 3, when I was talking about feelings, I described a model for how thinking, feeling, behaviour and our physical selves are all linked. The same model fits very well for stress. The more we worry, the more stressed we feel and then the more it will give us a sensation of worrying. Our thinking becomes a little less rational as a result and tends to zone-in or become over-focused.

DEALING WITH EXAM STRESS (STUDY-RELATED)

Dealing with exam anxiety takes a number of avenues. The first step is to try to help your teenager work out the source of the stress that they feel. Is it more about feeling overwhelmed with the enormity of the information to be learned, or is it about fear of failing or of the unknown?

> If it's fear of failure, **it may be possible to lower or clarify expectations for your teenager so that they feel more able to achieve the expected outcome. Whatever their own expectations, it is really not helpful for you to put unnecessary pressure on them. Once you have given them enough of a push to get them started, then pull back from reminding them of how critical and important the exams are. With the hype that is around, they can't fail to be aware that these exams are important and that doing well matters.**

> If it is fear of the unknown, **then practice with past exam papers will lower that anxiety, as will the experience of the mock exam where, hopefully, the exam hall layout will match the way it will be in the summer.**

> If the task of preparing and studying is overwhelming, **then between now and the exams you can help your son or daughter to break down what needs to be achieved so that he/she has clear targets for what to cover each week.**

> Study plans (timetables of study) are a good idea because once it is all written down, **it can be very reinforcing to put a line through what has been done and see your progress building towards the exam. Get your child to set realistic targets for how long they will study and break down each study session into twenty-minute segments, with a five-minute break in between. I have included a typical daily study plan for holidays or non-school days below.**

TYPICAL STUDY PLANS FOR TEENAGERS

This section and the next are directed at teenagers, to make some suggestions directly to them about studying. A typical study timetable for a full day will involve two to four study periods, depending on your energy and enthusiasm. Start with a minimum of two study periods and after getting into the swing of it (within two to three days of starting to study), up it to at least three periods a day. Stick to four subjects per day, spread across the study periods (two in each period), even when you do more than two study periods in a day (i.e. repeat the subjects).

Make sure to have all the books, copies, notepads, pens, etc. that you think you will need ready before the period begins so that when you get down to work, you can be really focused. Don't leave your room for the five-minute breaks, only come down for tea/coffee/milk/smoke, etc. for the fifteen-minute break halfway through the session. Time your long break to coincide with food!

Remember that you are studying because you want to achieve some (or all!) of your potential, not because anybody else is studying or not. Study because you want to prove something to yourself or to others and because you know the outcome will be worth it.

Typical Study Period (about two hours up to a big break)			
Subject	**Period (mins)**	**Focus of Study**	**Break afterwards (mins)**
French	15	Learn	5
French	15	Recall (make your own notes of what you just learned)	5
French	15	Recap/Check Recall	15
Subject	**Period (mins)**	**Focus of Study**	**Break afterwards (mins)**
English	15	Learn	5
English	15	Recall (make your own notes of what you just learned)	5
English	15	Recap/Check Recall	30

For some subjects the focus I have suggested may not work and you might be doing three fifteen-minute slots of practice (like doing maths examples). The important thing is that you make use of the time you are devoting to a given subject and that the system works for you, so adapt it as you need to. I would suggest that you break up a four-study-period day as follows:

> 8.30–10.30
> 11.00–13.00
> 14.30–16.30
> 19.30–21.30

At the end of your day treat yourself to something nice like a bath, a foot rub (if you can persuade someone to give you one), a good book, some time on the computer, a long phone call to a friend or such like.

DEALING WITH EXAM STRESS (BODY-RELATED)

There are also a range of different ways to relax that will help with the physical sensations of stress and anxiety and that in turn will have a positive knock-on effect in feeling less stressed or worried.

> The easiest one to explain and to try is abdominal breathing. **Also called deep breathing, this is where you deliberately slow down the speed at which you breathe in and out and try to get the breath as deep into your lungs as possible. Breathe deeply by imagining trying to expand your ribcage at the base, just above your abdomen. Count to four as you breathe in, hold your breath for a count of one and then breathe out over another count to four. As you practise you will be able to breathe slower and slower.**

> You could also suggest that your teenager follows one of the many guided relaxation or meditation CDs that are available. **These work in two ways. As your thinking is focused on the meditation, it brings you away from the focus on study and exams and, at the same time, the meditation or relaxation exercises that are being described will allow your body to relax. In Chapter 10, on Depression, Suicide and Self-Harm I have included the text of a typical guided relaxation that I use with teenagers.**

> Exercise and diet are also really important for teenagers to help them feel more in control of their anxiety and stress. **This is the one area in which parents can be very helpful as we can direct our energies, usefully, to minding our teenagers with cups of tea and wholesome food. Eating well and regularly and getting outdoors every so often will counteract the negative physical effect of the stress and improve your teenager's mood. Sleeping is also very important. Late-night studying doesn't give the body a chance to recover and also makes it hard for the brain to switch off when they do try to get to bed.**

IN CASE OF EMERGENCY . . . KEY POINTS TO REMEMBER

→ Moving to secondary school can be an easy transition for some. However, it is definitely a transition and so the change involved can be stressful and difficult to cope with for others.

→ The start of secondary school is usually a chaotic social melting-pot in which all of the pupils are trying to make sense of the social order in their new peer group.

→ Those first couple of years of secondary school are often the most challenging as young teenagers come to terms with the physical tumult of puberty and the emotional and psychological shift into adolescence.

→ For those youngsters who earn a negative reputation early on, school can quickly become a progressively more punitive and demotivating environment.

→ If you are aware that your child has a learning or behavioural difficulty, speak with the principal or vice-principal of the secondary school in which you are enrolling your child to see what resources will be available to your son or daughter.

→ Teenagers with ADHD often have trouble controlling their impulsivity and tempers can seem to flare up more easily. To help them stay healthy and to provide needed structure they should be given rules that are clear and easy to understand.

→ Get to know your child's year-head and some of their subject teachers. Find out who your teenager seems to connect with best and show yourself to be willing to work cooperatively with those allies in the school.

→ Bullying tends to be at its peak in the twelve to fifteen-year age groups and the jockeying for position, socially, can be very hard to navigate.

➤ Your teenager may not be open about being bullied and so you have to be alert to signs such as fear or anxiety about going to certain places or about certain people. Unexplained cuts or bruises or 'missing' items could be another sign.

➤ If they are being bullied you have two main tasks: help them to understand their feelings about being bullied and give them strategies to help avoid being bullied in the future, or at least to come and seek help sooner if it does happen.

➤ Explain to them that bullies are usually covering up their own feelings of inadequacy and are trying to make other people feel as bad inside as they do. Explain to your teenager that it is not their fault that this has happened.

➤ Your teenager may not feel confident to stand up to the bully themselves and so sometimes you have to intervene, with other adults, to make the bullying stop.

➤ In addition, however, help them to build their self-esteem and get them to practise being assertive.

➤ Unless teenagers are internally motivated to study because of a desire to achieve in exams it is very hard to motivate them. However, most teenagers take exams seriously and consequently can get quite anxious in anticipation.

➤ Preparation (by following a study plan) and active relaxation are the keys to coping with exam stress.

9. ALCOHOL, DRUGS AND EATING DISORDERS

learning the skills to cope with the tough decisions

As is probably clear by this stage, one of my strong beliefs is that teenagers will use some very negative behaviour to effectively 'self-medicate' or cope with the stresses, struggles and traumas that they experience. Essentially they are trying, at times, to opt out of their current world. They may not like the reality of their lives and if they can escape that through alcohol, drugs or eating disorders, then they will. Each of these are, unfortunately, very effective blocks to reality. This means that they are highly reinforcing for any teenager who wants to zone out and who doesn't want to deal with what is going on in their life.

This is not the only dynamic at play or the only reason why teenagers will use and abuse alcohol, drugs or food. Some of the issues associated with alcohol use amongst teenagers have their roots planted very firmly in societal attitudes and behaviours that are perpetuated by us adults. I think it is a true hypocrisy for us to be critical of teenagers' abuse of alcohol without looking at how adults regularly and at times 'celebratedly' abuse alcohol.

Teenagers have always experimented with alcohol and with other drugs. In many respects we take this experimentation to be a natural part of the developmental process, much as other experiments related to clothes, make-up, hair and friends are also undertaken. The worry for parents comes when experimentation seems to end and habitual use or abuse takes over. The fears are real and justified.

This chapter will distil knowledge for you about alcohol and various drugs, to better inform you to be able to make choices for, and ideally with, your teenager. I will identify the signs of abuse of alcohol or drugs and suggest ways of approaching the issue with your teenager.

Similarly, I will show you what to look out for if you suspect your teenager (usually, but not always, your daughter) has an eating disorder. Although the dynamics of why eating disorders may develop are often different from why teenagers abuse alcohol and drugs, there is some overlap. Eating disorders, of which anorexia nervosa and bulimia nervosa are the two main kinds, are very serious and potentially life-threatening illnesses. For example, about 6 per cent of people who develop anorexia nervosa die; approximately half the deaths are from suicide and the others are linked to the effects of malnutrition. In this chapter I'll look in detail at anorexia and bulimia. I'll explain how they are diagnosed, what their impact is and what you can do to help your daughter to return to normal eating. With eating disorders, more than with most teenage issues, external professional help is usually required.

THIS CHAPTER LOOKS AT . . .

Alcohol

 * *The views of teenagers about alcohol*
 * *The effects of alcohol on teenagers*
 * *Factors associated with teenage drinking*
 * *Encouraging responsible drinking or no drinking!*

Drugs

 * *The most common drugs out there*
 * *Drug addiction*
 * *Signs of your teenager using drugs*
 * *Responding to your teenager who is using drugs*

Eating Disorders

 * *Understanding anorexia nervosa and bulimia nervosa*
 * *Causes of eating disorders*
 * *The physical impact of eating disorders*
 * *Warning signs of an eating disorder*
 * *Preventing eating disorders*
 * *Responding to an eating disorder*

ALCOHOL

Practically, alcohol comes in several forms. Typically, it is found in beers, ciders, wine, spirits, liqueurs and alcopops (ready mixed spirits and soft drinks). The amount of alcohol is measured in standard units. A standard unit of alcohol equates to a half pint of beer, a small glass of wine or a single pub measure of spirits. The broad guidelines for safer levels of drinking are up to 14 standard units per week for women and up to 21 standard units per week for men. Obviously it isn't safe to be drinking all those units at the one sitting! Indeed, binge-drinking is classified as an occasion where we drink more than 6 standard units in one go. This means that a lot of times when we go out could probably be classified as binge-drinking occasions. Binge-drinking increases the risks of accidents, injuries, fighting and alcohol-poisoning. The physical effects of alcohol will be noticed, generally, within five to ten minutes of starting to drink and it takes one hour for each standard unit to pass through our system.

The influences for our teenagers' use of alcohol are not, primarily, their friends. It is much more likely that they are influenced by television, advertising, their family and even the broader community. Some research that was done shows that even by the age of five most children will have formed basic attitudes and opinions about alcohol. Teenagers will use their own experiences with alcohol and their observations of its effects on family, friends and in the community to draw their own conclusions about how to use or abuse alcohol. One very significant factor, I believe, is that in Ireland the attitude of most teenagers to drinking is that you drink to get drunk. This can be seen in a European report that showed that alongside teenagers from Denmark, the Netherlands and the UK, Irish teenagers are the heaviest drinkers in Europe. But then, is this a surprise given that Irish adults are also amongst the heaviest drinkers in Europe? A Youth ID survey of Irish teenagers, reported on in March 2009, showed that one in four sixteen- to seventeen-year-olds claim to drink alcohol at least once a week.

Consumption, in the overall consumerist sense, has been at its highest over the ten years up to the end of 2008. This is reflected in alcohol use, too. Although there was a drop-off in alcohol sales in pubs, it was more than matched by the increase in off-licence sales. There is little point, therefore, in looking at and being critical of teenage drinking habits unless we are to take a very critical look at, and then change, the societal attitudes to drinking.

The influences for our teenagers' use of alcohol are not, primarily, their friends. It is much more likely that they are influenced by television, advertising, their family and even the broader community.

THE VIEWS OF TEENAGERS ABOUT ALCOHOL

In 2007 the Irish government conducted a national consultation with teenagers aged between twelve and eighteen and asked them about their solutions to the problems that alcohol creates for teenagers. The two main suggestions were to reduce the legal age for drinking alcohol and to have more affordable alcohol-free facilities.

A small number of youngsters who took part favoured raising the legal age limit to twenty-one years, while the majority favoured allowing sixteen- to eighteen-year-olds to drink in moderation under the monitoring of a 'safe-limit' card. A 'safe-limit' card would allow young people over the age of sixteen a 'safe number' of alcoholic drinks of any type per night. They also recommended allowing those under the age of sixteen to drink alcoholic beverages with less than 5 per cent alcohol content. The teenagers in the consultation reported that it would be more sociable and safer for young people to drink in pubs rather than having to congregate to drink illegally 'under cover' in public. They felt that this would facilitate supervision of their drinking and reduce the 'buzz', which is enhanced by the illicit nature of drinking in secret.

The teenagers spoke of the necessity for an enforced system of identification for twelve- to twenty-five-year-olds. It was felt that only one form of identification should be accepted, such as the Garda Age Card, and that there was a clear need for tougher penalties for under-age drinking.

They also wanted more affordable, alcohol-free facilities. The suggestion of youth cafés was put forward, but the teenagers were very realistic in their view that while this might reduce the demand for alcohol, it would not get rid of it entirely. They recognized that there is already a culture developed that sees alcohol as an integral part of social gatherings and recreation. So they felt that even if cafés were to be developed, it would have to be in consultation with teenagers to make them more likely to meet their needs.

It was clear, too, from the consultation that teenagers did want information about alcohol and drinking, but they wanted it delivered by neutral professionals rather than by teachers. They also wanted the core message to be about responsible drinking rather than about abstinence.

THE EFFECTS OF ALCOHOL ON TEENAGERS

Alcohol is so pervasive in Irish life that I would guess most of us don't ever think about what it is and how it impacts on the body and the mind. When we adults use it, we drink to relax, have a bit of fun and as part of a social experience. People can feel more carefree or excitable when they are drunk and so we usually perceive alcohol as a stimulant, believing that it 'gets us going'. The reality, in fact, is that it is a depressant. The more you drink, the sleepier or more drowsy you will become. It is a drug, like any of the other drugs described in this chapter. The only difference is that it is legal. Because it is legal, its easy availability makes it more likely that users will become addicted to it. Alcohol affects the central nervous system of the body. This means it will have an impact on breathing, heart rate, thinking, feeling and behaviour.

It is the effects on thinking, feeling and behaviour that most of us like it for. Alcohol loosens the tongue, reduces inhibitions and can increase feelings of confidence, strength or power. It tends to numb emotions some of the time; other times it can exacerbate those feelings. Because of its depressant effect it can make emotions more labile, i.e. more prone to change and sometimes more volatile. Generally, though, moderate amounts of alcohol will give a bit of a buzz and a feel-good factor when we are going out to have a good time and so that is why most of us drink it. Our teenagers, of course, are just looking for the same buzz.

> Alcohol loosens the tongue, reduces inhibitions and can increase feelings of confidence, strength or power.

The longer-term effects of alcohol use by teenagers are hard to predict. But we do know that teenagers are still developing physically, socially, emotionally and intellectually. Research shows that heavy use of alcohol by teenagers does lead to loss of memory and can impair brain development and other skills.

How the alcohol itself will affect each individual teenager is also hard to predict because many things will influence how the body metabolizes the alcohol. So things like their age, weight and whether they are boys or girls will make a difference (alcohol affects girls quicker than boys). Similarly, how quickly they are drinking, how much they are drinking, what they have eaten before or since drinking and how strong the alcohol level is in the drink will also change the experience of drunkenness. Also, as I mentioned above, their mood when going to drink can also be a significant influencer on how they experience the alcohol. If they are in a great mood and going out to have fun, they will feel differently when drunk than if they are depressed or are trying to block out distressing events from their lives.

They will, however, get hangovers, which are an indication of alcohol-poisoning. Physically they are dehydrated and can feel nauseous and have headaches. The timing of their drinking and their subsequent hangovers are also important. Being hungover will have a serious impact on a day at school, leading them to miss out on aspects of learning. As I mentioned earlier, drinking can also affect their memory. In some cases alcohol use can be the result of difficulties at school. A youngster who feels bad about the trouble they are having in school may decide to drink to get away from these problems. Drinking under these circumstances sets up a cyclical problem as the more they drink, the greater the difficulties they may have in school. Many parents that I have spoken to also complain about the after-effects of drinking and the bad mood that can hang around their son or daughter for even a few days. Irritability with a hangover is very common.

Many of the anti-social behaviours, such as fighting on the streets, destruction of or damage to property and even abusive and threatening language to passersby are associated with, or worsened by, alcohol. Teenagers in groups can be threatening, but drunken groups of teenagers are even more threatening because they are less in control of their behaviour. I spoke earlier about how we can lose our inhibitions when we drink. For some people this is a positive loosening of social inhibition, which allows them greater confidence to function in a group. But we also have moral and ethical inhibitions that stop us from, for example, engaging in illegal activity, from hurting other people or from certain sexual practices. If those inhibitions get lowered, then we may place ourselves or other people at greater risk. It is good if our teenagers feel inhibited from engaging in some things. When it comes to sex, alcohol will always lead to riskier decisions being made. We don't put the same level of thought into sex when we are drunk and researchers have shown a definite link between drinking alcohol and being less likely to use contraception in subsequent sex. The danger of unplanned pregnancy and sexually transmitted infections is therefore greatly increased.

FACTORS ASSOCIATED WITH TEENAGE DRINKING

Some interesting facts about teenage drinking show that those teenagers who first drink before the age of fifteen are four times more likely to develop alcohol dependency than those who wait until they are twenty-one to start drinking. Those same early drinkers are seven times more likely to be in a car crash where alcohol is involved.

The decision a teenager makes about when to start drinking is, therefore, very important. Whatever the influences from society and the media, it is vital that we parents try to promote the message of waiting as long as possible before drinking alcohol. It is easier to do this if you give both very clear direction and a very clear example in your own life. There is no point in being half-hearted about the message you give in relation to alcohol. You are either in favour of teenage drinking or you are not. Similarly, you cannot rail against the dangers of drunkenness while regularly getting drunk yourself. You must be responsible in the way in which you use alcohol. As ever, the strength of your relationship with your teenager will play an important role in how able they are to accept what you say and do. Generally, though, the more connected they are to their family, to teachers and even to good friends, the greater the likelihood that they will delay their drinking.

Despite the messages we give our teenagers, we also need them to have good social skills that will allow them to withstand some of the peer pressure that may be brought to bear on them to drink. The more involvement and sense of responsibility they have in extra-curricular activities, like sports clubs or youth groups, the more likely they are to delay their drinking.

In contrast, teenagers who feel alienated from close family and have problems in school are more likely to drink at a younger age. If your son or daughter is exposed to high levels of alcohol consumption within your family (including older siblings), then this too might be a factor in their decision to drink young. In true confusing fashion, allowing teenagers unsupervised time with their friends is important for their development but it also increases the risks that they will drink at a younger age, especially if their friends are drinking.

Research has also identified risk factors for early drinking, such as parental separation, living in a disadvantaged area and a history of problem behaviour. It may be that these factors are all associated with a level of emotional distress, greater instability in a family and less control or limits on behaviour. In such circumstances there may be greater reasons, greater opportunities and less obstacles to drinking.

ENCOURAGING RESPONSIBLE DRINKING OR NO DRINKING!

There are a number of things you can do to actively influence your teenager's drinking habits. I know the teenagers that took part in the National Consultation I reported on above don't want to hear about not drinking, but I believe it is worth starting with an abstinence message. Given the overwhelming societal attitude to alcohol in this country, I think it is unrealistic to expect your teenager never to drink. Ultimately, therefore, your goal, for as long as alcohol is legal, should be to make sure that they drink responsibly and safely. Based on the research, I would suggest that every parent should be trying to delay the time at which their teenager starts drinking. It gives them the best opportunity of having a lifelong responsible attitude to alcohol.

Talk about alcohol

The first suggestion I have is that you talk about alcohol openly and knowledgeably. Know the facts, some of which I have included earlier in the chapter. An additional fact that may surprise your teenager is that not 'everyone is doing it' when it comes to drinking – over 50 per cent of schoolchildren in Ireland have never drunk alcohol. In Ireland there has been a positive reduction in the last few years in the number of youngsters under the age of fifteen who drink.

Begin talking about alcohol and drinking from when they are small. Always try to maintain a calm and matter-of-fact approach to the topic. If you talk about things in this way, you are much more likely to hear what your teenager's views about alcohol and drinking are. They will have had their own experiences, picked up their own stories and have their own views on the subject. Worrying though it may be to discover that your teenager is drinking, it is better that you hear from them how they approach alcohol. This also allows you to then be more influential for them in becoming responsible in their alcohol use.

A typical scene for many parents is the first night that their teenager returns home drunk, or clearly smelling of alcohol. Their use suddenly becomes undeniable. If you haven't acknowledged the issue before this, then you must address it now. However, don't address it on the night they return. Make sure they are safe (i.e. not about to puke and inhale their own vomit, or in the extremes of alcohol-poisoning) and then let them sleep. The next day, despite their hangover, is the time to deal with their behaviour. Don't assume that they were fully complicit in their drunkenness. Make sure you get to hear their side of the story. Remind them of your family rules and expectations, set in place any consequences and be patient. This is a scene you might revisit on many occasions. Your aim is to remain firm and fair and to make it clear that you are always available to sort things out calmly.

You may find that you can use situations like speaking to your own friends, in the presence of your teenager, to talk about alcohol. This means you can make explicit your views and values about drinking without coming into head-to-head conflict with your son or daughter. If you try to advise them directly about their drinking, they may reject your opinion. By sharing your opinion with your own friend, you can hope that some of the message will be heard by your teenager without their 'parent advice radar' being activated.

Being able to communicate effectively is a tricky business and in Chapter 2 I have given you lots of hints and tips for strategies you can try. Having great communication skills comes to nothing, however, if you are not with the person you wish to communicate with. So try to spend time with your teenager; one way is to maintain an interest in their sports or hobbies. Even though we have busy lives, we also need to make ourselves available to talk and to listen.

Be aware of your teenager's whereabouts

You may recall that one of the risk factors for teenage alcohol use is frequent unsupervised time with their friends. To combat this you need to try to have an awareness of where they are and what they are doing. This is a delicate balancing act. If you try to overcontrol them and their movements, you will encounter resistance and that might push their behaviour further into secrecy and lead to greater efforts on their part to conceal their true activity and to dupe you into believing that they are elsewhere doing other things. Nonetheless, having family rules about alcohol is important as a reference point for them. For example, are they allowed to go to house parties where there is no adult supervision or where alcohol will be served? Do you allow them to drink in a moderate, supervised way at home or not at all?

Be clear about what consequences you will impose if they break the rules. For example, if you have a curfew in place for them, what will happen if they are late? If they go overnight to a friend's house and you later discover that there was no adult in the house, what will you do? For younger teenagers you might have different rules and different consequences than when they are older. Typically, the level of supervision they will tolerate and that you can impose might be greater when they are younger. The kinds of consequences you might want to consider are things like earlier curfew or grounding them; docking some pocket-money or allowance; or the loss of some other privilege, like phone credit. Consequences are only as good as your ability to enforce them, so try not to have extreme or unrealistic consequences. If you don't keep to your word and follow through with a consequence that you had previously threatened, then all your teenager learns is that you can't be trusted and that they can 'get away' with things.

If your teenager is going to a friend's house, it always makes sense to talk to the friend's parent. Be explicit about any concerns you have about drinking and see what views or plans that parent has to try to minimize the risk (ideally regular supervision!). If your teenager is going out elsewhere at night, for example to a disco, have you a plan formulated with them for how they will get home? Do you know who they are actually going to be out with? Have you discussed their safety and your concerns and expectations around alcohol?

One of the safety concerns that you probably need to be talking about explicitly is the increase in knife-related incidents. Particularly over the last year, it seems to me, there have been many more media reports of knife crime which involve alcohol. Some of this is linked to the apparent 'knife culture' in which more young people carry knives, allegedly for self-protection. However, as with many other alcohol-induced misjudgements, the liklihood of arguments starting will always be greater when your teenager is out and about late at night and they or others have been drinking. Such arguments have the potential to be more dangerous if knives are involved so encourage your teenager to be alert and wary of fights.

Role-model responsible drinking

It sounds straightforward, but in reality we have probably all been guilty of occasions, on a frequent or infrequent basis, of being irresponsible with alcohol. The first time I heard about the criteria for defining binge-drinking, I was shocked. It certainly made me think about my own bingeing. I know too, from my own experience and from that of others, that we still celebrate occasions of extreme drunkenness. Stories about wild nights and cruel hangovers become the lore and legend in some families. Having a higher tolerance to alcohol, before getting drunk, is still perceived as an emblem of status. Sometimes we are careful with the stories we tell about our own or other's drinking. Sometimes, however, we present tales of irrational and irresponsible behaviour, associated with being drunk, which minimize personal responsibility and give a clear message that 'sure, when you're drunk, it isn't your fault'.

If you know and accept that your teenager drinks

Once you realize that your teenager is drinking, and that your power to prevent them is limited, you might want to change your tack in terms of influence. Rather than preaching an abstinence message, you can shift it to a safe drinking message that includes these kinds of points:

> - Drink slowly so that your body has a chance to metabolize the alcohol
> - Count how many drinks you have so that you can stay within your tolerances
> - Eat before drinking to delay or reduce the drunkenness
> - Drink water as a spacer between alcoholic drinks
> - Don't drink alone, be in safe company
> - Don't leave friends who are drinking, or are drunk, alone

DRUGS

In an Irish survey that was reported at an international conference in UCD in 2008, over 40 per cent of the 462 fifteen- to nineteen-year-olds who were interviewed admitted to smoking cannabis. If you generalize these results, it means that at least two in every five youngsters have at least tried smoking dope. Similarly, the study showed that 30 per cent had inhaled solvents, 11 per cent had taken cocaine and 9 per cent had used ecstasy. So, the drugs are out there and our teenagers are using them. Despite this, many parents adopt a 'head in the sand' approach to drugs and their teenagers. Sometimes this happens because of a genuine and complete ignorance about drugs, the prevalence of drugs or an assumption that your teenager won't experiment or use drugs.

Anecdotally, I regularly hear that when schools or parents' associations in schools organize talks about drugs, they get low numbers of parents attending. For example, just recently I heard of a rural school with over 300 pupils that had a turnout of ten parents for its drugs information night. This is blissful parental naivety at best, or neglect at worst.

Other times we can acknowledge that drugs are out there, but we don't actually want to believe that our child might be using and so we are happier to find and accept logical explanations for any evidence that might be appearing. Part of the reason we may do this is because recognizing that our teenager is a drug user will often bring about guilt and feelings of responsibility for letting this happen. We fear that we are bad parents who have neglected our children.

I also think that most of us feel quite powerless to act in response to news that our teenager is using drugs. Sometimes this is linked to our lack of knowledge about drugs. If we have had little or no experience of drug use ourselves, then the extent of our knowledge may be the very frightening stories of serious abuse that make it to the media headlines. It may be the first arena of our child's life where they know significantly more than we do and we may feel that puts us at a disadvantage when it comes to discussing drugs or trying to give advice and guidance. So what follows is designed to give you a crash course in what drugs are out there, what their effects are and what the psychological and emotional impact is of sustained use. I'll also look at how you can help your teenager if they are using drugs.

THE MOST COMMON DRUGS OUT THERE

Cannabis – *also known as hash, dope, weed, pot, grass, marijuana and blow.* **Cannabis usually comes as a brown or black lump (block of resin) or, less usually, as the stalks or leaves of the cannabis plant. It is usually smoked either in a pipe or rolled with tobacco using cigarette papers (Rizla is the most common brand). Cannabis is very prevalent in youth culture. Most teenagers will have easy access to it and some will smoke it to the same extent as others smoke cigarettes. It has the effect of relaxing the body and can make you feel more talkative, dreamy, giddy or philosophical. On the downside, it can leave you feeling paranoid and anxious and can affect your memory and concentration.**

Solvents/inhalants – *also known as huffing.* **These can be any kind of aerosol (hairspray, deodorant, adhesives, thinners, some household cleaning products). Part of the reason for the popularity of huffing is the easiness with which teenagers can find materials to inhale. It is impossible for parents to remove the potential items that can be inhaled from the house. If somehow you do manage to remove all such potential inhalants, you will find that the same products will be available in their friends' houses or can be bought anywhere. The aerosols are sprayed directly into the mouth or onto cloth (or for liquids just poured onto cloths) and then inhaled. Their use leads to drunkenness similar to alcohol use. They can cause sudden death, even on first use. They can lead to suffocation from inhaling vomit and unconsciousness.**

Cocaine – *also known as charley, snow, coke.* **Cocaine usually comes as a white powder and is sniffed up the nose through a tube or rolled-up banknote. It can also be rolled in with tobacco and smoked, or it can be eaten directly. Cocaine is often mixed (or cut) with other powdered substances so you never really know what you are taking. It leads to feelings of confidence, alertness, aggression, a willingness to take risks and a reduced appetite. Long-term use can lead to paranoia, hallucinations, memory loss, depression and anxiety.**

Ecstasy (MDMA) – *known as E, disco-burgers, doves, alphabet sweeties, Mitsubishis.* It usually comes as a pill with a logo on it and combines the effects of amphetamines with hallucinogens. It leads to feelings of warmth and calm, mixed with increased energy, greater intensity of feeling and well-being, which is why it is also known as the love-drug. It is most commonly associated with nightclubs and discos, where it is often easily and cheaply available. The dangers of ecstasy are heat-stroke due to the body's heartrate and temperature rise, which combines with the heat of a nightclub. You can also suffer palpitations and, later, depression and exhaustion as you come down from them.

Amphetamines – *also known as speed, whiz or sulph.* Amphetamines usually come as a grey, white, pink or yellow powder or tablet (pill). It can be taken in a wide range of ways, including by being swallowed, injected, smoked or dissolved in water. Speed will significantly raise your heartrate and brings feelings of confidence, sociability and energy. On the downside, it can also lead to depression, sleeplessness or restlessness and irritability.

Heroin – *also known as smack, gear, skag or junk.* It is usually a brown or white powder and is derived from morphine. It is smoked, sniffed or injected either under the skin (skin-popping) or into a vein (called main-lining and producing the greatest high). It has a strong pain-killing effect as well as an initial feeling of elation, followed by a relaxed dreamy state. It is highly addictive and its effects wear off with repeated use, leading to a chronic spiral into needing greater and greater amounts to feed the addiction. There are really strong physical side-effects from coming off the drug and users frequently suffer from depression and anxiety.

Addictions that serve to avoid something bad are sometimes the most powerful and difficult to cope with.

DRUG ADDICTION

Sometimes we think of addiction as the power of the drug to ensnare a person. The drug's effects are so overwhelming and enjoyable that we have no power to resist going back for more. It is true that many of the drugs do have intense chemical effects that make us feel good. In certain cases (heroin especially) there is also a physical addiction where our bodies become used to a certain level of a substance and then we get physical cravings for more and more of the substance just to feel 'normal'. It is the withdrawal from this physical craving that many of us associate with dealing with drug addiction, in particular. Withdrawal symptoms, such as feeling shaky, shivers, cramps, sweating a lot, headaches, flu-like symptoms or sickness, can occur if you are physically addicted and you stop taking the addictive substance. The withdrawal symptoms are different for each drug.

In fact, though, the physical addiction is only part of the story. With most drugs it is the psychological addiction that is far more powerful and more damaging. Psychological addiction is usually experienced as a compulsion to use substances or to continue with certain behaviour in order to feel good or to avoid feeling bad. This need dominates your teenager's mind and keeps them coming back for more. The trouble for most teenagers, however, is that even when something stops being fun or enjoyable and instead they start taking or doing it because they need to, they don't necessarily recognize that they have an addiction.

Sometimes, of course, teenagers don't have an addiction, they are just abusing the drug. That is to say, their occasional use of the drug is not compulsive or habitual and indeed it is being misused simply for the buzz, the feeling of having a good time and perhaps the sensation of feeling 'in' with a particular friend or group of friends.

Addictions that serve to avoid something bad are sometimes the most powerful and difficult to cope with. The emotional running away or dissociation that I described in Chapter 3 is a crucial part of many addictions. The fear of having to expose ourselves to bad or troubling feelings leads us to continuously find ways to block them out. The success of drugs in fulfilling this role makes them potent reinforcers.

SIGNS OF YOUR TEENAGER USING DRUGS

The indications that your teenager may be using or abusing drugs fall into three main categories: signs at home; signs at school; and physical or emotional signs. Bear in mind that many of these signs are also typically elements of adolescence and so this makes the task of identifying drug use harder. So look out for a pattern or several signs from across the three areas.

Signs in the home

There are many things to look out, for such as loss of interest in family activities or sudden disrespect for family rules. This can happen anyway as teenagers seek to be more independent, so be more alert if the change is sudden or is associated with a shift in their friendships. Teenagers who shirk their responsibilities or start lying about activities might also alert you, particularly if you notice the lying is associated with where they say they are or have been.

There are other, more practical physical signs that you might come across in your home. If you find cigarette rolling papers (especially with torn packaging, or other kinds of ripped cardboard), pipes, roach clips, small glass vials, plastic baggies, remnants of drugs (seeds, etc.), then these are significant warning signals. Just because your child denies ownership doesn't make it any less likely that these items are associated with their own use of drugs. Keep a nose out for smells of things like cannabis or unexplained burn holes in clothes.

Drugs cost money; some are cheaper than others but your teenager is going to need a regular supply of cash to meet any habitual usage. Be wary of requests for increased pocket money or allowances. Be alert, too, if your teenager doesn't buy the clothes they claim to be going shopping for. Look for any cash back from them if you have given them extra money for items they didn't get to buy. If you notice things like money or valuables disappearing from home, that is another sign. On the flip side, having more money than you would expect them to have would also be noteworthy. If you know what they should have from a part-time job and they seem to have more, do question where the additional cash is coming from as they may be selling drugs to supplement or pay for their own use.

Changes in appetite can be linked to some drugs, for example, getting 'the Munchies' after smoking cannabis is very typical. This can be hard to judge, however, because some teenagers have vast appetites anyway that are just naturally part of their growth and development needs.

Signs at school

Some of the school signs may only be alerted to you by their teachers, year-heads or principals, so pay attention at those meetings! Look out for a sudden drop in school results or a loss of interest in learning. Again, you do have to be wary of immediately associating this with drug use because there may be other factors, such as a sense of failure as the course work gets harder. Youngsters falling asleep in class or having significantly reduced memory and concentration span might be another sign. General defiance of authority in the school and truancy might set off the alarm bells for many reasons and it is wise to at least consider that drug use is linked to these changes.

Physical and emotional signs

A shift in friendships is often the first worrying sign for parents. I mentioned just above that who your son or daughter hangs around with can be a significant influence on their use of drugs. In fact, this fear of our youngsters having their heads turned by peers is a very significant one for parents. Don't be afraid to do a bit of sleuthing locally to see what you can find out about their friends and the kind of culture those friends promote. If the accepted view is that the group of friends your teenager hooks up with is into drugs, then it is much more likely than otherwise that your son or daughter is also mixed up in it.

Shifting friendships and joining a new peer group can be followed by a real change in attitude, with big swings in mood or behaviour. Look out for your teenager becoming more argumentative, paranoid, anxious or destructive. Some of this might be in response to the attitude they pick up from their friends, but it might also be linked directly to the effects of the drug or the withdrawal from a drug. If, overall, they seem unhappier than before or maybe even depressed then make sure to consider talking to them about drug use while trying to work out from where the depression is evolving.

RESPONDING TO YOUR TEENAGER WHO IS USING DRUGS

> **Make sure you seek help and support for yourself. There is no denying the shock that you might experience if you discover that your teenager is using drugs. Most of us are left feeling helpless and responsible. So it is vital to get some support for yourself, perhaps by talking to other parents or by ringing helplines or parent support groups. One really excellent internet site, www.drugs.ie, is filled with all the information about drugs and how to help your youngster. It really is important to be clear about what you want to achieve and what you are prepared to do. Don't ignore their drug use or hope it will go away without intervention. By accessing support, you will probably be able to decide at what level your teenager is using and this becomes important in deciding at what level you need to intervene.**

> Let them know that you care about them and are concerned. **They will undoubtedly minimize their use of drugs and the impact of their use. There is little point, early on, alienating them and so at this stage you are simply acknowledging that you are aware they have been taking drugs (be clear about what you think they are using) and that this scares you because you know how dangerous drugs can be. Remind them that you only want the best for them.**

> Use any facts you have gathered, like poor reports from school, smells in their bedroom and so on, to solidify your reasons for suspecting their use and to try to overcome any denial. **At this stage use your knowledge of the drugs they have used to identify the harm it brings to them or the family. Again, don't be too disillusioned if they seem to reject or minimize the risks involved. A strong discussion at this stage may be enough to dissuade them if they are still in the trial and experimentation stage. If their use has progressed to something more habitual, then you must continue with further intervention.**

> Hold your teenager responsible for their own behaviour. **The days of you having the power and authority to change their behaviour by the force of your will are probably gone by now. So, if you are not responsible for managing their behaviour, then they must take responsibility for themselves. It is good to be clear with them that they are making the choices to use, or to get into debt, or to damage their health, or to disrupt the family with their post-use moods, or to neglect their future by not studying. By holding them responsible, it also means that you recognize that you can't rescue them from the harm; they must make a decision to change their behaviour themselves. If they do make that decision, then you can offer practical support like helping them to break from a particular group of friends, or finding other things to occupy their time and so on.**

> Identify the supports or sanctions you will use to try to influence their behaviour; these will vary depending on the severity of the problem. **You will still persevere with trying to influence them, even though you know that stopping or changing must be internally motivated. Your sanctions for their behaviour may be to ground them, or restrict their access to their friends, or reduce their allowance. These sanctions may or may not be meaningful depending on the stage of independence or conflict that they have reached in the family.**

> Seek treatment if the problems are significant. **If their drug use is habitual or motivated by addiction, then look to get direct support for them and for yourself from a drugs counsellor or a treatment programme. There is a real desire, sometimes, to hand the drugs issue over to that counsellor to fix. Your involvement and your family's involvement will still be necessary to support and, if needed, to reintegrate your son or daughter into the family and help them to maintain a drug-free life.**

EATING DISORDERS

We all expect our teenagers to be self-conscious about their appearance at some stage, or even regularly, throughout their adolescence. As I described in Chapter 1, their bodies are undergoing very significant changes that can affect both their appearance and consequently their self-confidence. They are also facing new social pressures, perhaps to fit in or just to be like their peers. For some teenagers these pressures can develop into an obsession that can become an eating disorder. The two most common eating disorders are anorexia nervosa and bulimia nervosa. However, binge-eating disorders, food phobias and body image disorders are also becoming increasingly common in adolescence.

Current estimates of the prevalence of eating disorders suggest that 1 to 2 per cent of children and teenagers will develop eating disorders. In the majority of cases it will be girls who develop eating disorders, although more rarely boys can be affected (there are four girls with eating disorders for every one boy with an eating disorder). It's really important to remember that eating disorders can easily get out of hand and they become very difficult habits to break. Unfortunately, many teenagers can successfully hide eating disorders from their families for months or even years. Once an eating disorder is established, it becomes a serious clinical problem that will require professional treatment by doctors, nutritionists and therapists. The goal of parents, therefore, should be to help to prevent their teenager from developing an eating disorder by nurturing their self-esteem and encouraging healthy attitudes about nutrition and appearance.

→ Anna: Responding to the loss of control

Anna came to see me, aged fifteen, two years after she had developed an eating disorder. She had already seen another therapist who had helped her to regain a normal body weight and in many ways she seemed to be coping well in lots of areas of her life. However, she quickly described to me, in the first session, that while on the surface she seemed to be coping she felt in turmoil emotionally.

She recognized that she no longer had anorexia nervosa but she still felt that she never understood how it had developed in the first place. So we talked, for many hours, over a period of weeks and months. Her initial thinking was that it was due to the fact that in her school many of the girls were highly body conscious and extremely pass-remarkable about any girl who they believed to be 'fat'.

What also emerged, however, was that just around the time that she moved to that school her parents split up. The separation was acrimonious and she and her three younger brothers had been treated as pawns in the legal battles over custody and access. For a full twelve-month period her life was chaotic as her parents tried to establish two separate homes and it was never clear where they would be living in the longer term.

On top of this Anna described that her new school had a very high level of academic expectation. She felt completely caged in by these expectations, but internalized them to her own high standards. She described herself as a perfectionist and would never tolerate any drop in her own performance even if she felt exhausted trying to achieve all 'A's.

We began to formulate the understanding that her restriction of her diet was an effort to exert control, along similar perfectionist lines as her schoolwork, in a situation where she felt totally out of control as her parents caused chaos for her and her brothers. I felt the reason that she chose an eating disorder as her means of trying to exert this control was because, indeed, it fitted with the pressure from her peers to be thin.

What was interesting was that despite having changed her eating habits back to normal she still had never dealt with any of the feelings she had about her parents' separation. It came as no surprise to me that while her eating was now normal she instead relied upon binge-drinking of alcohol to deal with the difficulties thrown up by the separation. Coming to terms with the separation and finding healthier ways of dealing with it became the focus of our work together.

UNDERSTANDING ANOREXIA NERVOSA AND BULIMIA NERVOSA

As they are the most common, I am going to focus on anorexia nervosa and bulimia nervosa in this section. However, it is fair to say that eating disorders generally involve self-critical and negative thoughts and feelings about body weight and food. The dramatic weight fluctuation that is associated with eating disorders will also affect eating habits and can disrupt normal bodily functions and daily activities.

Anorexia nervosa is characterized by a striving to maintain a very low body weight. People with anorexia have a distorted view of their body size and shape. Some restrict their food intake by dieting, fasting or excessive exercise. They hardly eat at all and often try to eat as few calories as possible, frequently obsessing over their food intake. Even the small amount of food that they do eat becomes an obsession for them. Anorexia is classified in the *Diagnostic and Statistical Manual of*

Mental Disorders (DSM-IV-TR) published by the American Psychiatric Association. According to that classification a person with anorexia nervosa:

> **weighs much less than he/she should – 15 per cent or more below their ideal weight**
> **normally has a body mass index (BMI) of 17.5 or less**
> **has missed three consecutive menstrual periods**
> **has a preoccupation with body shape and weight**
> **has a severe fear of putting on weight**

The most obvious physical indicator of someone with anorexia is that they are very thin and underweight. You may also notice that a teenager with anorexia is often a perfectionist who sets herself targets beyond her reach. She may have an exaggerated fear of losing control (which is tied in to her low self-esteem and constant self-criticism), such that she can appear to be over-controlled in many situations. So the control over their food intake (one of the areas over which we usually can exert control) becomes crucial in an attempt to reduce their anxiety about being out of control more generally.

Bulimia nervosa is characterized by habitual binge-eating and purging. Someone with bulimia may undergo weight fluctuations and rarely experience the low weight associated with anorexia. The person will have regular bouts of serious overeating, which are always followed by a feeling of guilt that can then lead to extreme reactions such as crash dieting, doing lots of exercise and deliberate vomiting. According to DSM-IV-TR, people with bulimia nervosa must show the following four symptoms:

> **binge-eating repeatedly, i.e. eating much more than most people normally do, together with the feeling that they can't stop or control their eating**
> **repeatedly and inappropriately compensating for the overeating by, for example, over medicating with laxatives, fasting, exercising to exhaustion or making themselves vomit**
> **binge-eating and inappropriately compensating repeatedly at least twice a week for the last three months**
> **overly judging themselves in terms of the weight and shape of their bodies**

As there isn't the same dramatic weight loss, bulimia nervosa can be much harder to identify. A teenager with bulimia is not usually underweight. However, because of the shame and guilt associated with their eating, such teenagers can become very skilled at masking the symptoms.

Both these conditions tend to develop in young teenagers. Indeed, researchers describe that 81 per cent of ten-year-olds are afraid of being fat. It is no surprise, therefore, that further research statistics show that over three-quarters of eating disorders will start between the ages of eleven and twenty years, with the majority of youngsters beginning their disordered eating between the ages of eleven and thirteen.

CAUSES OF EATING DISORDERS

The causes of eating disorders aren't entirely clear. There are a whole range of factors associated with the individual youngster, their thinking and feeling and factors associated with society more generally. For example, some research suggests that media images now contribute to the rise in the incidence of eating disorders. Most celebrities in advertising, movies, TV and sports programmes are very thin, and this may lead girls to think that the ideal of beauty is extreme thinness. Boys, too, may try to emulate a media ideal by drastically restricting their eating and compulsively exercising to build muscle mass. Certain sports and activities, like gymnastics, ballet and ice skating, may put some teenagers at greater risk for eating disorders because of the idealized body shape that is associated with success in these pursuits.

Essentially, however, for youngsters with eating disorders there is a large gap between the way they see themselves and how they actually look. People with anorexia or bulimia frequently have an intense fear of gaining weight or being overweight and frequently think they look bigger than they actually are. This distorted body image can be very difficult to challenge. Other cognitive problems, like anxiety disorder and obsessive–compulsive disorder, are also commonly found in youngsters with eating disorders.

But the most consistent factors linked to eating disorders seem to be emotionally based. The disorder often develops slowly over time as a response to upset or distress in a person's life. This upset is likely to be caused by a specific traumatic event or a series of traumas and stresses. Examples can include sexual abuse, loss, significant change, bullying, critical comments about size and weight, constant general criticism or an overload of stress. So, for example, teenagers who feel out of control in an area of their life due to one of these traumatic experiences may use their eating as a way to assert control. Stress and pressure caused by things like conflicts at home or school expectations can put youngsters at higher risk of problem eating behaviours. As I mentioned earlier, low self-esteem is also a contributing factor to the development of eating disorders as teenagers strive to feel better about themselves while also, probably, feeling unclear about exactly who they are and trying to fit in with their peers.

Essentially, however, for youngsters with eating disorders there is a large gap between the way they see themselves and how they actually look. People with anorexia or bulimia frequently have an intense fear of gaining weight or being overweight and frequently think they look bigger than they actually are.

THE PHYSICAL IMPACT OF EATING DISORDERS

While eating disorders might develop as a response to or a coping mechanism for dealing with trauma, the distorted thinking that is involved becomes extremely resistant to change. Unfortunately, this particular method of coping is ultimately self-destructive in a very seriously debilitating physical way. I have listed below the many ways in which the body is affected by an eating disorder. Be under no illusion that in addition to the physical problems listed below, anorexia or bulimia may cause dehydration and other medical complications like heart problems or kidney failure. In extreme cases, eating disorders can lead to severe malnutrition and even death.

The starvation and lack of nutrition induced by anorexia can lead to:

> a drop in blood pressure, pulse, and breathing rate
> hair loss and fingernail breakage
> loss of periods
> lanugo hair, a soft hair that can grow all over the skin
> light-headedness and an inability to concentrate
> anaemia
> swollen joints
> brittle bones

The constant vomiting and lack of nutrition in bulimia can lead to:

> constant stomach pain
> damage to the stomach and kidneys
> tooth decay (from exposure to stomach acids)
> the salivary glands expanding permanently from throwing up so often (gives the appearance of swollen cheeks)
> loss of periods
> loss of the mineral potassium (this can contribute to heart problems and even death)

WARNING SIGNS OF AN EATING DISORDER

As soon as you become aware of the dangers of eating disorders, it can be very tempting to panic at the first indication of your child or teenager talking about dieting. However, being self-conscious, comparing themselves with others and even dieting are very normal parts of ordinary teenagers' lives. It is certainly the case that a youngster with an eating disorder will show all of these features, but you need also to witness some features that are not the norm for most teenagers. With anorexia, specifically, you might be looking out for:

> **excessive weight loss resulting in your teenager looking emaciated or frail**
> **an apparent obsession with food, portion control or weighing themselves**
> **excessive exercise**
> **extreme or 'crash' dieting**
> **withdrawal from family activities like meals or celebrations involving food**
> **complaints of feeling fat despite extreme thinness**
> **depression and lethargy or frequent complaints of feeling cold**

Signs for bulimia (some of which might also apply to anorexia) include:
> **a severe fear of weight gain**
> **trips to the bathroom immediately after meals**
> **an intense unhappiness with body size, shape or weight**
> **regularly buying laxatives or diuretics (things to make you wee)**
> **excessive exercise or other ways to try to work off calories**
> **withdrawal from family activities like meals or celebrations involving food**

PREVENTING EATING DISORDERS

I strongly believe those theories that suggest that eating disorders develop as a reaction to or a coping mechanism for trauma. Earlier I listed some of the kinds of experiences that your child or teenager may have that they may find traumatic. Obviously, one way of preventing eating disorders is to prevent the trauma occurring in the first place. However, this isn't always possible. But if you are aware that your child has experienced difficult situations like bullying, abuse, or conflict within the home, then you can try to address those issues by helping them to connect to the feelings in a meaningful and congruent way. Use the strategies and tips that I describe in Chapter 3 to empathize with them and help them to process those difficult feelings.

If you do have to talk about eating habits, always focus on and emphasize health rather than weight. The ideal message for them to get is that their bodies are healthy and strong and that you love them for who they are and not how they look.

It is possible, of course, that they may choose other unhealthy and potentially self-destructive methods of dealing with difficult feelings. But an eating disorder is more likely to develop if they already have unhealthy attitudes to food and body image. So it is really important for you to take on a positive role in your teenager's development of healthy attitudes about food and nutrition. Be aware of the influence of your own body image and the comments you make about how you look, and how you feel about your body. If, for example, you constantly say, 'I'm fat,' complain about not exercising enough or practise a whole series of diets, your teenagers may get the wrong message about their bodies. Indeed, they may feel that a distorted body image is normal and acceptable.

Unfortunately, there has been an upsurge in obesity amongst children and teenagers and so there is a corresponding concern in society about children and their weight. It can be tricky for parents to talk to their youngsters about their eating habits, even though we may well have to address these issues at some stage. If you do have to talk about eating habits, always focus on and emphasize health rather than weight. The ideal message for them to get is that their bodies are healthy and strong and that you love them for who they are and not how they look.

It may be that you have to work hard to create a healthy lifestyle for your family. You can try to involve your teenager in the preparation of healthy and nutritious meals; you can let them know that it's okay to eat when they're hungry and to refuse food when they are not. You can also build exercise into the fabric of your family by taking regular walks or trying to go swimming regularly. The aim is to make exercise a fun, rewarding and regular family activity rather than a means to an end.

It's also important not to panic about your child's or your teenager's eating habits. Faddy or fussy eating is very common. Teenagers often make decisions like becoming a vegetarian or choosing to restrict what they perceive to be fatty foods. Even if you disagree, your aim is to avoid getting into a power battle as this might feed directly into any control issues that your teenager might have. Try to support the food choices they make while continuing to encourage healthy eating. Do also set some limits about family mealtimes and the social aspects of food.

RESPONDING TO AN EATING DISORDER

If you do suspect that your teenager's attitude to or behaviour in relation to food and eating is disordered, then intervene. Try to gain their perspective on food by talking to them about what is going on in an open and non-judgemental way. You may find that your teenager reacts in a defensive or angry way the first time you suggest that something about their eating is not normal. Many of them have trouble admitting, even to themselves, that they have a problem.

Your teenager may be more receptive to a conversation if you focus on your own concerns and use 'I' statements, rather than 'you' statements. For example, steer clear of statements like 'you have an eating disorder,' or 'you're obsessed with food,' which may only prompt anger and denial. Instead, try, 'I imagine that it's very stressful to count the calories of everything you eat,' or 'I'm worried that you have lost so much weight so quickly.' Cite specific things your child has said or done that have made you worry.

Trying to help somebody when they don't recognize that they need help can be very difficult. However, if an eating disorder has developed, then you are unlikely to be able to deal with it alone. You will need to seek professional assistance, ideally from a team of doctors, psychologists, psychiatrists, other therapists and nutritionists. I would suggest that you start this process by making contact with your GP or family doctor.

There are many aspects to an eating disorder that need to be addressed. The two key areas, however, are getting a return to a more normal body weight and helping the person to change their thinking away from some of the distorted views that they had. I also think it's beneficial for therapy to focus on some of the core and underlying emotional difficulties and traumas that your teenager may have used the eating disorder to cope with or to block.

Generally, the earlier the intervention, the shorter the treatment period required. For example, youngsters who are severely malnourished may require hospitalization and ongoing medical care, even after their weight has stabilized. Similarly, the longer an eating disorder is in place, the more solidified the distorted thinking becomes and the more resistant it is to change.

> If you do suspect that your teenager's attitude to or behaviour in relation to food and eating is disordered, then intervene.

IN CASE OF EMERGENCY . . . KEY POINTS TO REMEMBER

→ Teenagers are trying, at times, to opt out of their current world. They may not like the reality of their lives and if they can escape that by using alcohol, drugs or eating disorders, then they will.

→ Teenagers will use their own experiences with alcohol and their observations of its effects on family, friends and in the community to draw their own conclusions about how to use or abuse alcohol.

→ Whatever the influences from society and the media, it is vital that we parents try to promote the message of waiting as long as possible before drinking alcohol.

→ Given the overwhelming societal attitude to alcohol in this country, I think it is unrealistic to expect your teenager to never drink. Ultimately, therefore, your goal, for as long as alcohol is legal, should be to make sure that they drink responsibly and safely.

→ Worrying though it may be to discover that your teenager is drinking, it is better that you hear from them how they approach alcohol. This also allows you to be more influential for them in becoming responsible in their alcohol use.

→ Having family rules about alcohol is important as a reference point for them.

→ Consequences for drinking, or getting drunk, are only as good as your ability to enforce them, so try not to have extreme or unrealistic consequences.

→ Many parents adopt a 'head in the sand' approach to drugs and their teenagers. Sometimes this happens because of a genuine and complete ignorance about drugs, the prevalence of drugs or an assumption that your teenager won't experiment or use drugs.

→ Educate yourself about drugs because otherwise it may be the first arena of our child's life where they know significantly more than we do and we may feel that puts us at a disadvantage when it comes to discussing drugs or trying to give advice and guidance.

→ If you discover that your teenager is using drugs you may feel helpless and responsible. So it is vital to get some support for yourself, perhaps by talking to other parents or by ringing helplines or parent support groups. One really excellent internet site, www.drugs.ie, is filled with all the information about drugs and how to help your youngster.

→ The two most common eating disorders are anorexia nervosa and bulimia nervosa.

→ Your goal should be to help to prevent your teenager from developing an eating disorder by nurturing their self-esteem and encouraging healthy attitudes about nutrition and appearance.

- For youngsters with eating disorders there is a large gap between the way they see themselves and how they actually look.

- Emotional stress and trauma are also consistently associated with the development of eating disorders.

- Teenagers who feel out of control in an area of their life due to traumatic experiences may use their eating as a way to assert control.

- Seek professional help from a team of medics, psychologists and dieticians if you are concerned that your teenager has developed an eating disorder, especially if they are resistant to acknowledging they have a problem.

10. DEPRESSION, SUICIDE AND SELF-HARM

finding a safe place to feel and understand emotions

We all think we know about depression. We regularly hear people say, 'Oh, I feel so depressed.' Anecdotally, we might understand depression to be about feeling sad and maybe a bit lethargic. Over the course of your life you may have felt depressed or you may have known family, friends or colleagues who have been depressed. It is estimated that at any one time there are over 400,000 people in Ireland suffering from depression. Given this huge prevalence, it is not surprising that we're attuned to the possibility that adults around us might be depressed. However, we don't commonly associate depression with adolescents. But the reality is that about one in ten Irish teenagers will experience a major depression during their adolescence. This is a very high prevalence rate.

So we need to understand depression fully. Specifically, we need to be able to identify the symptoms of adolescent depression and what similarities and differences are present in comparison to adult depression. Knowledge of what to look out for will make us more alert to changes in the mood, behaviour, thinking and physical health of our teenagers. We then need to know what to do to support them, individually, and ourselves and our families. A depressed teenager can be a weight and a worry for everyone. This chapter will look at the breadth of issues relevant to depression and give you a focus for helping directly or getting the right kind of help for your teenager.

One of the areas associated with the hopelessness that is felt and expressed in depression is an increased risk of suicide or self-harm. Much has been written in Ireland about the mental health of teenage boys and young adult males, who have had the most startling rise in rates of suicide in the last ten years or so. In contrast, deliberate self-harm is much more frequent amongst teenage girls than boys. But both suicide and self-harm can seem like a taboo subject for parents and teenagers alike. Our reluctance to talk about these issues pushes the thoughts, feelings and actions underground. I would guess that most teenagers have had at least a passing thought about suicide or self-harm at some stage through their adolescence. For a tragic minority, those thoughts lead to action.

In my experience of working with teenagers who have expressed thoughts of harming themselves or killing themselves, the acknowledgement of the psychological hurt that underpins their thinking and actions is the single most significant factor in reducing the likelihood of real harm occurring. But it takes courage for parents to broach the subject and for teenagers to engage with it. This chapter will discuss the dynamics of suicide and self-harm. It will look at the risk factors involved, the warning signs to look out for and the support you can offer. Hopefully it will provide you with a language and a confidence to address this issue if it seems relevant in the life of your teenager.

THIS CHAPTER LOOKS AT . . .

Depression
   Identifying teenage depression
   * *Warning signs of depression*
   * *Responding to depression in teenagers*
   * *Minding yourself while minding them*

Suicide
   * *Warning signs*
   * *'The American Dream'*
   * *Responding to suicidal thinking or suicidal behaviour*

Self-Harm
   * *Reasons for self-harm*
   * *Responding to your teenager who is self-harming*

DEPRESSION

In many of the other chapters I have referenced the fact that things like alcohol, drugs, eating disorders, school problems or conflict at home may lead to depression. But equally, it is just as likely that an underlying depression may in fact be the cause of, or at least a contributing factor in, all of these situations. Depression, it seems, may weave itself through so many of the challenging issues facing teenagers that it can appear as either the cause or the outcome of those problems. In many ways, it doesn't matter if it is the proverbial chicken or the egg. It still needs to be addressed and treated. If depression is the cause, then treating and resolving it will lead to a reduction in, or an elimination of, the problems it led to. If depression is caused by drug abuse, for example, then alleviating the symptoms of the depression may reduce the need to rely on drugs rather than the depression remaining a cyclical link in a spiralling drug problem.

In Chapter 3 on understanding teenagers' feelings, I referenced a model for understanding the link between thoughts, feelings, behaviours and our physical selves. I have reproduced the model here because it fits very well with trying to understand the myriad of ways that depression affects us. Depression is likely to have an impact on each of the four areas of thinking, feeling, acting and our physical bodies. It is also quite likely to be influenced by the environment and social pressures that surround us.

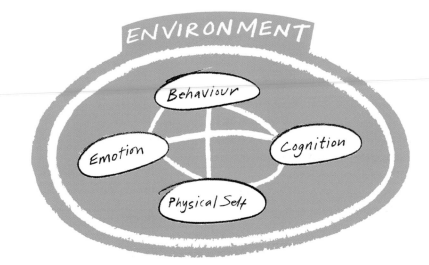

A model for thinking about the interconnection between key aspects of our being.

Thomas: Depression masked by anger

A client of mine, a boy aged fifteen, was brought to me by his parents, who were concerned about the fact that it was almost impossible to get him up for school, that he was constantly in trouble there and that he seemed really angry, generally. As they described his history, nothing seemed very out of the ordinary. He had an unremarkable childhood; if anything they felt that he was a bit hyperactive as a younger child and he had always been considered a bit of a messer in school.

When I met the boy, he was very distractible and seemed to find it very hard to stay focused on our conversation. He made almost no eye contact, spoke sparsely in a low mumble and initially denied that anything was the matter. He did agree that it was hard for him to wake up in the mornings, but he went on to explain this to me as 'What's the point in getting up when school is going to be shit anyway?' It turns out that despite having average intelligence, he was falling behind in a lot of subjects and had given up trying. He felt that all the teachers considered him to have a bad reputation and that nobody in the school seemed to think he had any potential. He described the only good thing about school as being the fact that he could meet up with his friends with whom he had 'a laugh' each day. The 'laugh' usually involved messing and he was constantly in trouble for things like being late for class, being giddy and distracting in class and occasionally for being disrespectful to teachers.

However, even at the weekends he found it hard to get up, despite playing for a local soccer club. As we talked some more it became clear that he was a very talented soccer player and that he was quite a fit and athletic person in general. Over the years he played many different sports, had been good at most of them, but gave them all up out of disinterest and lethargy more than any issue with the sport or the people.

I discovered that Thomas was having real difficulty getting to sleep at night. He spent most evenings slumped in front of the television or playing on the computer and would stay up until at least 1 or 2am because he felt too restless in his mind until then. Even going to bed so late, he explained, it might take him another hour to fall asleep. Suddenly, it was no surprise why he was finding it so hard to wake up and get up. More than that, however, Thomas described how he would get in a really bad mood because he felt so tired and bored for much of the day. He hated school and felt he had nothing much else going on in his life either. The bad mood was directed, usually in anger, as a tirade of verbal abuse to his mother when she tried to wake him in the mornings or to any of his family who ever seemed critical of him.

On the basis of the information that his parents gave when they rang to make the appointment, it had seemed that Thomas was likely to be another young person struggling with angry feelings and difficult behaviour. But as I made better sense of the bits of information above, it seemed to me that he was depressed. I noted, particularly, that symptoms such as his difficulty sleeping, his lethargy, his restlessness in his mind, his angry outbursts and his lack of direction were all indicators of that depression.

So when I worked with Thomas, I focused on getting him active and involved again in the community through the soccer club, where he took on coaching responsibilities for younger children in the club. It turned out that he was a natural coach and had a great rapport with the younger children, who really looked up to him. This gave Thomas a great feeling of being needed and valued, which was in sharp contrast with his school experience. We built on his sense of ability and being valued to challenge some of his negative perceptions about himself. I taught him relaxation skills to help him get to sleep earlier in the night with mixed results. However, at the weekends Thomas was always up early to get down for his coaching sessions.

The better Thomas felt about himself, the less angry he was with the world and the easier his relationship with his family became. By his nature he wasn't a talkative lad and I'm not sure that his parents ever felt that he became wonderfully interactive, but they could certainly see how much more positive and energized he became. Because they were on the receiving end of less aggression and nasty comments, they found it much easier to be positive with and supportive of Thomas, not just with the soccer but also with the fact that he still found school a bit of a drag.

Working with Thomas reminded me that it's almost impossible to achieve successful positive change in every aspect of a youngster's life. But, most importantly, by addressing his underlying depression primarily through activity and more positive thinking, Thomas achieved a greater sense of purpose in his life, a significant rise in his self-esteem and a reduction in his angry outbursts at home. His school life didn't improve, but he felt he was concentrating more in class and that he got given out to less, but nor did it get worse, with the result that he kept plugging away there.

the context in which the change is occurring is important in determining its relevance. Many teenagers who are depressed complain of difficulty in falling asleep as they can't get their minds to switch off. Depressed teenagers may also find that the quality of their sleep is worse and that they are more fitfully asleep than deeply asleep.

> Restlessness and agitation. **This is a common experience for many teenagers and can sometimes have been present from when they were a child. Restlessness alone, therefore, may not be an indicator but again must be taken in the context of other signs and symptoms.**

> Fatigue or a lack of energy. **Perhaps their exhaustion is fuelled by their difficulty sleeping or perhaps it is associated with a more general bodily malaise. Many depressed teenagers will complain of aches, pains and exhaustion. Typically, this element of depression is expressed in an unwillingness to get out of bed or in their physical, at times almost catatonic, sprawl on the sofa.**

As I was just mentioning above, the context in which any of these signs and symptoms occurs is crucially important in determining how meaningful they are in terms of depression. So, if you're unsure whether your teenager is depressed or is just 'being a teenager', then think about the range of symptoms that are present. Generally, depressive symptoms will be seen in each of the key areas of feeling, behaving, thinking and their physical self. Similarly, think about how long the symptoms have been present. The longer and more consistently that your teenager has been thinking or behaving in a particular fashion, the greater the likelihood that it reflects an underlying problem rather than reflects a phase of their development. Be aware, also, of the severity of the symptoms. What you are looking out for is dramatic, long-lasting changes in personality, mood or behaviour. It is the persistent and pervasive nature of the changes that are probably signals of a deeper problem.

Specific symptoms that are more likely to be present in adolescent depression, that differ from adult depression, are as follows.

> Irritable or angry mood. **Sadness, lack of self-worth, hopelessness or despair often get displaced as feelings of anger. I sometimes wonder if teenagers feel ashamed or embarrassed by appearing not to cope and so react angrily as a defence mechanism to mask their true feelings. Or, possibly, anger can be expressed more intensely and so letting it loose gives temporary relief from more vulnerable feelings of not being good enough or worries about having no future.**

> Unexplained aches and pains. **Stomach aches and headaches are the most common physical ailments experienced by depressed teenagers. It is worth having these aches medically checked out and if there is no obvious cause, then perhaps depression may be the latent reason.**

> Extreme sensitivity to criticism. **Most teenagers feel self-conscious at some stage during puberty, feeling like they look or sound ugly or different. It takes time to settle into a newly shaped body. Depressed teenagers, however, are so imbued with a sense of worthlessness that they are keenly aware of any criticism or apparent rejection. Even any perception of their own failure underlines their feeling of incapability or of being a bad and useless person.**

> Withdrawing from some, but not all people. **Adults tend to isolate themselves entirely when they are depressed, but teenagers will often maintain some friendships while pulling away from family, for example. It may also be visible in a marked reduction in socializing with peers, rather than a total detachment from others.**

WARNING SIGNS OF DEPRESSION

Some of the warning signs of depression will be seen in externalizing behaviours and some can be seen in internalizing behaviours. Essentially, externalizing behaviours refer to those behaviours that show in an external and visible way that a child or teenager is struggling with some kind of emotional pain. In contrast, internalizing behaviours refer to those behaviours where a child tries to cope on the inside in a less obvious way with similar emotional pain. Many of the specific teenage issues that I have talked about in greater detail in other chapters are examples of either externalizing or internalizing behaviours. As a broad generalization, in the main boys will turn to externalizing behaviours whereas girls more readily choose internalizing behaviours as their way of both coping with difficult feelings and trying to alert the world to the struggles they are having.

Typical externalizing behaviours are problems at school, running away, substance abuse, high risk or reckless behaviour and violence. Typical internalizing behaviours are eating disorders, deliberate self-harm and suicide. Another way of thinking about externalizing behaviours is that they tend to be outwardly destructive, whereas internalizing behaviours tend to be inwardly self-destructive.

Depression may well lead to your teenager 'acting out' or 'acting in' in any one or a number of these ways. That depression may well stem from low self-esteem and hopelessness in relation to change. All of the externalizing and internalizing behaviours are very effective reinforcers because, in the short term, they are effective at numbing or distracting from difficult feelings. This means that your teenager may repeat the behaviours, developing habits that become hard to break. But because of the negative nature of so many of the behaviours, they will also elicit negative responses from adults or feelings of self-blame, guilt and shame. So it is quite likely that engaging in all these worrisome behaviours, with such negative outcomes, will solidify depression or may lead to depression if there were other reasons that your teenager started engaging in the behaviours.

SUICIDE

Suicide is a significant problem in Ireland, with more people dying by suicide than in car accidents. Ireland has the fifth highest rate of youth (fifteen to twenty-four years) suicide in Europe, according to a 2005 World Health Organisation (WHO) report. Men under the age of thirty-five account for 40 per cent of all suicides. Suicide can be understood as a conscious or deliberate act that ends one's life. Suicide is usually perceived as a solution to some life problem for which no other solution can be found. The most common methods of suicide are hanging, poisoning (drug overdose of some kind) and drowning. In Ireland, men are at least four times more likely than women to commit suicide.

Estimates from the US suggest that for every completed suicide amongst the fifteen to twenty-four age group there are up to 400 attempted suicides. Clearly, therefore, not every youngster who attempts suicide intends to kill themselves. There is a very definite group of youngsters who are hoping to draw attention to themselves by trying to kill themselves. These youngsters are typically seen to be giving a 'cry for help' by their actions. Their attempt at killing themselves is not about a wish to die, but a wish to be noticed and responded to.

WARNING SIGNS

Bear in mind that most people who think about killing themselves may not actually want to die; they just want an end to some kind of emotional pain. Irrespective of the actual intention, however, most people who think about killing themselves will take some kind of action in the build-up that may give you a warning that they are thinking about it. Thinking about killing yourself is called suicidal ideation. The actions you take in killing or attempting to kill yourself are labelled under the umbrella term 'suicidal behaviour'. The warning signs come in both categories of ideation and behaviour.

Expressing suicidal thoughts

Such thoughts may be things like, 'There is no point in continuing, it is all worthless'; 'I'd sooner be dead'; 'There is nothing left to live for.' Many teenagers use expressions like these in a provocative manner and many parents don't know whether to take them seriously or not. Indeed some parents may feel manipulated by their teenager, who they believe has no intent to harm themselves but is trying to 'emotionally blackmail' them. This is especially the case if a number of threats of suicide have been made with no action. I hope you will be inclined to think of the fairytale of the 'boy who cried wolf' to the extent that you continue to take any threat seriously, even if they seem repetitive and manipulative.

Preoccupation with death

You may see this reflected in their reading, their music and the comments they make. Be very wary of comments that seem to glorify death or suicide. Sometimes a preoccupation with death can be apparent when you look at a history of websites that they visit too.

Changes in mood or behaviour

This can be tricky to associate with an increased risk of suicide as many teenagers are incredibly moody. But things to look out for are increased isolation or withdrawal from friends and depression. Similarly, increased abuse of alcohol or drugs are also associated with higher risks of suicide.

Making final arrangements

This is akin to tidying up one's affairs. Adults may draw up a will; but teenagers are likely to give away their possessions, like CDs, books, jewellery or even favoured clothes.

Suicide attempt or deliberate self-harm

Where a young person has tried to kill themselves before or has a history of intentionally harming themselves, it is much more likely that they may go on to commit suicide. Always treat self-harm seriously. It is usually the case that some significant emotional stress underlies any attempt to kill themselves or even any act of self-harm where there was no intent to kill themselves. The only exception to this may be a youngster who was playing 'The American Dream' game. I describe that in the next section.

'THE AMERICAN DREAM'

There is another phenomenon amongst teenagers that is sometimes confused with self-harm and, in the case of some deaths that are associated with it, also confused with suicide. The phenomenon is known here as 'The American Dream'. This name emerged because the game, such as it is a game, seems to have developed in the US and transferred over here. In the US it is usually called 'the choking game', but it is also known by numerous other names:

- > pass-out game
- > space monkey
- > suffocation roulette
- > fainting game
- > purple hazing

- > blacking out/blackout
- > dream game
- > flat liner
- > space cowboy
- > cloud nine

In the game, teenagers (and sometimes children) use a strap of some kind wrapped around their necks to temporarily cut blood flow to the head. One variation of the game involves holding your breath and getting punched in the chest until you black out. Yet another version involves bending over and trying to induce hyperventilation by taking deep breaths followed by someone giving them a 'bear hug'. Regardless of the method, the goal is always the same: to cut off oxygen until you pass out. Asphyxiation like this produces an adrenaline rush and sensation of being high. It is often described as a 'tingly' or 'floating' feeling. A second high is produced when the pressure is released and oxygen rushes back to the brain.

It is estimated that as many as 20 per cent of teenagers and preteens play the game. Sometimes it is played in groups. Both girls and boys are equally likely to try it. Part of the popularity of The American Dream is that the high doesn't involve drugs, alcohol or other substances, which makes it appealing to younger teenagers who may not yet have access to drugs or who are still too wary of trying drugs.

The game has actually been around for years in one form or another, but it appears to be spreading. One theory is that the internet has made it easier to learn about the game. A search of the internet can, comparatively easily, turn up several videos of people playing the game and explanations of how to play. Many youngsters are not aware of the dangers involved and some youngsters have died as a result of choking to death. Nearly all of the deaths were among younger boys in the eleven to thirteen year age group who tried the game alone.

The kinds of injuries that may result from the game include brain damage and heart attacks. Three minutes without oxygen is all it takes to do irreversible damage. Any activity that deprives the brain of oxygen has the potential to cause moderate to serious brain cell death, leading to permanent loss of neurological function. Problems can be minor, like a flushed face, headaches, bloodshot eyes, loss of concentration, slurred speech, agitation and aggression. But there can also be major health problems, such as neuro-muscular problems, memory problems, coma, concussion, fractures, as well as permanent neurological disabilities such as seizures as a result of the deprivation of oxygen.

Whatever you call it, there are a few warning signs that your teenager may be playing The American Dream or the choking game:

> **discussion of the game or its aliases**
> **bloodshot eyes**
> **marks on the neck**
> **wearing high-necked shirts, even in warm weather**
> **frequent, severe headaches**

> disorientation after spending time alone
> increased and uncharacteristic irritability or hostility
> ropes, scarves, and belts tied to bedroom furniture or doorknobs or found knotted on the floor
> the unexplained presence of dog leashes, choke collars, bungee cords, etc.

If you are at all worried, talk to your son or daughter about it. Because it is younger teenagers who are more likely to be playing it, the more knowledge you show the less likely it is that they will get involved or believe that they can keep it a secret from you. The key message to get across is the danger of death or serious brain damage that can occur from even one attempt. Even if they have tried blacking out already, with no apparent long-term damage, this doesn't mean that they are less likely to suffer serious injury another time.

RESPONDING TO SUICIDAL THINKING OR SUICIDAL BEHAVIOUR

Discovering that your teenager has attempted suicide is an enormous shock. It may be that your initial response will have to be to quell your own panic and your own distress. There is nothing wrong with panic; it is a very normal and appropriate reaction. However, your panic may prevent you from connecting with your son or daughter and may in fact leave them more isolated than they were before. Even hearing that your son or daughter has seriously contemplated killing themselves is terrifying. We can easily feel that we have failed them by not offering the right kind of support or understanding in the preceding months or maybe even years. The guilt associated with that sense of failure might also prevent us from connecting with them now.

Even hearing that your son or daughter has seriously contemplated killing themselves is terrifying. We can easily feel that we have failed them.

The most important thing, though, is to show them that you care. Put aside your own feelings of terror, guilt or panic and let them know that you're worried about them and that you want to help them. It may be that that help is direct or that you're encouraging them to talk to someone else. If it is the case that their suicidal thinking is associated with depression, then getting professional help may be the best solution. Even if you are encouraging them to go to talk to someone professionally, it is still not just okay but in fact a good idea for you to talk to them about suicide.

The most important thing, though, is to show them that you care. Put aside your own feelings of terror, guilt or panic.

Sometimes, we fear that talking about suicide will make it more likely to happen. In my experience, however, talking about suicide and the deeper feelings that lead young people to contemplate suicide actually reduces the likelihood and the risk of them going on to harm themselves. It is actually very supportive for them to know that somebody seems to understand and acknowledges the seriousness of the feelings that they have. The old adage of 'a problem shared is a problem halved' applies to suicide and suicidal ideation just as it does to other emotional difficulties. Be explicit in the language that you use when talking about suicide. I have included a representative conversation from a previous client of mine who was aged fifteen at the time. In the conversation you will see that not only am I encouraging her to talk about her suicidal feelings, I am also exploring the amount of planning and any action that she had taken to actually commit suicide.

> **Me:** *It sounds like it's been very difficult in your house over the last year or so. I'd say it feels like you're living in the middle of a war zone. I'll bet that in the middle of their fighting your parents never really think what it must be like for you having to hear them both having a go at each other.*

> **Jane:** *Yeah, it's pretty shit really. I don't think they ever think of me.*

> **Me:** *So how did they respond when you got suspended from school for hitting the girl who had been slagging you off for ages?*

> **Jane:** *They just gave out to me and then started blaming each other for how I had turned out as 'bad' as I have.*

> **Me:** *That's awful. You must have felt so alone as well as feeling bad about yourself.*

> **Jane:** *You get used to it.*

> **Me:** *Perhaps you do, but that doesn't stop you feeling lonely. When I hear of all the difficult things have been going on for you, I wonder if you've ever thought about killing yourself.*

> **Jane:** *(long pause) Well . . . maybe . . . but everyone feels like doing it sometime.*

> **Me:** *Maybe they do. What about you, though? Have you thought about killing yourself?*

> **Jane:** *(meekly, with eyes downcast) Yeah.*

> **Me:** *(short pause) It's a scary feeling. How often do you feel like that?*

> **Jane:** *Not much, just every now and then.*

> **Me:** *When was the last time you felt that way?*

> **Jane:** *Well . . . I dunno . . . I suppose last week when they were having that row about my suspension and screaming at each other that each was the worst parent who had created the worst daughter. I mean, if even my parents think I'm a complete waste, then what's the point?*

> **Me:** *It must be terrible to feel a complete waste. No wonder you'd rather be dead than have to feel like that.*

> **Jane:** *Yeah . . . whatever . . . but I did wonder if I was gone, would they care about me then or would they just keep blaming each other.*

> **Me:** *It sounds like you wanted to know if anyone would miss you or if anyone cared enough. So what did you do that night when you were feeling so bad about yourself?*

> **Jane:** *Nothing. I just went up to my room and turned on my music really loud.*

> **Me:** *Have you ever thought about how you might kill yourself if you did want to go through with it?*

> **Jane:** *Sort of. Some of the girls in school say that the easiest way is to take a lot of paracetamol because you just go asleep and never wake up. So I guess that's what I'd do. I'd never have the guts to hang myself or anything.*

> **Me:** *And have you ever tried taking paracetamol to kill yourself?*

> **Jane:** *No. I suppose it's never gotten that bad, I just feel I could sometimes. I don't actually think I'd want to ever do it.*

> **Me:** *Well, it's better to talk about it than to actually do it. It's pretty terrifying to even be in a situation where suicide seems like a good option. You've obviously got a lot of inner strength to be able to hold back from harming yourself. You are also trying to sort stuff out for yourself by coming here to talk to me. It seems like you've got a lot of determination to make life better for yourself.*

> **Jane:** *Well, I don't think so, but I do know actually that it's not my fault that my parents fight. If I didn't get suspended, they'd have found another reason to have a row. I'm more annoyed with myself that I got suspended because I want to do well in my Junior Certificate because I want to prove to them that I am good at something.*

> **Me:** *Okay. So it is good that we are talking about this stuff because it might free up some headspace to study for those exams. Before we finish today we need to make some plans for what you can do if you're thinking about suicide in the future. I understand that things can get so bad that it might feel like you would be better off if you were dead, but you deserve to feel better inside. So we'll agree an arrangement so that even if you feel that way, you won't act on it to harm yourself until we've had a chance to speak together.*

The rest of the session was focused on her feelings of worthlessness when her parents used her 'failings' as the trigger for their arguments. We also made a concrete plan for Jane to talk to her best friend, as a short-term measure until our next session, if she felt like killing herself. As well, I spoke to her mother after the session, with Jane's knowledge, about her suicidal ideation. Her mum was shocked and admitted that she herself feels so caught up in her conflict with her husband that she doesn't pay too much attention to Jane. She said that she too would talk to Jane about it. By the end of the session I had a clear sense that the risk of Jane harming herself was quite low because the act of talking about suicide and identifying some of the sources of her bad feelings had given her the hope that she could make things better. I was also hopeful that she and her mother might be able to open up a line of communication that would help Jane to feel more recognized and valued at home.

You may not have the confidence to talk so openly about suicide. But even the recognition and acceptance that suicidal thoughts can be present is support enough for most teenagers who have felt like killing themselves. By offering your help and your ongoing support, you share some of the burden that your teenager might feel and you lower the risk that they will ever act on any suicidal feelings. It is really important, however, that you encourage them to engage in counselling if you feel that your own support may not be enough, and you remain worried about any risk of suicide.

SELF-HARM

As the name suggests, deliberate self-harm is the act of hurting yourself on purpose. It can involve taking some action (like cutting) to harm yourself or ingesting a substance that you know will harm you. In a large Irish survey of over 3,800 students aged fifteen to seventeen years, about two in ten youngsters had thought about deliberately self-harming in the previous year and about one in ten had actually self-harmed in the previous year. That same survey showed that girls were three times more likely than boys to self-harm. Cutting was the most common form of self-harm, representing about two-thirds of all acts (66 per cent). Overdose was favoured by about 30 per cent. One-fifth of all acts of self-harm were carried out under the influence of alcohol. Other types of self-harm include:

> **hitting oneself (punching walls, head banging walls, beating oneself)**
> **burning oneself (using lit cigarettes or matches)**
> **pulling hair or picking at skin**
> **self-strangulation (usually this is an attempted hanging and is part of a suicide attempt. There are other forms of self-strangulation that are not linked to suicide or self-harm attempts; see earlier about 'The American Dream')**

Lisa: Emotional release through the release of blood

My first professional experience with self-harm was in working with a fourteen-year-old girl, whom I shall call Lisa. She was brought to see me by her mum, who was complaining that Lisa had become very withdrawn and argumentative with her mum's new husband. Lisa's mum described that Lisa had never accepted her new husband during the five years that they were together before they married. She had always been resentful and sarcastic towards him, treating him with scorn and fury in equal measures. The stepdad, Brian (not his real name), never came to the sessions. Lisa's mum initially explained that this was due to his work commitments, but later confided that he could be very angry and confrontational and she was afraid that he and Lisa would simply cause a big scene. It turns out that Brian adopted a harsh and punitive parenting style with his own children, which he also tried to impose on Lisa once he came to live as part of their family. Lisa's mum admitted that Brian was exceptionally critical of Lisa but, given Lisa's behaviour, felt that a lot of the criticism was deserved.

When I met with Lisa alone, she was initially very reluctant to talk to me. I noticed that she had a habit of staring intensely, almost provocatively, at me whilst refusing to answer any questions that I asked. It was only when I became more aware of the nature of her relationship with Brian that I guessed she was probably expecting me to be equally critical of her and also to try to stamp my authority on the sessions. Once we began talking about power and control, her resistance began to shift. I empathized strongly with her sense of the loss of her relationship with her mother, which had been so changed by the arrival of her stepdad. I also empathized about how difficult it was to live in the shadow of a very controlling and autocratic person. Slowly, some of Lisa's defences began to soften and to dissolve. She began to talk about how much she hated her stepdad and equally about how powerless she felt to make her mother see how bad he was and how unfairly she felt treated by him.

Then one day, by pure chance, she pulled up the sleeve of her school jumper to scratch an itch and I noticed a series of scars all along her forearm. I told her that I had noticed the scratches and asked her to tell me more about them. In fairness to Lisa, she was very open in describing how she sat in her bedroom late at night and deliberately cut herself using a razor she would normally use to shave her legs. She talked about how the impotence and rage she felt at being mistreated by her stepfather and misunderstood by her mother would boil up inside. Rather than have a blazing row with her mother or her stepdad, she would cut herself. She felt the pain of the cut, but enjoyed watching the blood flow and feeling a huge sense of relief and release as if the blood flowing was cleansing all of the hurt that she felt inside. She was incredibly articulate and made the process sound as if it was a sensible way of coping with the stress of her home life.

In the immediacy of that session I can remember feeling powerless to offer any alternative solution that might be as effective for her as she described the cutting to be. Thankfully, over the course of the next number of sessions we were able to continue to talk about the strength of her feelings about how she was treated at home and I did offer a number of practical alternatives to her to avoid actually cutting as her means of psychological release.

However, being able to talk with Lisa and her mother together about Lisa's self-harming was the real beginning of positive change in that family. Her mum immediately 'got' what the cutting was about and the reality of life for her daughter began to hit home. She became more of an advocate for her daughter and became a practical support in improving the quality of communication between her husband and her daughter. By the end of our work together I was satisfied that Lisa no longer relied upon cutting and felt much more securely connected to her mother and fought less with her stepdad.

When I think of Lisa now, I realize how representative she was of many youngsters who deliberately self-harm. She never had a desire to kill herself, indeed her cutting was kept hidden and private and didn't even reflect a 'cry for help'. Instead, her cutting was a clear coping strategy that she felt gave her at least temporary relief from a build-up of troubling feelings.

REASONS FOR SELF-HARM

If you remember in Chapter 8 on school, I listed a range of different life events that have a significant impact on teenagers and may also be traumatic for them. In that chapter I made the point that any of these factors may be complicating or even causing the difficulties that youngsters have in school. I have repeated the list here because the same life experiences may also be critically important in understanding why some teenagers will turn to self-harm. For those teenagers, self-harm may be a tool that they are using to cope with a specific problem:

- > **eating disorders**
- > **depression**
- > **smoking, drinking and drug use (marijuana, ecstasy, etc.)**
- > **suicidal ideation (thinking about suicide)**
- > **anxiety disorders**
- > **grief and loss**
- > **divorce or parental separation complications, custody battles**

- > **early sexual experimentation**
- > **physical, emotional and sexual abuse**
- > **bullying at school and in their neighbourhood**
- > **low self-esteem**
- > **sexuality**
- > **social phobia**
- > **learning difficulties**
- > **poverty**
- > **homelessness**

With this range of complicating and distressing life experiences in mind, it is easy to see how teenagers can become stressed and overwhelmed. On the assumption that they are struggling to find helpful ways of expressing their feelings about these issues, we can take it that emotional pressure will build as these problems remain unresolved. For some teenagers who self-harm, the level of emotional pressure becomes too high and the self-harming acts as a safety valve to release and relieve the tension. This, for example, was the key to Lisa's cutting in the anecdote I described earlier. There is a sensation of the blood, in this instance, taking away the bad feelings. Unfortunately, it is only temporary relief and so the cutting can become a habitual response to the build-up of emotional pressure.

Another reason given by some who self-harm is that the hurt makes the person feel alive; it is a present and conscious experience of pain. This is especially the case for some teenagers who may have experienced significant physical or sexual abuse. If their coping mechanism for the abuse was to emotionally shut down, they may be feeling numb or dead inside. Cutting or other forms of self-harm allow them to reconnect with their bodies when their normal experience in the aftermath of the abuse was to feel detached. Guilt and shame are also strong feelings that teenagers may feel in the aftermath of abuse and sometimes they describe self-harming as their attempts to punish themselves.

The need to feel in control, if you remember, is one of the dynamics that leads to eating disorders. It is also a dynamic that leads to self-harm. Where teenagers feel radically out of control in aspects of their life (like living in the midst of parental conflict, the separation of parents or moving house against their desire), self-harming gives them back some elements of control.

Others will use self-harming as a 'cry for help'. They may feel unable to talk to anyone or to acknowledge their difficulties. The self-harm then becomes a covert communication that they are in distress. The challenge for parents is to correctly translate and understand that communication.

Sometimes self-harm is the outcome of a failed attempt to commit suicide.

RESPONDING TO YOUR TEENAGER WHO IS SELF-HARMING

Be aware that your son or daughter may not have intended for you to find out about their self-harming and they may feel so ashamed, guilty or bad that they can't face talking about it. The most important response, therefore, is to be understanding. You can assume that if they are harming themselves they are struggling to cope and they need help to deal with what is going on. Let them know that you see that they are distressed and struggling in whatever way is most obvious. Sometimes the reason for their distress may not be obvious, in which case you use all of your communication skills, which I identified in the chapter on communication and in the chapter on dealing with feelings, to encourage them to express both the distressed feelings and, if possible, the causes of those feelings.

It may be that their problem-solving skills are not great and you can help them to solve a problem they may be facing. By staying calm and offering a reassurance that the problem can get sorted, you might give them the confidence to see that they can learn to cope with, or even resolve, that difficulty.

Simply by taking the issues seriously you will find that your teenager is supported. You might also want to explain to them the dynamic of self-harm and that your understanding is that their self-harm is actually a coping strategy for dealing with or relieving an underlying problem. By expressing your confidence that they won't need to turn to self-harm if they sort out the problem, it can give hope to your teenager. Where you don't feel confident that you can help them to sort out the issue (like with abuse, or a bereavement where you too are grieving), then get professional help from a child and adolescent mental health team or a child and adolescent clinical psychologist.

One of the suggestions that professionals might make to your teenager is that they start to keep a 'mood diary' in which they record their feelings on a daily basis. This can help to identify the times when there is greater or lesser distress. It might also help to pinpoint the source of the distress. For example, regular experience of anxiety at school, or in anticipation of school, will help to clarify that some aspect of the people or the environment of school is putting pressure on your teenager. They will also, probably, be trying to identify the predominant feeling your teenager has just prior to harming themselves.

As a distraction from the hurting behaviour they may suggest that your teenager rings a friend, goes for a walk, or practises deep breathing or a guided imagery task. I especially like guided imagery because I think it serves the dual purpose of allowing a teenager to relax and giving their mind an absorbing task to distract them from negative thoughts. In their relaxed state they can also feel more in control of their thinking and may even be able to overcome their urge to hurt or harm themselves with thought-stopping. I have given you, below, the guided imagery script that I use with my teenage clients. I use this script (or slight variations of it) with many kinds of anxiety, stress and pressure responses that teenagers are struggling with. The key is to employ as many of the senses as possible to bring the scene alive in their imagination. As I speak it, I speak slowly, pausing regularly to allow them to experience the scene. When we are done I encourage them to practise it regularly at home.

Sit comfortably in your chair. Rest your hands loosely in your lap. Close your eyes and focus on the scene that I am going to describe. Let yourself be part of the scene and try to imagine it in as much vivid detail as you can. Along the way, I'll be encouraging you to focus on what you can see, what you can smell, what you can hear and what you can touch. If at any point you feel that you're distracted, just bring your mind back to the scene and focus on the objects that are around you and think about what they look, sound, smell, taste or feel like. And so we begin.

Imagine that you're standing in a large field. The sun is shining and the day is warm. There's a slight breeze that causes the grass in the fields to sway and ripple. As you look around the field you notice that there's a big wood over on one side. You walk over towards the wood. As you come closer you notice that a trail begins between two large oak trees. You walk into the wood. As you walk in, notice what is different. Perhaps the sun is now shaded by the branches of the trees. Does it feel cooler inside the wood? What has the grass of the field been replaced with on the ground between the trees? Perhaps as you walk you're conscious of crunching on twigs or shuffling through fallen leaves. What sounds can you hear in the wood as you walk? Maybe the breeze causes a particular rustle amongst the branches of the trees, or maybe you can hear the sounds of birds and other animals. What does it smell like in the wood? Is it the fresh smell of pine needles, perhaps, or a deep earthy smell?

Continue to walk along the trail, noticing the kind of trees that you pass by, keeping alert to different sounds.

As you walk deeper into the wood, notice the sound of running water. Perhaps it is the faint tinkling and gurgling of a small stream or maybe it is the rushing sound of fast-moving water. It may even be the cascading, crashing noises of water tumbling over rocks or a small waterfall. Follow the trail towards the sound of the water. Continue to notice what you can see, what you can hear and what you can smell. As you come closer to the water you come out into an opening or a glade in the wood. Here the sunlight has the chance to break through. Perhaps, again, it is warm and bright.

What else can you see in the clearing? What does the water look like now that you're up close? Go right over to where the water is. Perhaps you might reach down to touch it. You may even feel spray or mist hitting your face and hands.

*Find a big flat rock that is near to the running water. This rock is bathed in sunshine and is a warm and inviting place to sit. Sit on the rock and feel comfortable. Pay close attention to the noise of the water. Be soothed by it. Be reassured by it. Be strengthened by its constant presence. Enjoy the feeling of the warmth of the sun on your face and know that this is a good place to be. **This is your safe place; this is your good place**. Everything about being here is positive. This is a place where you can truly relax and be safe. This is your place and it is private. Look around; discover all of the sights, smells and the sounds of your safe place.*

If, while sitting on your rock, you get distracted by other more negative thoughts then deliberately put them to the side and focus again on the running water. Watch closely the way it moves . . . perhaps reach out and touch it . . . let its power or its gentleness reassure and soothe you. Any time that other thoughts intrude, put them aside and focus on what you can see, smell, touch or hear.

Rest here.

Be here.

When you have had a chance to feel rested, warmed and relaxed by your safe place then get up from your rock and walk across the glade to the trail that you came in by. Begin to walk along the trail knowing that you're heading back to the wide-open field. Notice again, as you walk up the trail, if it is cooler or darker in the wood. Perhaps there are wild flowers growing in amongst the trees or maybe there's a blanket of pine needles underfoot. Notice any birds and animals that you can see or hear nearby. Keep walking towards the field. See the gap between the trees filled with bright sunlight that you're heading towards. As you come back towards the field we will be finishing this exercise. As you walk out into the field I'm going to count backwards from five through to one. As I get to one I want you to open your eyes, feeling refreshed, and be back present in the room here. 5 . . . 4 . . . 3 . . . 2 . . . 1 and your eyes are fully open and the exercise is over.

Occasionally, as professionals are working with your teenager to help them to understand and deal with their core feelings, they may suggest alternative, less damaging things that your teenager can do instead of their normal method of hurting themselves. Examples include: putting a rubber band on their wrist and snapping it; using a marker to mark their body instead of cutting it; rubbing ice on the part of their body they want to injure; or covering the part they want to injure with a plaster. These are temporary alternatives that are safer and less self-destructive, but that might meet some of the needs that the harming met.

As you respond to your teenager who is harming themselves, be patient. Sometimes the experiences they have had that have led them to the point of self-harm can have been present for a long time. Changing their understanding, perception and coping strategies in relation to those problems can also take a long time.

IN CASE OF EMERGENCY . . . KEY POINTS TO REMEMBER

→ Depression is likely to have an impact on each of the four areas of thinking, feeling, acting and our physical bodies. It is also quite likely to be influenced by the environment and social pressures that surround us.

→ Along with a range of symptoms in each of these areas, depressed teenagers will often exhibit anger, extreme sensitivity to criticism, unexplained aches and pains and withdrawal.

→ If you are worried that your teenager is depressed then seek help, initially from your GP to rule out medical causes, and subsequently from a child and adolescent mental health team or a child and adolescent clinical psychologist.

→ Support any therapy with encouragement to your teenager to keep active and involved in social and sporting activities.

→ Caring for a depressed teenager can be wearing so try to care for yourself by eating well, getting enough sleep, taking some exercise and making some space and time to do things that you enjoy.

→ One of the areas associated with the hopelessness that is felt and expressed in depression is an increased risk of suicide or self-harm.

→ In my experience of working with teenagers who have expressed thoughts of harming themselves or killing themselves, the acknowledgement of the psychological hurt that underpins their thinking and actions is the single most significant factor in reducing the likelihood of real harm occurring.

→ Discovering that your teenager has attempted suicide is an enormous shock. It may be that your initial response will have to be to quell your own panic and your own distress. The most important thing, though, is to show them that you care. Put aside your own feelings of terror, guilt or panic and let them know that you're worried about them and that you want to help them.

→ It is really important that you encourage them to engage in counselling if you feel that your own support may not be enough, and you remain worried about any risk of suicide.

→ Deliberate self-harm is the act of hurting yourself on purpose.

→ Girls are three times more likely than boys to self-harm. Cutting is the most common form of self-harm, representing about two-thirds of all acts.

→ For some teenagers who self-harm, the level of emotional stress from other things in their lives becomes too high and the self-harming acts as a safety valve to release and relieve the tension.

→ You can assume that if your teenager is harming themselves they are struggling to cope and they need help to deal with what is going on. Simply by taking the issues seriously and letting them know that you see that they are distressed and struggling you will find that your teenager is supported.

→ You might also want to explain to them the dynamic of self-harm and that your understanding is that their self-harm is actually a coping strategy for dealing with or relieving an underlying problem.

→ Where you don't feel confident that you can help them to sort out the issue (like with abuse, or a bereavement where you too are grieving), then get professional help from a child and adolescent mental health team or a child and adolescent clinical psychologist.

AFTERWORD

When I was writing this book I deliberately chose to include lots of information about the difficulties and struggles that teenagers experience and that they present to us parents. Given that this is the reality for many of you reading, I reckon this is a good thing. It meant that I got to express my wisdom, such as it is, about how to understand and deal with these issues.

But, when I re-read the book as part of the editing process, I was struck by the fact that I may not have expressed fully my enduring faith in the goodness of humanity and that includes my faith in teenagers and in families. Teenagers are complex beings. Parents are equally complex beings and it is no wonder that in the face of so much physical and emotional change those merging complexities will throw up lots of conflict and stress.

But the developing individuality of our teenagers also throws up wonderful creativity and opportunity. Their greater insight and maturity can be provocative, challenging and consequently energizing. We can experience great pride in their achievements and in their ability to do more and understand more (hopefully matched by their own pride). Because our love for them doesn't diminish, our desire to protect them as they move more independently through the world is activated. This is a good thing.

You work hard for your teenage son or daughter. You have invested hugely in them and their potential future. The fact that you have taken the time to read this book is testament to your caring and your commitment to doing the best for them. They may never fully appreciate the lengths to which you have gone to look out for them and to mind them.

It is no wonder that we can feel a bit hard done by and unappreciated if they take all of this for granted and never seem to give anything in return. It is yet another selfless act of parenthood to let them move into adulthood without guilt but with the confidence to know that they are loveable and valuable.

For sure our teenagers will reject us and our beliefs at times. For sure they will be disrespectful and betray our trust. But we are the adults. We are the ones who pick ourselves up, each time, and have another go at reconnecting. We never give up on our children, and especially not just because they are suddenly teenagers. My real hope is that this book will support you to stick by your teenager and to help them to keep moving safely forward in their development.

Your teenager is worth it, so celebrate the good things, plug away at the bad things and if in doubt always be the one to reach out to them. This is the time to enjoy your teenager. By the end of their adolescence they will still be your son or your daughter but they will never again be your child.

ACKNOWLEDGEMENTS

I would like to thank Michael McLoughlin of Penguin Ireland for prompting me to write this second book. I would like to extend this thanks to the rest of the Penguin team, who have all contributed to the production of this book to the quality you see today.

I would like to thank especially Patricia Deevy, also of Penguin Ireland, Rachel Pierce and Fiona Brown for their encouraging words and their editing, all of which helped me to write the best book possible, despite myself. Thanks, too, to Anna Hymas for her great illustrations throughout.

I would like to thank my manager, Noel Kelly, and the team at NK Management, who have kept me solvent over the last number of years. Special thanks go to Niamh Kirwan, who has fielded so many queries destined for me and who has organized so many other aspects of my working life, freeing me up to write.

My biggest thanks go to my family. I would like to thank my eldest son Conall, my daughter Megan and my youngest son, Éanna. You have all been exceptionally patient while I worked. I know it was more tantalizing because I was working from the little office upstairs and, despite my proximity, I was even less available to you than I normally am. You may not appreciate it now, but I valued every minute of time that you gave me to focus on the book. I am sorry, too, that I snapped at each of you at various stages as you bravely came to warn me of useful things like dinner being ready or the fact that you were going out. I love each of you and thank you. Yes, I am coming out to bounce on the trampoline now.

I know there is a saying about the sweetest wine coming at the end (or something along those lines). Of all the people in my life, my wife Michèle has given and done most to support my career and this book. You have the generosity of spirit that I aspire to. You are my little-known editor who vets not just this manuscript but everything that I write for public consumption. I love working with you, but not as much as I love living with you. Thank you doesn't seem adequate, but it will have to do. Thank you.